The Anxiety Conversation

How to live the life you were meant to live – and become the person you're supposed to be

Psychotherapist Wayne Kemp & writer David Hurst

Acknowledgements

Melica Richards for transcription.

Nonso Udechukwu for video subtitles –
https://www.youtube.com/channel/UCqAIULCnE8uloUuzk_Nw
COw/videos

Published by The Immanent Press.
London - Manchester - Malaga

David: For Debs, Daniel & Darley.

Wayne: For my kids Billy, Sam, Joe, Hannah
& Charlotte.
For my dad Lionel.
Also for Norman Shaw and Nick Godsall,
without whom I wouldn't be here.

And for all those who are still suffering.

"There is a principle that is a bar against all information, which is proof against all arguments, and which cannot fail to keep a man in everlasting ignorance – that principle is contempt prior to investigation."
– Herbert Spencer.

"We shall not cease from exploration
And the end of all our exploring
Will be to arrive where we started
And know the place for the first time
Through the unknown, remembered gate
When the last of earth left to discover
Is that which was the beginning."
– T.S. Eliot.

Wayne Kemp is a leading psychotherapist with 30 years of experience in successfully treating thousands of clients in Britain, Ireland, Spain and around the world. He has helped people suffering from every known mental health illness, including severe stress, anxiety, alcoholism, drug addiction, sex addiction, PTSD, gambling addiction, OCD, bipolar, ADHD, schizophrenia, depression, and he has seen many suicidal people who have told him they wanted to end their lives – yet none of these people ended their life while seeing Wayne and as far as he knows since. Wayne has five grown-up children. He has lived in England, Ireland, the Middle East and Spain.

David Hurst is a writer who has written for newspapers and magazines around the world. He has two young sons. The death of his best friend by suicide led to a life change that saw David travelling with his family in a motorhome for the past few years around 13 countries covering 40,000 miles and visiting more than 350 friends and family. He has lived in Sweden, Australia, England and Spain.

When the student is ready, the teacher will appear...
After 15 recovery years with the support of others, writer David Hurst suffered a summer of extreme emotional and mental torment when he'd tried to do things his own way again for a few months. He was driven insane and found himself literally on his knees in his lounge, a grown man in floods of tears like a lost child in the supermarket.

With face turned to the heavens he cried out for help. He surrendered.

He came out the other side by seeking the help of psychotherapist Wayne Kemp after reluctantly sitting next to him in a group of people who were having coffees the next day. It was the only free seat left.

They got chatting and David told Wayne about ending up on his knees crying out for help. "Life feels like I'm trying to climb a vertical cliff face made of jagged glass – and I'm still waiting for that prayer to be answered."

"But what are you doing here then?" replied Wayne.

Wayne explained that he'd been where David was and he knew not only a way out but a manner of living that would change his life – to ensure the best years of his life were ahead. He promised that.

Over the next year, in a weekly series of sessions on Wayne's balcony in Andalucia, David heard so much that made so much sense – words and actions that Wayne had seen in his own personal life as well as his professional life working successfully with person after person.

David also now witnessed his own transformation: he felt the most relaxed and happiest he had ever been, a state of being that continues to grow. As a writer he knew he had to share this.

Wayne and David have had 30 years of successful experience in their respective fields. Now they come together to bring you a life-changing read, a method for living that will reconstruct and revolutionise everyone who is here and alive today.

Contents

There is no way to happiness; happiness *is* the way

Spiritual sickness of judging skin

If we don't look within we'll never change

More on anxiety – do you believe the negative or do you believe the positive?

Question why you keep taking the tablets

Everybody's got talent!

Rip up your blueprint – rip it up and start again

Why pain is the communication to change

You and your free will

Is suicide selfish? (Asking for a friend)

Don't worry. Relax.

Grow old greatly

Forgive or die

Led by your head

A thinking problem

Ongoing stigma of mental health

Can talking about mental health problems ever just be attention-seeking?

Forever pain or infinite change

Sadness & anger

God doesn't want any of us to be slaves

"Fuckin' God!"

"Good morning, God" or "Good God, morning"

Don't hang on to your shit

Smoking, gambling and the integrity of the false self

Search for the hero inside yourself

The root of our troubles

Acceptance is the key

Our faces are the same

Ten thousand times the size of us

Focussing on abundance

The Ten Commandments are not for keeping

Growing up or dragged up?

Dedication to meditation

The secrets that keep us well

Genetic complications

This hostile beautiful world

Panic dying

God up

Help or Hell, the choice is ours

Wayne: The majority of people are never going to get well. You've got to accept that. When somebody comes and is there in front of you, you have to see whether they're open to getting well. Some people are totally resistant to it. Others are more open and they want you to give them more information, they want to be filled with hope.

If somebody comes looking for help, however tentatively, whether they believe there is any such thing as help, then the idea is to sit that person down and to build a relationship and some trust with them. The first thing is to give them some hope. You have to be absolutely confident in yourself that you have a solution and that you can give them a message of hope, that you know it works.

This is the same whether it's somebody suffering with anxiety, an alcoholic, addict, someone depressed or any of the mental health illnesses.

If you can't give them hope you give them nothing.

Most people who come to me have usually been from pillar to post and run the anxiety gauntlet of seeking help. They are usually desperate... desperation is wonderful for opening the mind – but, of course, it certainly doesn't feel that way at the time.

David: Bestselling author Matt Haig wrote in a popular tweet: "I hate that distance. You know – when you look into someone's eyes and you know they are in that place, that hell thousands of miles away but also right there. In the pain you once were trapped in. You wish you could reach them but they are so far away they need to find it alone."

How can you reach someone like this?

W: Do they want to be reached? Of course, some people do not want to be reached because they're not ready or they're awkward or they're blocked or stubborn – they think they know all the answers. The first commandment is always: "Thou shalt be right!"

So if somebody wants help, the first thing is they've got to be open to the idea that they can be helped. Many people will keep that look in their eyes that Matt Haig writes about until they're ready.

As a psychotherapist I know that the personality of the counsellor or person they've sought for help is extremely important, the confidence and the enthusiasm from the counsellor or person they've asked to help, and the ability to connect with another person. You know, anybody can be helpful, but you have to be guided to that one person who can help you.

D: What makes someone ready: when the pain is big enough?

W: When you're sick and tired of being sick and tired.

D: And that can go on forever with some people: they can be sick and tired until they die, yet never sick and tired of being sick and tired.

W: For the majority it will go on forever. That's why psychiatrist M Scott Peck called his bestselling book The

Road Less Traveled. Because the majority will not recover. They refuse to travel the road.

D: Those who do are those on the road less travelled... So most people who need this will not get this. Most people like this are still led by the sick part of their mind. And of course it does not want them to get well and be happy. That would be its loss of power and possibly lead to its near-death. It never completely dies until the death of its host.

So you have to cut through this voice in the head, this "thinking", if you want to beat the illness, if you want peace and happiness. That's often why it's useful to speak with someone who understands the process. Some may say this is not a solution for everyone, that it won't work for some, so it is not then a solution – but it is, for any of us with the human condition. We are made this way.

There is a solution and the solution is the same and always has been and always will. It's like if I know there's a huge thick wooden gate and if you open it there's a pot of gold there that is yours to have, but you say you don't want to open the gate, then the pot of gold is still there. That pot of gold is always there.

W: Exactly, and it's understanding what that pain is about. Pain attracts your attention to a problem, an issue.

D: Always, as I see it – whether that's physical or mental. So we are given pain to show we need to do something different.

So there is always a reason for pain, and that goes for mental pain in the form of such as depression or debilitating anxiety and so on. There is always a reason, and so the pain is there to tell us to make a change, to do something different, to move away from something and sometimes that can be the way we're living or a relationship, be that a so-called romantic one or with some of our family or from someone we're working with on a regular basis.

Some people say that anyone struggling with such as anxiety or depression could simply choose to be positive. But is that really a choice?

W: No. If you've got it, you've got it. It's like being an alcoholic, you can't help it. It's a disease, it has a pathology. The choice you have is that you can choose to recover.

It's a message to you telling you that spiritually you're dying, you need to fix this. It's getting your attention so that you look inside, and then you'll seek what you need to seek and you will begin to fix it, you go on the journey.

D: So the choice of getting well is ours, but the choice of having the illness isn't?

W: The choice of seeking a solution is yours. But it must be emphasised, that solution must not be on your terms. That's very important and that requires trust. Remember that the first commandment says: "Thou shalt be right." It has to go.

D: So you have to ask for help, explain the problem honestly and thoroughly, then shut up to listen and get on with what you're advised. Take the cotton wool out of your ears and stick it in your gob, as was put to me at the start of my recovery!

W: Firstly, you've got to know that you don't have the answer. Even though the answer is within you, presently it's a complete mystery to you.

D: Because otherwise you wouldn't be in the place you are, you would be in the place of the answer.

W: Look at a coal fire that's burning brightly. If you take a piece of coal off and put it to one side it just goes out. And one of the things mental health issues such as depression do is that it begins to isolate us and separate us from others – and if we cannot connect with other people, then we can't connect with ourselves.

It's useful to know the warning signs too, but most people don't. We don't learn this in schools yet. For instance, with depression one of the first warning signs is usually disappointment.

D: Why is it then that some people get mental health illnesses and others don't?

W: Everybody gets something, just that some people are better at hiding it than others. Of those who don't get mental health issues, their problems often seem to manifest physically sooner or later. Everybody gets something, it just depends whether it affects you mentally or physically.

D: And you are saying that a mental health problem will lead to a physical issue?

W: Doctors will tell you that if you're depressed your immune system won't work as well as it's supposed to work. Conversely, when you are happy your immune system works better. So obviously mental health issues are going to reflect physically.

D: So, really, every human being has a mental illness of some sort?

W: Every human being has issues that manifest mentally or physically. Or both.

D: M Scott Peck described addiction as "the sacred disease", saying that addicts, including of course alcoholics, were lucky because as drug-taking and drinking excessively is one of their symptoms, it's much more obvious they have a problem and so more of them will seek help than others.

W: Well, lots of people seek help. For example, most people who are depressed sooner or later are seeing their doctor or a psychiatrist. But whether they're prepared to do the work that it takes and whether they get the proper information, that's another matter.

A lot of the time if they go to the mental health services they're not going to get the proper information on what their depression is about and the best ways to treat it. They'll be given a tablet and some form of counselling will be recommended, but if that counselling is ten sessions with a counsellor who may not be that well educated in affairs of depression, then it's merely sticking-plaster stuff.

The problem is that pain tells someone that something's wrong, so they go to their doctor and the doctor may say:

well, you can't possibly be depressed for any reason because you're happily married, you've got wonderful children, you have a great job, you live in a beautiful place, your health is good – so you shouldn't be depressed. So therefore we'll give you some tablets because it's obviously chemical imbalance. But I think that's a load of nonsense. Psychiatrist Peter Breggin wrote on this in his book Toxic Psychiatry.

If you really want to recover from such as depression, depression is there to change you – that's what it's for. It's attracting your attention. It's pain. Pain is always attracting your attention to something.

This is the modern world

D: How does our modern world play its part in this? Is the world insane?

W: Of course the world is insane. Just turn on the news, read the newspapers.

D: And the world is insane because individuals are insane that makes a collective society insane or a nation insane or...?

W: Why is the world insane? Because we lack information. We lack information about the spiritual, physical and mental laws of life. Our insanity is always because of lack of information.

For instance, when people started doing surgery and they didn't wash their hands that was insane, but it was because they lacked the information that there was such a thing as bacteria. So just because you can't see something doesn't mean it's not there.

The more information you have the better you will be. But if you're resentful and full of pride and you're awkward or you're very fearful, then how are you ever going to be happy? It doesn't make sense and yet people go around with those attitudes all day long and think that one day they'll wake up and everything will be all right.

The passage of time alone will not heal the problem. It will progress it. You will practise being depressed or anxious and you will become a genius at it.

Nothing stands still in this world, everything is progressing... for better or for worse. Any disease – and such as anxiety is a disease – will get worse if not treated.

D: Additionally, these days such as social media, newspapers, TV news and so on rouses and intensifies fear and resentments. The word "resentment" comes from words meaning to "re-feel deeply". So a resentment is anger and indignation repeating itself as a bad feeling inside us, and a resentment can go on for years, blocking a person from more positive things and feelings.

W: Yet our world is a far safer place than it's ever been. If you read United Nations statistics on poverty and travel safety and crime you can see there's been a huge improvement. I'm not saying it's great, but there are great improvements.

So the world has become far safer, but we now have an avalanche of news and people become addicted to the drama that tells us how bad everything is. I would include TV programmes such as some soap operas in that. You turn them on and it's an assault on the senses – and how do people watch that and think they can be at a decent place afterwards?

D: Because people copy, and so they see all the drama on TV and think this is how it is then and I want some of this.

W: Lots of people love drama. I remember watching The Sopranos and I really enjoyed the drama and thought it was a fascinating programme – yet I always felt awful at the end of it. Every time I had this horrible feeling because the main character I was identifying with, that I was supposed to have some empathy towards, was such an obnoxious person.

D: Why is it that some people create more drama than others?

W: Because it's addictive, because it helps them escape from their problems. It develops patterns of thinking and behaving. We drag our dramas around with us from the past and constantly seek, subconsciously, to recreate them. Our drama is like our evil destructive twin – therefore we have to take great care with our internal conversations because they dictate our lives.

D: So it means they don't have to think about themselves? To get out of it, to get away from the bad feelings and get away from themselves?

W: Exactly. And they are addicted to it. It's practised, it becomes compulsive and automatic. But it's only making them sick. People even get addicted to such as anxiety – sometimes your fears become very comfortable because they're so familiar.

It goes back to what I said before about not understanding the spiritual, physical and mental ways of life. They do it because they lack information. But when you tell someone like this the information, they don't believe it because of: "Thou shalt be right."

Psychiatrist Carl Jung said, and I'm paraphrasing: If you believe something go and check it out, then you won't have to believe it any more, you'll know.

D: Do you think rates of stress and anxiety are rising?

W: Depends on where you live. But in the Western world, such as Britain and America, the rates of stress and anxiety are rising because people are less taken care of in many ways.

We used to have more communities, such as in Britain with the shipyards, car-working areas and with the miners. People knew each other in these communities. There's increasingly less of that, and the fact that more and more pubs are closing down.

D: And perhaps the community of going to churches too – less and less go. I'm sure connection helps people.

W: Of course. People used to have jobs for life, but there is no such thing any more. People don't even get contracts and some people are expected to work for nothing to "prove" how good they are... Then we're constantly assailed by adverts and by the people in the world who've got more than us, and we're told we're less than unless we have these things. So stress and anxiety are going to go up because less people are looking out for you, and there's more pressure.

In the 1980s everyone was encouraged to make lots of money – make sure you've got plenty of money and everything will be all right... and the British Prime Minister then famously said: "There's no such thing as society."

D: But that's surely not a normal human state to be on your own, to just try to live it alone?

W: Go back to what I said about taking a piece of coal from a glowing fire and watch how it goes out. Human beings need other people: we're not designed to be an island, we need to be in relationships.

People grow with relationships. The problem is if you get in the wrong relationship, whether it be parents or partners, then you begin to grow in a way that's very unhealthy.

So finding the right relationship is always difficult if all you've got in the past is bad relationships – because that's your pattern. That's in your blueprint, and that's what you'll act out.

D: That's what you seek then, the familiar?

W: You will always seek what you know. You'll keep repeating what you know. That's why recovery depends on finding somebody who doesn't think like you, because if you keep going off what you know you won't get anywhere. If you try to use the same sort of thinking that created the problem in the first place you're making a big mistake.

D: A bit like someone trying to bite off their own teeth. Or when self-will is running riot and you're trying to fix your self-will you're always just going to be led the wrong way because it's the damaged will that's doing the leading…

Do you think life has just got harder?

W: You could say in one way we've got better because overall in our society now we've become a little more correct, such as that it's quite rightly frowned upon to make jokes about people's size or age or whatever. It still happens to some extent, but it's got better. I mean not many people go around today calling other people racist names.

Of course, sadly some people do, but at one time it was just normal everyday stuff and you even had programmes on British television that did it. Thankfully we don't any longer.

Pain, the touchstone to growth

D: Do you think mental health issues have got bigger in the past century?

W: We've probably always had tremendous mental health problems, but what we have now is more openness to discuss them.

D: Do we have less spiritual life, less spiritual growth? Because M Scott Peck said in The Road Less Traveled that he thought all mental illness was caused when the gap between our conscious will and our unconscious will becomes too far apart – the conscious will being our ego and the unconscious will being God's will. He wrote: "It is because our conscious self resists our unconscious wisdom that we become ill."

So a major, if not the major, part of his job as a psychiatrist was to bring that closer together – so that people are living by "God's will". It's the same process that the 12 Steps achieves if they are done thoroughly and honestly – just look at the first words in Step 12 for proof: "Having had a spiritual awakening as the result of these steps…"

W: I agree with Peck's analysis, which is very similar to Carl Jung's: we all live to some extent in illusion about our lives. For example, we see things in others they don't see themselves and therefore the same condition applies to ourselves. Illusion and reality living in the same space causes our complexes, our restlessness, our disturbance. When the illusion and the truth become so far apart that they are no longer containable in the same space, this leads to a mental breakdown, which is characterised by overwhelming anxiety, chronic fear, paranoia and depression.

But this is where the great paradox comes in – if dealt with properly the pain becomes the gift of desperation, the prerequisite rock bottom that leads to surrender – so that the urgently needed psychological reorganisation can take place.

D: Of course, you can see why some people say: I don't believe in God, in any god, because why would any sort of god let this shit happen to me?

W: Exactly, the god, God, doesn't intervene. Great love never intervenes unless it's invited. That's important.

Life is a set-up. Everything is governed by laws: laws of the universe, the seasons, health, cooking, driving, how to walk, talk. We learn laws, we keep them, we prosper.

Or you can keep the law of fucking up, one that's characterised by fear, selfishness, pride, resentment, self-pity, greed and suchlike. All of these laws work too, and bring their own "rewards".

So spiritual and mental laws of life are no different. If we break the law we suffer. We may get away with it for a while, but eventually we suffer.

The suffering is the key to change... or death. Your relationship with a higher power will follow the laws that are fixed in that area. There are rules of engagement.

Because no matter how bad it gets, God doesn't intrude because great love never intrudes – it has to be invited. This is why I emphasise so much about surrender. This process of surrender is vital... to surrender to this Higher Power that some people call God, some people call Jimmy, some people call the Universe. But it's important that you seek that higher power so that you eventually find who or what it is.

A spiritual law. If you seek me with all of your heart you will find me.

The reason we need a Higher Power is because the first step to recovery is to admit that we're actually powerless over what is happening to us. We're not stupid, we're not imbeciles, we can be very intelligent people – but whatever we're in the grip of, whether it's chronic anxiety, chronic depression, alcoholism or whatever it may be is far more powerful than we are. So if we are admitting that we are powerless and that no human power can save us, then we need to find an alternative source of power if we are going to live successfully at all.

The whole concept of a Higher Power is how can we find a power greater than the disturbance that is within us.

You have to seek, and it's a process of seeking throughout your life. And God reveals more and more of Himself as you go along.

D: You use the word "Himself" there?

W: You can use anything, capital H or small h or no h – it's just the way it works for me. It's God as you understand Him, Her or It. Remember it doesn't have to be God, it could be Jimmy or Jenny.

D: But you've also got people who say if there is a God why did God let my friend die of cancer, why did God let that war happen?

W: Because think of it purely and simply like this, you have a free will, we all have a totally free will and we are put on this planet and we're given opportunity: do you want to carry on living your life your way or would you like it to be different? Better? Is there a plan for me?

Living your own way out of your blueprint may very well be the root of all your problems. Or do you want to be saved? That's the choice you have. It's a spiritual set-up.

It is always difficult to understand why bad things happen to good people. But I suspect it's about the laws of existence, how we live brings consequences not just for ourselves but also for the generations that follow.

Stem cell research biologists have some interesting things to say on this with epigenetics where they talk about a part of our cell that rewrites our DNA in response to the environment and that if we suffer from stress or anxiety that is going to affect what we pass on.

We are all going to die of something. In fact a good friend of mine used to say it would be a shame to die of nothing. He died young from smoking and drinking.

Some people arrive at that point where they realise they'd like salvation. Salvation means every area of your life from your sex life to your mental illness to your prosperity to everything, needs to be saved, to be dragged out of the water, to be pulled out of the mire because we all live in the mire. That's what God is saying, do you want me to get you out or not?

D: Why are we living in the mire?

W: Just look around you. Isn't there so much shit for most people, on the inside as well as the outside? People might have lovely children, a fantastic partner, live in a beautiful place – yet they are constantly worried about everything. So is that the human condition? There is another part of us that needs to be born to develop. Most mental illness is the resistance to that part.

D: So we are born and there is this other part waiting to be born.

W: Of course.

D: And if we pray, meditate...

W: It's been called "the self" and "the self" is like any other birth: it's painful and it's difficult. It's like creation all around – volcanoes and earthquakes and floods, thunder and lightning, they create the planet that we live on and the new life that comes from it. There's a second person within everybody that has to be born and that's why Jesus spoke about being born again. He was saying that you have to understand you are a spiritual being on a psychological journey.

D: And this is the spirit being born and then growing.

W: The spirit has to be born within you.

D: And do we have to lose ego to get that?

W: Yes, you have to lose ego to get it. You see the ego doesn't understand, the ego only understands what it sees round about it, like the ego doesn't understand how to keep your heart beating or the blood flowing or your digestion or any of these things, but you're doing that. You're doing this amazing thing keeping this incredibly complex system going all the time, regeneration of all the cells and everything that we are doing is incredible.

So within you there is something that is created, that's being born, and your body is nothing more than the shell that contains the essential you. If you think of your mind as the size of a beach ball, your ego is the size of a marble – but it thinks the rest of it doesn't exist.

So the subconscious makes itself known. It's a bit scary because you don't understand it and don't know where it's coming from. And what will happen is the ego will resist it because it will think that something's wrong.

D: Or could it be when you have these thoughts of: this is my ambition, I can do that and then you get another thought coming in and saying: you can't possibly do that, that's too risky, you're too old, you're not experienced enough, not you, you're shit?

W: That's something else, that is the negative, the satanic – remember it's symbolic. Satan means "the opponent, the adversary, the one who is plotting against you". It's a direct translation of the Hebrew. But the opponent isn't a guy with a pitchfork and a tail – it's that undermining voice in your head.

D: So why do you have that against you inside you; why do we all have this to varying degrees?

W: Because the battle between Heaven and Hell takes place in your head. You know, as soon as you were put into that body you were crucified, because nobody – no matter how much money you've got – nobody can eat your dinner for you, nobody can go to the toilet for you, nobody can feel your pain or your disappointments, your hurt, your rejections… nobody but you. You're crucified in the body, but there has to come a time you have a resurrection and that's when the self develops.

D: Are the self and the ego different?

W: The ego is the servant of the self, but through childhood problems or trauma the ego can disassociate from the self. Then you have a collision course.

Carl Jung talked about how he found "the self". And how did he find the self? Two mental breakdowns. But it was very important that when Carl Jung had his mental breakdowns he was kept in a loving, secure environment and there was no medication to block growth. So it took him somewhere.

If you look at all shaman throughout the world, they usually had a period where for ten to 15 years they went through severe problems. Some of them just rested on a bed and never spoke to anybody. Then one day they got up and all the tribe went to them and treated them as a wise person because the tribe recognised they'd been somewhere, that this person had acquired wisdom, this person had started to understand something about life that we don't usually have – and that's what a lot of mental illness is.

If you take an everyday person, when they suddenly get depression or they start developing different types of mental illness, it's usually about the self trying to be born because what they do is that they resist it. Now there are lots of other options we can go into about this, about why depression is good because it's a message to make a change, to do something differently, to look at finding part of you that's not yet developed.

But when it happens, first of all it's bloody painful and terrifying – so the ego fights: it will try to suppress it. It will try to pretend it is not happening. The ego will always use suppression of feelings, denial of feelings and the idealisation of situations.

D: I read that Jung spent about six years during his breakdown and inner disturbances on working to prevent his conscious mind from blocking out what his unconscious mind wanted to show him. So going off what M Scott Peck said – that the conscious mind or will is the ego and the unconscious mind or will is God's will – does that mean our ego fights against us living the life that we were born to have; that it stops us becoming the person we're supposed to be?

W: Often – by idealising the situation. That's the ego's defence. I once idealised a relationship I was in and for a long time I made her into something she wasn't. I knew all the time that it wasn't right, I wanted to make it work – so I covered up a lot of things.

Idealisation is always a form of denial, it's just a technique to blatantly deny stuff and push it away and pretend it never happened because you don't want to face the reality. So you create an alternative one and you become your own spin doctor, because you were taught by experts.

D: Like you once asked me if I enjoyed secondary school and I told you I did. Then you asked me how I used to feel on Sunday evenings, and I remembered that I frequently developed nausea.

They used to show That's Life! on television on Sunday evening and if my memory is ever jogged about that programme, I still get the exact same feelings I did as a teenager. It's not the programme of course, but the association with Monday morning, and the following four mornings too. That dread of being shackled to a desk forced to listen to lots I wasn't really interested in.

W: Or such as someone who says: "I had a fantastic childhood, it was wonderful. I got smacked lots, but it didn't do me any harm, in fact it did me good... You know, my mother was a saint, she was the most wonderful person. She only hit me in the afternoons."

I had a client once and she said to me: "Oh my father was a lovely man" and it turned out he kept a cane over the fireplace and not only did he keep it, but this "lovely man" used to sit there with a knife putting notches in the cane so it would hurt her more when he hit her – and yet she was idolising him, she was idealising the situation.

D: Why do we idealise?

W: It's denial, because someone can't face something, such as they can't face the fact that they're really immensely angry and they hate what happened to them. If they have been abused they may have incredible hatred towards someone – but it may be a family member and they fear exposure and the calamity for the family it may bring, or the sickness in the loyalty is too great.

Maybe they don't hate the person, but they hate what happened, and the suppression of that anger is the depression.

With a lot of people who are depressed, the problem is they've turned all the anger in on themselves, and then they say: "Well, I don't feel angry..." But they feel depressed. If they could feel their anger, they wouldn't be seeing me.

Remember that depression can develop due to many complex reasons and in a multitude of ways, but it always involves the repression of the self. We practise repression as a subconscious behaviour and become experts at it.

It has even been suggested by psychiatrist William Glasser to turn it from a noun into a verb and ask: what is it I am depressing? That is instead of someone saying "I am depressed" to say instead "I am depressing" or "I am choosing to depress".

This doesn't mean you can snap out of it. Depression is a painful illness. But it gives you a handle on a beginning of a solution.

D: Is this to do with ego again?

W: The ego should always, always be the servant of the self. It's like a TV, and a TV is a machine that can take in information out of the air, decode it and then present it to you. Your ego is the same. We can take in information out of the air, we can hear it, see it, taste it, feel it and we bring it all back in for you, the operator, to make decisions.

So think of your brain as your computer. That computer is like, say somebody hurt you, you think: "I'm going to kill them, I'm going to have their family kidnapped, I'm going to burn their house down" or "Well, they didn't really mean it, I'll forgive them, they're quite nice, I want to be friends with them..." Then you choose one of these options. The ego acquires information; the self is the decision-maker.

Which do you choose, we get that all the time. But unfortunately lots of people think their thoughts are them rather than a set of solutions that we have to choose between. So that way you can step to the side of your thoughts and look at this person within who's making the choices. The ego fights back with repression, denial and idealisation. But then when that doesn't work it will use drink, drugs, food, sex, work, shopping – whatever it can.

So the self will fight back with panic, anxiety, depression and fear because it wants your attention. If it doesn't do those things to you it won't stop you dead in your tracks. Once you turn round and ask where is this coming from and start to look at you, when you start to give yourself time and you begin to get honest with yourself and look at yourself then it begins to change, but it takes time. It's not instant coffee.

It begins to change because that's what it wants, but it won't let you go running off quickly because if you fixed it quickly you go running off and the same thing will happen again. It's like with a child who is sick, they are on the sofa all day, then suddenly feel better and go running round and – bang! – they're sick again. It takes time because it has to be developed within you. It develops over time.

You begin to experience something totally different than you ever have before. Sam Shoemaker, a priest and great spiritual writer who was a significant influence for the founders of Alcoholics Anonymous (AA) said: I can take you and I can put your hand on the door, but I cannot turn the key, you have to do that.

So all the information I've given is getting you to that point where you say this is possible. We can show you that there is an experience in life beyond what you've ever felt. It's like trying to explain to somebody what drugs or sex is like, but it's only when they have really experienced it themselves that they will really know.

It's the same with spirituality. Think of your body as a pod that contains the seed inside. Like Jesus said: a seed has to die, and if it dies much fruit appears. A seed has to die in the ground and then the whole plant comes from it. And that's what's happening within us – these bodies, when you're born physically that is your first birth. But throughout this life, the sole purpose of this life, is for that second person to be born.

D: So we are the seed and what grows out of the seed is...

W: What grows out of the seed is the second person.

D: Which is a beautiful, blooming plant, a flower.

W: My opinion is that it's like a sci-fi movie where the planet is dying and we've got a short period of time to work out how do we survive beyond the planet's death... To me what it's saying as well is that this is the second part of life, that we are to understand that there's a second person within us and that person is eternal.

If you look at Robert Lanza's work – and he's considered one of the best scientists on the planet, one of the cleverest men in the world – his theory is that it's impossible for a human being to die.

Run into the trouble – for the disturbance is the answer

D: What about when people say things such as that they hide inside themselves sometimes, that they suffer from shyness?

W: Shyness is always about ego because you think everybody's looking at you and that you're the most important person in the room because everyone's attention is on you. You want to be the footballer, you want to be the film star, you want to be that person when you walk in the room that it just lights up…

But the problem is your opinion of yourself is so negative that you project this onto others. So it becomes excruciatingly painful… as if everybody can see your shame. Everyone can see an ego problem when a person has an overinflated view of themselves, but the flip side of the coin is when you believe you're a pile of crap.

Now a lot of people won't admit to that, but that's what it is: shyness is a pure ego problem because you're not connected to who you are, and your opinion about yourself is so fickle.

D: So again the solution is to lose the ego by growing spiritually? Let me say here too that I know part of your job as a psychotherapist is to confront people, that without that they won't change… Sometimes this is very uncomfortable, even though it might be done with love and knowledge. I know that from personal experience with you! But I'm grateful as I'm ready to change because I want to move as far away as possible from the extreme torturous insane pain I experienced. So is this type of confrontation essential for change?

W: If you could develop a better sense of yourself, of who you are, on the way to this new birth, then you won't care what other people think. It's the same thing that keeps somebody locked in their house, because they're absolutely dreading what other people think and that leads to subconscious tension where the mind begins to project into disaster.

People become riddled with impending doom. They are scared to death of everybody else because of the opinion they have of themselves and therefore of others.

It's the self-perception that is critical. Many people carry toxic shame.

If we are judging others in our internal conversations, we are judging ourselves. Judging is a defect of character. This type of judgement always has a guilty verdict passed by the high court in our heads on ourselves. A sentence is passed: guilty. Self-condemnation follows. How the hell can you not be anxious in that environment?

D: Then there's the problem some people have of going to the local shop or like you had a problem getting on a bus or a plane.

W: It's self-perception. You feel ashamed. Counsellor and author John Bradshaw's work on toxic shame is very good.

D: What is toxic shame?

W: Toxic shame is where you carry shame that doesn't belong to you. Usually it has been passed to you by parents, guardians, teachers.

For example, it comes from abuse in all its forms, especially sexual, and is always accompanied by huge amounts of criticism, such as what happens from living in a house full of conflict. So these sort of phrases are sadly all too familiar to people who carry toxic shame: look what you made me do; we're getting divorced because of you; there would be no arguments if it wasn't for you, and suchlike.

It is parents blaming children for their own faults and failures, parents who refuse to apologise, continuing to blame others for their own behaviour. It leaves a person on the receiving end of it feeling flawed as a human being, with a programme playing in the background 24 hours a day that's saying: there's something wrong with me.

With it all, your world begins to close down – such as because you have a panic attack in the supermarket you don't go shopping any more; you have one at church so you don't go there again; you have one at the bus stop, so you don't even go out again…

You don't understand what's happening to you, you don't understand it's coming from within and then you start living your life trying to accommodate it. So you get very good at not being able to go out and you get very good at being agoraphobic. It's the same with depression – if you keep allowing depression to possess you, you become an expert at depression.

D: Like anything, the more you practise it the better you get.

W: It's like if you're a footballer and you keep missing penalties. After a while you're practising missing.

D: Anything you focus on gets bigger, it grows.

W: Of course, your little magnifying mind. Life and pathologies are progressive, so they either get worse or better depending on what you're practising.

D: People distract themselves when what they really need is to know themselves.

W: Of course, they're distracting themselves from the pain. But the disturbance is the answer, resistance to the disturbance is always the problem. When you can see, you see.

The first thing I have to do with anyone who's depressed is to tell them it's okay to be depressed. Because they keep saying to me, I shouldn't feel this way, I shouldn't be like this. But you know if you're in Dublin or London and you want to get to Paris you have to accept you are in Dublin or London. It would be ridiculous to keep insisting you're not.

It doesn't mean you want to stay where you are, but acceptance is the key.

By accepting you're depressed it doesn't mean you want to stay depressed forever. But you have to accept you are depressed and there is nothing wrong with that. This is part of the human condition: by accepting it we can begin to move from it. It's like being an alcoholic and until you accept that, you are going nowhere.

D: That's why then Step 1 of the 12 Steps in AA is: "We admitted we were powerless over alcohol – that our lives had become unmanageable." And why people introduce themselves at meetings saying: "My name's John, I'm an alcoholic." If they are called John!

W: Many people live in delusion, and one of the things that causes mental or nervous breakdowns is when the delusion of your existence – what you want to believe about yourself and about life – gets so far away from the reality that it's no longer containable in the same space. That's when people crack.

A lot of the time, within the person, that delusion and the reality are in total conflict, which causes a lot of these problems and we then call them complexes – a group of repressed or partly repressed emotionally significant ideas that cause mental conflict leading to abnormal mental states or behaviour – and that's when the breakdown comes.

D: This reality of life is I think connected, often strongly connected, to one of the many great things Carl Jung said, a point he made about family and culture.

W: Until you leave your family and your culture behind you'll never find out who you are.

D: So you'll never find your true self. Because there's this pressure and an inflexible expectation of who and how you should be, of what you should do and achieve.

W: It's programming, it's belief. "Because my dad did" sort of stuff.

D: Then you've got such as celebrity stories in the media and people see this celebrity's massive house and their flashy car and they think that's what I should have. And our society tells you that you need to own your own home, you need to be this or that... In order to be happy, to be someone.

W: A lot of people look at that stuff and will totally accept that it's not for them. But others will aspire to it and go on to work at it. And then others will just feel dissatisfied because they'll feel less than because they don't have it.

D: People get anxious about this. Is being scared what anxiety is all about?

W: Totally, it's fear. So you have to ask, what am I afraid of?

D: What are they afraid of, anyone that's anxious?

W: They are afraid of their own demise.

D: That's it, really – of dying or not existing?

W: To the demise of themselves – you know, the world is a scary place. When you're born, you know very soon, within a few years, you get this concept of you are not going to be here at some stage. No matter what people want to do, they will get old and die, or they get sick or they have tragedy before then or whatever it may be. So the world's a scary place and there are lots of reasons for people to be scared.

Lots of people for instance come to the end of their lives and they're absolutely terrified because they've never taken on the fact that they're going to die. In The Tibetan Book Of Living And Dying it says that until you have accepted your own death you'll never live. But lots of times people are panicking because they're killing themselves by the way they're living.

D: In what way?

W: Their spirit is dying. The thing that tells you you're happy or sad is your spirit – nothing else. People try and find pleasure and that doesn't necessarily make them happy or otherwise rich people wouldn't kill themselves. So your spirit is the only thing that can tell you whether you're happy or sad. But when you're depressed it's far from it being a chemical imbalance – it's that your spirit is fucked. And people say: but you can show it in the brain. But you can show you're thirsty in the brain, and what do we do? Give you drugs to take away the thirst or give you a glass of water?

D: How do you make the spirit happy then, how does the spirit become happy?

W: That's what we have to find out. Obviously we don't know what's good for us, so someone has to ask: why is my spirit unhappy? It could be that you are in total denial about your past or in total denial about who you are now, total denial about what you believe in or what you would like. It could be that you're a very successful businessman and you are making loads of money, but really you should be teaching kids with disabilities to play basketball instead.

You climbed the ladder of success but found it was up against the wrong building.

D: So you're not the person you're supposed to be?

W: Exactly. You have to find the design within.

Alcohol, drugs and social media

D: If anyone tries at some point to cut down on alcohol, is that usually a sign that deep down they know they have a problem with it, that it causes them problems? Maybe they are at that point where they can't imagine a life with or without alcohol.

W: Yes, it's usually because they found they had problems with it. They got into trouble when they were drinking or the next day they felt the pain. You see, if you have a problem with alcohol one of the first symptoms is that instead of just feeling sick after alcohol – a bad stomach or headache – you start to have this very uneasy feeling… usually remorse or you begin to feel a little depressed and this is the beginning.

Drug use is the same. Some people take illegal or prescription drugs and have a happy time on them, but then feel remorse. Why do we feel that remorse? Because we've created a short circuit of our brain to induce a spiritual feeling. But we did it with chemicals.

D: So like Carl Jung said about alcoholism: it's a low-level thirst for God.

W: It is definitely a low-level thirst for God. Some drugs and definitely drink imitate spiritual experiences – that's why people enjoy them… they give us a glimpse of what we are looking for in this world. Take a drink or some drugs and you feel like you belong, no anxiety about tomorrow, you're relaxed, unafraid, the world is in its right place.

D: Because you're losing ego? Your fears go with your ego because it's the ego that creates fear? That's why maybe people think they can dance brilliantly when they're drunk!

W: You lose your inhibitions, not ego. Your ego is getting a boost. It's a chemical illusion, but the first thing is that it makes you feel like you're okay, confident within yourself, you belong, that everybody is your friend.

You're losing the barriers that you've put up, you feel that the future is bright, you don't have any anxiety. It's all about creating a spiritual experience. When you begin to allow the second person to be born all of those things begin to happen naturally because they are all in us.

Your body was designed for pleasure – and now some of the religious people will go fucking bananas when you say that! But you were given taste buds to taste wonderful food, you were given eyes to see beautiful sights, you were given ears to hear beautiful sounds such as birdsong and music, touch to feel warm water on your body or a waterfall or a caress, a sense of smell to smell such as flowers, and your sex organs to feel pleasure too. These are all wonderful things, you are designed for pleasure!

Many religions deny this fact about our bodies, leading to many complexes based on the guilt concerning our natural desires. When I worked in Ireland the amount of sexual abuse I encountered was huge and I believe that sexual repression imposed by the state and church through guilt, condemnation and the degradation of men and women led to repression of a powerful human need, twisting it into many types of abusive behaviour.

Conversely, allowing our desires to control our lives denies the spirit – as the disease of selfishness robs us of joy, drowning us in a pool of our own greed, lust and avarice.

Our sex life is like anything else: if we use it selfishly we will never know its true ecstasy.

D: So alcohol affects our spirit?

W: Drinking alcohol fuels the ego. You know, when I took a couple of drinks I thought everybody thought I was fucking great. When I left the pub I'd be walking home and thinking they're all still there saying what a guy that Wayne is... when they were probably saying I'm glad that bastard has gone!

So when alcohol acts like this on someone, it's boosting ego. What it's doing is changing the opinion you have of yourself and everyone else. But the next day I always felt so bad that I'd go from thinking everybody thought I was great to feeling totally ashamed and that everybody thought I was really bad. So it was constant mood swings.

That's the chemical nature of it and that's why people seek it. People want a boost, they want to feel good, they want to relax or in many cases they want freedom from fear, such as because they're too afraid to socialise without it.

D: So addicts need this or alcoholics need this, a search for God as Jung described it? Is it that they sense there's something missing more than other people, they feel the spiritual emptiness more starkly?

W: I don't know if the alcoholic can be able to quite put it in those terms when they're drinking, but they know that there is something missing, that something is wrong. One of the reasons the 12 Steps work for alcoholics who work them thoroughly and honestly is because they are spiritual-based creatures and they are looking for that sort of answer. That obviously doesn't suit everyone: some people kill themselves rather than do the 12-Step programme.

D: Aren't we all spiritual-based creatures? Isn't this the human condition?

W: Our spirit guides us through this world, and it tells us if we are happy or sad. When it's sad it puts us on the search for happiness... We seek to feel better from changing the channel on the TV, to playing sport, shopping, holidays, a partner, food, alcohol, drugs – increase the list yourself.

We need to feed our spirit, but most of us don't even realise it's our spirit that's hungry.

I've seen hundreds of people over a few decades and in fact I think everyone needs a programme exactly like the 12 Steps as it gives the spiritual growth that everyone needs for happiness and peace in their lives. It's what everyone needs, but few ever find. Anxiety is the motivating disturbance that pushes us to spiritual fulfilment... but so many refuse the path.

Alcoholics who do the 12 Steps usually feel very fortunate, and you hear many say they are "grateful recovering alcoholics", because the only way they were ever likely to find a solution was because they were in deep trouble, terrified and mentally bankrupt to such an extent they were ready to let go of their old ideas. They found AA and asked for help.

One of the things about alcoholics is that they are very sensitive people. Anxious people are very sensitive too. Sensitivity is very important spirituality, to be sensitive in your mind to the touch of God, to what the world is about, thinking about the bigger picture.

I was always thinking about what's the meaning of life and death and why we are here and all that sort of stuff. Many anxious people are searching for meaning.

But it's only when we've had enough pain that we let go of our own prejudices that we find the road to meaning, fulfilment and purpose.

"I'm here in here..."

W: Working with people is a very serious business, a great privilege and responsibility. I only use what works, what I know works. People have to be given the best.

I have to know when a client walks out the door that I have given them absolutely everything – their lives, the course of their lives and often the lives of their family members depends upon it.

Through my interaction with other professionals in various settings I saw that everything I had learned professionally was from my observation, and though hugely beneficial didn't have the life-changing and sustaining power that I had found in my own recovery.

So I realised I needed to blend a 12-Step programme that had transformed my life with my professional training. I have been applying this process to clients who are open to it for more than two decades. The clients who accepted this route had far better rates of recovery and quality of recovery than those who didn't.

That's not to say those who didn't accept the 12-Step programme didn't change or work hard, it's simply that they didn't develop the deep-down grounding, enthusiasm and sustainability that the 12 Steps give. A big plus with the 12-Step programme is that it gives clients a framework to live by when they finish therapy that's not usually found elsewhere.

I've adapted the programme to help clients with such as chronic anxiety, depression, OCD, schizophrenia, bipolar – all with remarkable success. Even the result it had on people with psoriasis amazed me... I had no idea how profound the connection was between anger and the skin disorder because in many cases we were walking through virgin territory together.

A young lady in her mid-20s from England attended me with chronic anxiety. It had got to the stage she could no longer continue her studies at university and she had left. She was now out of work, anxious and living back with her mother. Her self-esteem due to her perception of herself as a total failure was on the floor and this was exacerbating her already chronic anxiety.

She was very nice, very polite; her persona, her false self was in full flow: despite her anxiety everything was wonderful... When she talked she reminded me of an English country vicar.

She was covered from head to toe with psoriasis, for which she had been receiving medical treatment including hospitalisation for the past eight years.

We went through a 12-Step programme and she talked about and allowed herself to experience her deep-seated resentful anger towards her particularly violent alcoholic father whom she lived with into adulthood. Her psoriasis cleared up – totally.

It was also the beginning of the end of her anxiety. She was able to resume her studies and go on to a successful career.

Her demeanour was polite and gentle, hiding all her pain, hiding the little girl deep inside – but the psoriasis was a symbol of the self, while she talked like an English country vicar her psoriasis was screaming: "I'M HERE IN

HERE AND YOU WILL FUCKING SEE ME BECAUSE I AM FUCKING FURIOUS!!!!!"

Of all the therapies there are, none can claim the success of the 12-Step programme: millions of people are walking around with changed lives because of it. No other area of counselling, psychiatry or psychotherapy can claim anywhere near the same level of success.

How do we stay human in a technological world?

D: In general, anxiety levels seem to be increasing. What about social media such as Twitter, Instagram or Facebook causing it? I've read of this happening to lots of people.

W: Because people want to get it right. It goes back to the first commandment again: "Thou shalt be right."

D: Something that I always try to remember on that is what author and philosopher Wayne Dyer, a real favourite helper of mine over the years, a life-saver at times, said: Most arguments are basically one person demanding to the other – and vice versa – "Why can't you be more like me…?"

W: Of course.

D: Good to know. Although of course we do also have that inside knowing of what's morally right and wrong. Some people seem better than others at ignoring it though, or so it seems, but I'm sure it eats them up.

W: But arguing is often childish too – because you get a child who goes to school when they are six and the child puts their hand up and tells the teacher she's doing something wrong because the child's mother doesn't do it that way… Unfortunately a lot of adults do the same. They don't realise it, but they are still unquestioningly trying to do things the way their parents did.

D: Or I've seen something like that in national newspaper offices when a few journalists are arguing about the certain way to write something and it often comes down to what they were taught at school all those years previously. Now that is the whole truth and any other way is wrong and a lie! These debates over such as the use of a comma, have become quite heated.

W: I've seen it in relationships. The man is judging his wife by how his mother would do things. And getting quite angry because she's not washing the pots immediately after the dinner or she doesn't look after the children this way or she doesn't go out to work or she does go out to work or whatever... Then I've seen it the other way when the woman could be looking at the guy and thinking that he's not doing it like they did in my family or he's not doing that like my father did it.

D: A lot of people will relate to that.

W: So with social media, people are going out there, they're putting themselves at the mercy of other people's comments. Basically they want people to approve of them and like what they share, so it creates tension, anxiety and adrenaline. That's what they're looking for, that's their escape.

D: Is that addictive then?

W: Anytime you get adrenaline it can be addictive. People can even get addicted to panic attacks.

D: Because their adrenaline is flying?

W: We bring it on ourselves – you can sit in a chair and give yourself a panic attack or an adrenaline high. So they come from our thinking. I'm not saying that people necessarily do it as a choice, but they do create it. We create it by our own thinking.

D: So to avoid a panic attack we need to learn to think differently?

W: To avoid a panic attack you have to change. It's not something you can just snap your fingers and do as it's a progressive thing. You have to practise being different and somebody has to teach you and show you how to be different and that comes from within.

D: And what would that be − to trust in the world, the universe, a higher power?

W: And yourself.

D: And yourself?

W: You need to find a higher power to be able to trust that you're being looked after.

D: That you're not going to get run over on the way to the shop?

W: It's when you don't care whether you get run over or not, that you'll be better. Obviously you do care, but − the last time I had a panic attack I just said to it: "I don't care if you kill me, I'm not running." That's what I said and it never happened after that.

D: Also, your advice to me was very good when I wrote you the very long WhatsApp message full of my worries and woes when you were in South Africa. It would've taken ten minutes to read it! After ten minutes you replied, saying simply: "Don't worry. Relax."

I was angry at first as I thought you were not taking all these massive worries I had at all seriously! But about an hour later your three words started to float to the top of my thinking, dissolving all my worries into a nothingness, back to the nowhere wherever from which they came.

I have come to realise it was some of the best advice I've ever been given. It goes along again in trusting that we're here for a reason, with good plans for us, that we're being looked after, loved and approved of, and so we shouldn't worry and we can relax.

W: Anxiety is created by our thinking. You're not going to feel anything until you can think: "But that's very unlikely or impossible." The problem is we don't catch all thoughts quick enough, so we just catch the feelings and then we get the feeling and we go: "Oh my God, why am I feeling this?" and that increases the thought pattern and that makes the feeling worse. As a man or woman thinks so they will be.

It's all about how you think. Your mind is a fantastic creating machine, your imagination creates your world. If your imagination is out of control you'll scare yourself to death.

Then when somebody comes up to you, especially in a spiritual context, and they say: well, you've got to look at reality, you've got to keep it real, we all need to keep our feet on the ground – what they're really saying to you is: don't you dare believe the impossible. If you believe in reality then you will only ever believe in what you can see and what you can choose. But what you want to achieve is something you have to imagine. Everybody who has achieved something had to imagine it to see it.

D: How do we stop the bad things coming in our head and crushing us to the point where we get a panic attack and don't want to go out the front door, and even when we stay inside we get worried that the ceiling is going to collapse?

W: The first thing is that you have to trust you're being looked after.

D: By?

W: By whatever you deem will look after you. For most people when they're having panic attacks they are having an experience of their child identity.

D: Really?

W: A lot of the time it's because you realise you're a child in an adult's body and you're getting overwhelmed because you're in an adult situation and you just can't handle it.

D: Like in a supermarket and shopping centres, where a lot of people seem to have panic attacks.

W: Yes, but anywhere really. Just imagine if you're a little kid and you go running off from your parents and then you can't find them again, you can't see anybody... Then you're screaming and shouting "Where's my dad?". It's the same thing. A panic attack.

So you need to say to yourself: "I'm having an attack of my child identity, I'm feeling overwhelmed." Feeling overwhelmed is a huge psychological condition.

Somewhere along the line the person has stopped themselves from growing, so that emotionally they're not growing and that could be through trauma or addiction or whatever it may be. It can be dealt with over time by dealing with those issues.

Lack always leaves us wanting

D: I found it very significant when I discovered that the word "want" derives from an Old Norse word meaning "lacking". Are adverts designed to make us feel like we're lacking something?

W: Every advert in the world uses the idea of lacking. In any society on the planet if you look at the idea of nirvana or Valhalla or Shangri-La, every society has this idea of paradise. And what adverts do is they are selling it to you, that if you buy this you will never see a sad day again… if you get our mortgage your life is sorted… if you smell like this every woman in town will want to have sex with you, all that sort of stuff.

So every advert keys into what you haven't got and that your life will be better if you have it, that it's going to be an improvement in your life. So yes, adverts focus on the lack in your life: the lack we feel in ourselves – and remember life is about hunger. We are always hungry for something, we are looking to be filled and will be anxious until we find it.

D: And if you allow that in, you're going to focus on it.

W: But we do allow it in, nobody's not going to allow it. But it's understanding spiritual laws and the spiritual law says you must not compare yourself to somebody else.

D: And having gratitude for what you have got.

W: Along with gratitude, which is the essential ingredient. Then we have a desire to change. But we need persistence because if you haven't got any persistence, the desire won't get you anywhere.

D: Persistence to change?

W: To get out of the shit you're in, you need to have desire. You know, if you want to be a professional footballer and you went to City or Arsenal or some team like that, the first thing they look at is how fast your feet are, and the second thing they look for is desire. Because no matter how fast your feet are if you have no desire you will never be a professional footballer.

I always look at people when helping them get sober and ask if they have that desire. My greatest desire was I wanted to get well, I wanted to be able to live without fear, without panic, without depression, without drink or drugs. I had an incredible desire and I was very persistent in doing what I needed to do.

But I had to reach that point of personal bankruptcy before I could change.

That's why still today I regularly go to places where I can help people with a desire to stop drinking and do my 30 minutes of prayer and meditation every morning – because that doesn't change, that's how I live. You have to live like that, there doesn't come a time when you pass the test. You just get the next one.

My anxiety recovery means I have to work at my life. I can't rest on my laurels otherwise I will go backwards and the default settings of the blueprint will return. So paradoxically this gives me the best life possible, progressing on a daily basis.

D: The test, or spiritual set-up as you also call it, is to help us grow – or at least to give us the opportunity to –

and by growing we move away from the pain that we can, and do, often give ourselves as human beings, or that's given to us to illuminate that we're going the wrong way.

For instance, temptation to cheat on a partner; and is this because someone has excessive lust, the capacity to be dishonest and is self-centred? Or someone who finds themselves always infuriated by the supermarket queue – is this a test of impatience, intolerance and self-centredness, self-pity and also pride? Pride being in this case, how dare they do this to the great me! Although pride can also be in the form of: what would people think if they knew I'd done or said or thought this?

W: Life is always about maintenance. You can buy a new villa and it's absolutely beautiful – but if you don't look after it... soon it's going to be a dirty mess with a stagnant swimming pool. I mean, it's great you get the swimming pool, but then you realise you need to clean it every day.

D: And a lot of us don't do that with ourselves.

W: No, many people are extremely sloppy with their lives. It's like a lot of people have routines and that's why so many people are pleased when Christmas is over, so they can get back to their routine. Because when we lose our discipline we don't feel good.

D: Does mental well-being count as much as physical well-being, indeed don't they go together?

W: Yes, they go together. A majority of doctors will tell you that many physical illnesses that people get have come from their thinking. It's like if you look at stomach problems, it's often because someone's angry inside.

D: But what about the thing that people always say: what about a child with cancer then?

W: We've got to think about genetics, and epigenetics is looking at how things are passed from one generation to the next. Experts are saying now that there are parts of the cell that will actually rewrite your DNA in your response to life. So how the generations lived before us is going to condition the health and well-being of the children we have.

D: So something hereditary, an illness, a bad heart for example, could be caused by your great great great grandfather because he was angry all the time?

W: Yes, their interaction with the environment, their DNA. Cells do two things – they protect or they grow, and so if your cells are constantly switched on to protect all the time because you're tense or anxious, then your cells are not growing, they are not regenerating as they should. Cell structure is so complex – they're all like little humans, like little beings on their own. They have a respiratory system and digestive system and defecation system and they are so complex – and there's a trillion of them making you up.

D: So if enough of them are affected badly it's going to cause an effect?

W: If you look at what scientists are doing for a cure for cancer now, they take cells out of the body, increase their ability to fight the cancer cells, then put them into a virus. Next they inject them into the cancer cells as the virus helps to penetrate the cancer cells and the treatment they gave the body's cells helps to kill the cancer cells. I'm not a scientist, I'm just trying to explain the basis of this.

So how we deal with our cells is hugely important. That's why stem cells work: they become whatever culture you put them in, which totally blew the whole idea of genetics.

D: Is this anything to do with it all? In the Bible it says: "I lay the sins of the parents upon their children; the entire family is affected − even children in the third and fourth generations of those who reject me."

I mean, even for someone who doesn't think much of the Bible, isn't it simply saying here that if you have a lack of love in your heart and soul, that you will pass that on and teach it to your children, and that it can take generations − surely even more than three or four, let's go right back to humankind's cave-dwelling days − for the cycle to break.

To my mind, it is only going to get broken when someone comes along who probably suffers so much pain, anguish and trouble in their life that they are actually given that gift of desperation to make a change, to be able to realise that what they know isn't the best way of living, in fact that it's a disastrous way of living and they are just making the same mistakes as their parents and grandparents. I mean, how often do you hear about someone who marries the carbon copy of one of their parents, even when that parent was an abusive drunk.

So anyway, once that person is given the humiliation that brings on enough humility for them to say they have got it wrong, that they need help, then they are able to start work on ripping up that family blueprint that's been passed down for generations on how to think, behave and react. As they start to rip that one up and shred it, they can start to gain and then have a new blueprint for life.

The hugely important thing here is then that can help their children and go on for generations. A loving blueprint will work for as long as a blueprint of fear and anger. This is true for mental, emotional, spiritual and physical aspects. What do you think?

W: One person who turns their own personal trauma from a liability to an asset, from a curse to a blessing, will affect positively the generations that come after them, provided the nurture as well as nature sides are dealt with too.

Why we're still at war

D: It seems that many mental health problems are rising and so shouldn't we as societies urgently look at what could be the cause of this increase?

W: Years ago mental health was hidden. For example, we see lots of programmes about soldiers coming back from Vietnam with tremendous problems and how Vietnam was horrific. But when these soldiers went to Vietnam, when they'd been fighting for a few days, they'd go back to the barracks and they had everything they needed: doctors, painkillers, morphine.

I'm not minimising it, it was horrific. But what happened to all those people that were in the trenches for years with not even painkillers for their wounds in the First World War, then Second World War? These are the people that brought a lot of us up, or brought up our parents or grandparents, the survivors of this. They passed down the blueprint, and that contained trauma. Nobody got any help, nobody got any counselling – and yet don't think for one minute there weren't any mental problems. Indeed there were.

D: I've often thought about this as well. The generation of my parents weren't actively fighting in the Second World War, but their parents were and it certainly had a huge impact: a lot of them lost a parent, or their dads were away for five or six years and even when they returned of course many were not in a fit state mentally, emotionally or physically... So my generation was also brought up by people who had been traumatised as children by the Second World War.

W: Of course they were affected by it. My parents were in Manchester when they were children. My two grandfathers fought in the First World War in the trenches. One saw his brother killed next to him. My grandmother's brother was killed when he was 19, her father died of tuberculosis when he was 40. That was a very common killer, and she had a brother who died when he was five as infant mortality rates were very high.

All of these things affected everybody. My mother's eldest brother was in a German prisoner of war camp for five years, another of her brothers was at Dunkirk. Her eldest brother's best mate was in a Japanese prisoner of war camp and took his life when he came home because he could not live with it. At one stage my grandmother had two sons missing in action, believed killed. As a young girl my mother witnessed my grandmother collapsing when she received the telegram. Fortunately both survived.

More soldiers have ended their lives who fought in the Falklands War than actually died in it... Approximately 7,000 American soldiers have died in the Iraq and Afghanistan wars up till now. Yet according to a report published by the US Department of Veterans Affairs that analysed 55 million veterans' records from 1979 to 2014, 20 veterans died by suicide each day – that's 7,300 every year. Since the start of the Iraq War in 2003, up to date that works out at more than 100,000 soldiers and former soldiers ending their lives...

So we've always had huge mental health problems, but they were hidden because there was so much shame about it. In Britain we had huge psychiatric hospitals all over the country that were closed in the 1980s, and people were given huge amounts of tablets instead, so we had what we called "care in the community". Chemicals are the new straitjackets.

Of course, if someone's taking tablets they need to seek professional advice to lower their dose or come off them. No one should go cold turkey from drugs.

D: So a lot of those people that it was recognised had a mental health problem were basically locked up, and then in the 1980s they were put out on to the streets?

W: They didn't just lock up people with mental health problems either. When my mother was a social worker I used to go with her sometimes to a psychiatric hospital near Blackburn in Lancashire, England. We used to visit a guy who'd been in there since he was 12. He was put in because he stole sweets from the cinema and he had what we call today learning difficulties. But when I met him he was in his 60s and he'd never been out since he was 12 – there were a lot of people like that put in psychiatric hospitals.

We could say we have different types of mental health problems today. But what I'm saying is that by giving you the examples of the two world wars that we certainly have had post-traumatic stress disorder (PTSD) for years now, and we certainly have had people who suffered from depression. But a lot of it was hidden and a lot of that was, and still is, about shame. Remember, it used to be that you went to jail if you tried to take your life and survived.

D: Thinking back to the world wars, obviously there was lots of extreme anxiety – among the people going to fight in the war, but also with such as children who had fathers fighting in the war because not only were they apart from their dads – but also they probably knew of a lot of other children who had never seen their dad again after he left for the frontline.

W: But remember that communities were far stronger then. People helped each other more. If somebody was sick next door, then people made some soup and dinners for them, and looked after them. Community strength was a lot stronger. Much of that has slipped away. In Britain it was in the 1980s when the government shut down industries where people used to work and socialise together.

D: That is different from country to country. For instance, in such as Spain it seems family is still more together and there's more community, and consequently people seem happier and less stressed. I know lots of people say it's just the sunny weather – but I've seen it is like this even in the north of Spain, known as España Verde or Green Spain because it rains so much there. So I can see how the attitude of a government and the actions it takes can greatly affect a nation.

W: When people were poor in Britain they all lived in the same area. My mother didn't see a cow until she was 30! When the poor people in our society were all together that's all they knew as they didn't see middle-class people, they had no television, so they didn't know how everybody else was living. People really didn't travel anywhere near as much and many never left their communities.

D: And that knowledge of others has increased so much now because even within an area where people don't have much money there will be television showing how others live.

W: Wherever you are in the world today, even if you're in some remote village there's probably one TV somewhere that everybody can watch...

D: You can see what some people have got in terms of material things.

W: That's why you get people moving more, with such as migrants from parts of Africa coming to Europe, because they can see there's a world that looks better somewhere else, one they didn't know existed before.

That's why when everyone in the Western world wakes up in the morning a part of their gratitude needs to be "thank God I live in a society where there are doctors and there's an ambulance that will come if needed and there's a dental service for if my children or I have a toothache". So many places in the world still don't have that and people die of very minor diseases because they can't find or afford to go to a doctor.

Why we're made to feel pain

D: There are treatment centres that treat people with gaming addiction. Now social media addiction too because people go on, for example, Facebook or Twitter all the time. They get totally addicted. Some people are aware of this and are talking about having or needing a "digital detox".

W: You're only going to digitally detox because you know that it's driving you insane. It's like somebody making a decision to give up drinking for a month – nobody really decides to give up drinking for a month unless they've got a problem of some description, or else why would you?

Anything that can change the way you feel, anything like that has got the power to get you addicted. You could get addicted to green tea if a part of your head keeps saying this is making your life better, if it changes something.

D: And such as cleaning, and that's why some obsessively clean, often connected to people with OCD (Obsessive Compulsive Disorder)?

W: People can compulsively clean, tidy, rearrange their bodies, homes, environment in a desperate attempt to clean up their internal problems. They are trying to manage the chaos within by imposing order on their outside world.

In the 12 Steps, Step 4 is called the housecleaning step. It says: "Made a searching and fearless moral inventory of ourselves." People get rid of their shit.

People don't realise that inside ourselves, if we don't clear stuff out from there, it's as if you've not been to the toilet for the past 50 years… That would be pretty messy wouldn't it?

D: For sure!

W: But what if you've not been to the emotional lavatory for 50 years, the brain-cleaning process or the processing of the situations in life because all those things – everything that we process – develops us, that's how we mature.

And the funny thing is with people, just while we are on the toilet analogies, is that you know when you go to the toilet your own waste products usually don't bother you, but you go after somebody else and it fucking stinks! That's how we are, our own defects of character don't usually bother us, but other people's bother the fuck out of us!

D: That's true, although your own defects can bother you when you have an awareness. Such as I know I can get into a place of self-pity and it really bores me these days, and so I can get myself out of it quickly enough. However, in the past I didn't know of the tools to do that and it was kind of just what I knew to do, the poor me, poor me, pour me another drink – so much my middle name should have been Self-pity!

W: Other people's defects get on your nerves a lot more than your own though.

D: I can see that. I've heard some people describe what the 12-Step groups describe as "defects of character" – as our "sins". These are our natural instincts for survival blown up way beyond anywhere as they were intended or are needed for our survival.

So such as excessive pride that causes the person to punch another for a minor comment; extreme lust that causes the marriage break-up; total gluttony that makes the person unhealthy; uncurbed greed that makes the businessman worship the love of money so much he forgets about his love for his children; envy that makes us feel furious as well as full of self-pity; intolerance that makes someone hate another person before they've even seen them just because of that person's skin colour or the land they were born in or their religion.

So by defects we are talking about what the 12-Step programme describes perfectly in its Step 4 explanation from the book Twelve Steps And Twelve Traditions, which is great reading for anyone: Creation gave us instincts for a purpose. Without them we wouldn't be complete human beings... Yet these instincts, so necessary for our existence, often far exceed their proper functions. Powerfully, blindly, many times subtly, they drive us, dominate us, and insist upon ruling our lives...

So, it's that we all have a certain amount of tolerance and also intolerance, as a natural protective mechanism to, for instance, cause us to be able to ask the person in our face to politely get out of it. But then excessive intolerance leads to racism, you know prejudice, pre-judging someone simply because they look different to the intolerant person. Connected to this is excessive pride, wrath and greed too.

These are what the deadly sins are, and they are called deadly because they are deadly – to the individual, and often to those around that person as well.

It's the things that stop us achieving our full potential, the natural human traits gone so extreme that they stop us from getting any sort of spiritual connection. I used to think the seven deadly sins were merely a list of the most fun and best things in life and it was that religion wanted to stop me enjoying my life! But I now know they are a list of those things that mess me up if I have too much of them.

W: Christianity institutionalised guilt. But what sin really means is to "miss the mark, to go the wrong way". It means to think you know where you are going when you actually don't. To live your own way unaware of the laws of your very being.

It's like when I was sober in my early days and I lost those crazy dreams of having a yacht full of women in the South of France, and realised that I was happy washing up in my small house in Manchester with my young children around. It was then that I suddenly realised I hadn't ever known what was good for me. I thought I did, but I actually didn't because I was listening to my ego, and my ego tells me lies because it definitely doesn't know what's good for me.

My ego always wants instant gratification, it wanted to feel good all the time. The ego is about maintaining the integrity of false self.

As my drinking descended into ever-increasing displeasure for an ever-increasing craving, my self-esteem hit rock bottom. I felt like shit, but the instant fix was another drink – and bingo! I would feel like I was back on top again.

D: But I've realised that I don't want to carry these excesses, these defects of character. They get on my nerves and I wish I didn't have them. They block me. As the 12-Step group literature puts it, again perfectly, they "block the sunlight of the spirit".

W: That's Step 6 of the 12 Steps too: "Were entirely ready to have God remove all these defects of character." Then if your defects of character didn't get on your nerves you'd never do Step 7, which is: "Humbly asked Him to remove our shortcomings." You know, if your drinking didn't hurt you you'd never stop. So we change because of pain. Then pain is a good thing. Pain is the touchstone to all growth.

D: You were saying earlier that we're made for pleasure, but we're also made to feel pain.

W: Because that's what guides us. Pain is when we can't see the path, so when we start doing things that cause disturbance, it's the pain that pushes you back on to the path. Pain is guiding you back on the track.

D: Or trying to guide? Because a lot of people don't change directions, they just live in the pain, keep struggling along the painful route.

W: What happens is we have a thing called temptation, and that word comes from Latin meaning "test". That's what the story of Odysseus is about when on his return from Troy he sails past the Sirens, and the Sirens are the women on the rocks who sing their song. Sailors want to meet them because the song is so beautiful, but they are being lured on to the rocks to their deaths.

So Odysseus wants to hear the song so much that he gets all his men to block up their ears with wax. Then he orders them to strap him to the mast and then they're all in the ship and they can't hear anything, but he can and even though he's strapped to the mast he's screaming at his men, screaming at them to release him because he wants to go to these women – even though he knows that will kill him, that he knows the whole idea of the song is to bring him to his own destruction.

You know, that's just the wrong relationship – and that's the drink, that's the drug, that's the big mortgage, that's the new job – you know, all of these things. For a man to be unfaithful to his wife he's not going to do it with some 80-year-old woman... but if Miss World turns up and he even knows she may destroy his family and his relationship and everything he has, he still might not get past her. Even though it will destroy everything. That's temptation, so that is a reality of existence.

D: So why do we have temptation?

W: It's part of the spiritual set-up. If you look at this life and you ask why we are here, what is this life about, think of life as a game show, that you're down here, you're in this game show, and here are the rules: you've got to get from being born to dying without destroying your own soul... If you get to the end of your life and you've developed your soul you'll continue to exist; but if you don't, then you just disappear. Temptation is all the problems and all the things that will come against you, that will make you or destroy you.

You've heard that what doesn't kill you makes you stronger, which is true – but what I'm saying is we come to a point when we see we can't resist temptation as much as we want to... It's more powerful than us – sex, food, money, drink, drugs, the power of anxiety, the power of our ability to generate fear...

All these issues bring you to a point where you are humbled enough to know you need help, that you can't resist them. You need a higher power. Unfortunately at this point some see death as a higher power.

D: But if you handle them okay, you're growing?

W: Well, none of us are going to handle them right, none of us – and that's why we need a higher power. We cannot resist temptation, there's no human being on this planet that's going to completely resist temptation. For instance, you have all these priests who have decided to be celibate, but look how many of them are drunks or gamblers.

D: Isn't Christian Lent and Islamic Ramadan partly ways to show that a person has good control over temptation?

W: I think what they're doing is they're going through a time of penance and trying to get closer to God, which is fine... but the problem is with a lot of religious festivals the people who do them are not spiritual, they're not living the rest of their lives in harmony with God. It's like a lot of people go to church on a Sunday and come out and then immediately tell lies or go to hassle their neighbour for the money they owe them. We have to learn that life is about love.

D: Or the politicians who go to church on a Sunday, then go and lie and declare a war on Monday that causes so much pain and suffering.

On the subject of pain, why do some people self-harm?

W: The first thing with self-harm is the physical pain becomes comforting because it substitutes for the emotional pain. It's also a plea for help, a way of expressing and demonstrating emotion, but mainly it's signalling the person's inner rage.

Love is everything

W: We have to learn that life is about love, then we have to learn what love is because most people have no idea what is love.

D: What is love?

W: Read Chapter 13 in Corinthians in the Bible. It's probably the best definition of love I've ever read. "Love is patient, love is kind. It does not envy, it does not boast, it is not proud. It does not dishonour others, it is not self-seeking, it is not easily angered, it keeps no record of wrongs. Love does not delight in evil but rejoices with the truth. It always protects, always trusts, always hopes, always perseveres. Love never fails."

I think when I first learned about love was when I had a child. Up until that time I thought I knew about love and the philosophy of love. And basically I knew about Hollywood romance or biology, but when I had a child for the first time I began to understand the whole idea of love.

D: Can it be that you know when you have a child that without a doubt you would jump in front of a bus to save them from breaking a fingernail – so you would give yourself for someone else, completely and unconditionally?

W: It's like when you get up in the middle of the night to go and help a child with a leg ache or a bad dream or an earache and every part of you just wants to scream to them to go back to sleep, but you don't do it. Instead you smile and you're as kind as you can be because you love them. Not because it's a feeling.

D: Love is an action.

W: So many people talk about feelings. They say: well, I can't do that because I don't feel it. It's never about how we feel, it's about our intention, it's about motives. If I go to do something and I don't feel like doing it, but I do it because it's the right thing to do at that moment, then I am going against my own desires, for another, I'm seeking to be selfless.

Or I tell somebody I love them when I don't feel like saying it, but they need to hear it. Then I'm forgetting about me. And that's the most important thing. I think any parent has to make a decision when they have a child to give up their life. What happens then is they find another life with the child.

For me, the years I brought my five kids up, although they were tiring and they could be hard at times, those years were the best years I ever had. They were a load of fun because I wanted to have fun with my kids. But a lot of parents don't have that.

Anyone like you who still has young children really has to make the most of every second. Where my children grew up in Ireland we were lucky enough to have a garden large enough to have a small football pitch on. Almost every day there'd be me and all five of my children having a kick about. It was always such immense fun.

As they grew up, we carried on playing, but then there were five of us as the oldest of my children left home, then there were four…

One evening I went out there and it was just me and a football and that empty pitch.

So, just whatever you do, make the most of every second with your children.

D: It's exactly what we did a few years ago, when our children were aged just three and four. We kept having all these very lovely but wistful elderly people telling us to make the most of them, that they grow up so quickly. We'd lost a couple of people we loved unexpectedly. One of our boys had been in intensive care a week after they had been born for a week, and with the other my wife had complications a week after the birth and was rushed to hospital by ambulance for emergency treatment. Life had been put starkly into perspective...

So we sold our house to buy a motorhome and travelled 40,000 miles for a couple of years round 12 countries in Europe plus Morocco. It was unbelievable and we didn't miss one single thing that we'd left behind in storage.

M Scott Peck wrote a fantastic definition of love in The Road Less Traveled: "I define love thus: the will to extend one's self for the purpose of nurturing one's own or another's spiritual growth." Then Matt Haig wrote a chapter in his bestseller Notes On A Nervous Planet simply titled Love and the one sentence of that whole chapter is the axiomatic: "Only love will save us."

W: As you know, not only the love of others but the love of ourselves can be difficult. With so many of my clients over the years I've said to them, sit in a chair for five minutes and ask yourself how you feel, don't move, just sit in the chair. I say to them, ask how does my stomach feel right now, what are my legs feeling – are they heavy or light, is my chest heavy or light, how does my stomach feel, how are my arms?

That sort of attention is practice. Becoming more aware of the shape of you and the outline of your body, then when you're brushing your teeth just be aware.

The whole idea of being aware of yourself is that you are giving yourself time, you are listening to what your body has to say. You cannot love anything if you don't give it your attention.

Children seek attention because they need it like they need food and drink. As a child you see these big tall strong people who can do everything that you can't, such as feed yourself or dress yourself and all this sort of stuff, and if they tell you you're wonderful but not just tell you you're wonderful, if they then act out that you're wonderful by spending time with you and doing things with you, then your self-esteem and your value, your perception of who you are, which is everything, will grow positively.

Then when your self-esteem grows your confidence will grow. If your confidence grows you can give birth to the plan of your life. There's a plan inside you, it's a desire. You may want to write, to do work in health, to be a fantastic parent, whatever it may be. But if you haven't got the confidence to go and be a writer or a doctor or a great parent, then you are going to have frustrations and you are going to develop complexes. Then these things are going to get twisted and perverted together and your life is likely going to be a painful mess.

So when we talk about love, you then as an adult – if you didn't get good parenting or emotional parenting as a child – you then have to learn how to become a parent to yourself, how to give yourself love. It demands something from you.

D: Confidence derives from the words "having full trust". So if you're saying a child grows up into an adult and they can't trust themselves, then this is when it's extremely hard work being an adult.

And with love it's no good just thinking it or saying it. We have to show it. So the parent that says to their child "I love you darling" and buys them lots of gifts at the weekend because they don't see them in the week and don't have any time to listen to them, that's not love.

W: No, and they are teaching them to solve their problems with pleasure. So that when you get older every time you've got a problem… As I did when I was a teenager – I would go out and buy myself a new album and that would take my mind off everything for a short while. Then I discovered drink, which not only took my mind off things, it took my mind.

D: And the modern world is making this happen – more and more people are getting sucked into it.

W: Of course. But it's a natural thing for people to want to do – you know, we all like to have a new house or buy a new sofa or buy a new car or whatever. That's totally natural. But proportionately more rich people kill themselves than poor people. The more we have time just to think about our own selfish desires, the more it damages us.

D: Also it seems to me that a lot of people are putting their material aims above spending time with their children. So it's nice to buy a bigger house or new car – but that's at the expense of not spending time with their children.

W: But not everybody wants children, not everybody values children in the same way. I've talked to many people who went to boarding school who hated it, who cried when they were there and felt rejected from their own home – and then they send their kids to boarding school because it was in their blueprint. And their children then have the same terrible experience.

D: Then there are some people who have children just because it seems to be the done thing, that everyone else is having two children, especially maybe this is true for the older generation.

W: When I worked in Ireland a lot of the farmers had children mostly to run the farm. They actually used the same word for their children as their animals, that they would "rear" children. I'd never heard of anyone "rearing" kids before, that word only usually applied to animals. The children would go to school and then work on the farm.

I spoke with one guy who came to me because he was depressed in his 50s. He had three children and he said at the end of the time that he was coming to see me that he'd learned that you're supposed to speak to your children. He never spoke to his children – he would take them to school, he'd get their clothes ready, he'd make their lunches, but he never spoke with them because he was one of 14 and nobody had spoken to him. One of his brothers didn't even speak until he was aged 10, yet nobody bothered and this guy had just thought it was amusing.

D: That's obviously going to have a terrible effect on the children.

W: Of course, because that's what they learn. It's like a lot of people come to me that are depressed, and a lot of them can be very quiet and they grew up in homes where they were constantly told to be quiet and their parents were quiet too. That's not always why people are depressed obviously, but I saw more than a few people like that.

Depression is always about depressing something down. But what are you depressing, what are you pushing down? Depression is the pushing down of the self. If you keep pushing yourself down and down and down, then it will really start to really hurt you.

D: That's because you don't like yourself or something about yourself?

W: That's because you are blocking it, you are refusing to grow.

D: To let the real self out?

W: Alcoholism is the same, an attempt to stop growing, to not change.

D: To push it down, with a drink, to drown it?

W: To stop change. Anxiety is the same: you cannot grow emotionally and therefore mature in a continuously anxious state – if we get in the way of our natural growth we will create pain... panic, fear, anxiety, depression.

D: I was thinking about the Corinthians Chapter 13 "Love is patient, love is kind" words and how I've lost count of the number of weddings I've heard it read aloud at... and yet divorces are booming.

W: Because many people don't understand it. They cannot put it into practice because of the blueprint in their own lives. Until we understand the blueprint that we get in the first seven years of our life, it's difficult.

D: This is the blueprint of how to live life that we're handed by our parents or caregivers?

W: If you think of your brain as the hard drive, then the software is put on in the first seven years. Then when you get to around seven or eight years of age the ego is developed enough to challenge or not believe some of the stuff you are told. But before that, whatever your parents say you will believe. The power of their example is life-changing.

It's what you're taught, what you see, what you believe and your own personality. So you get a belief system of what you believe about yourself and what you believe about the world, and that will act itself out. People think they are making decisions – but that blueprint will tell you what to do, how much money you can have, who you can marry, where you can go. For most people it will tell them for the rest of their life.

D: So if you have a parent that criticises you a lot and doesn't praise you, you're going to go out into the world feeling like you're worthless.

W: That's how you'll treat yourself. So even if you get the top job and you get loads of money it still won't make any difference. I had a lady came to me one time and she had every qualification I'd ever heard of, twice! And she was still looking for more. Because it was never enough as her parents never acknowledged her. She was still trying to prove she was of value, but it never worked. Her anxiety manifested in an eating disorder, chronic self-doubt, and depression.

D: What about indecisive people? Is this often because they were criticised as children so much and hardly ever asked to make or be part of a decision – and if, as a child, they did make a decision it was criticised as a bad one or the wrong one or just not even listened to in any way...?

W: If you got in trouble for constantly doing the wrong thing, often it can lead to you being indecisive or lacking confidence. Like when I went to school I didn't have much confidence with woodwork and metalwork, even though I came to enjoy the metalwork a little bit and the woodwork guy told me to go and do art because I was putting all the joints around the wrong way. Yet as an adult I suddenly realised I could do these things and I started making my own kitchen cabinets and different stuff that I wanted to do.

I remember my father brought me one of those Airfix model plane kits and he was very slow on getting around to do them with me and I was supposed to wait to do it with him. But one morning I got up and I started making it and the next thing I knew my father's downstairs standing next to me shouting because I'd wasted his money and I was doing it all wrong. So it didn't stop me in the future trying to do models or whatever, but it certainly damaged my ability where I could be trusted just to find things out.

As a result, with all my own kids I was the opposite. I always encouraged them to try everything and I would give them models or whatever or give them tools and say to them that they could just see what they could make. Whatever they did, I'd say it was great – so they could get used to trying things without fear of criticism.

Becoming what you hate

D: There are people, even if they know someone has had a terrible childhood, who say that as the person has been away from home for 10, 20, 30 years or whatever that they can't go talking about their terrible childhood and blaming it any longer. But it's not that simple is it?

W: I was in a relationship with a woman from South America who'd been sexually abused when she was younger by her own family. So we're in a relationship, it's very loving, we're getting on very well and then she starts having problems like I would turn up and she would say to me: "Oh I don't think I really love you, maybe we should just be friends or end it." We would chat, sort it out, carry on the relationship... then it would happen again. I started getting sick of this.

I tried talking to her about the sexual abuse. She was in a form of therapy that obviously wasn't working because she'd been in it for years and nothing was changing. She had a blueprint and her blueprint was that because she'd been sexually abused by her own family members she was thinking: if you really love me, how could you do this to me?

So whenever she met anyone that she loved or who loved her, she would push and push until the person walked away, as I did – and then she could say to herself: see, I knew he didn't love me.

The blueprint will prove itself. She wasn't doing that consciously. Yet she could dress it up in all sorts of ways such as: "Oh, this doesn't suit me, and that doesn't suit me..."

I had a friend who said the worst thing he could ever imagine in life was growing up to be his father because his father was a drunken, violent alcoholic – and he became the same and he killed himself.

D: Because he became what he hated?

W: Yes. It's astounding how many people grow up in alcoholic homes where their lives were ruined by their father's or mother's drinking – and what do they do? They start drinking.

D: And they follow the same pattern of relationships, including the so-called romantic ones. I've seen that to an exact replica version.

W: When you're younger you build up in your blueprint the pattern of attraction, so when you go to get a relationship you will be extremely choosy – but that doesn't mean you'll make a good choice. You are though very careful who you choose and you will choose what is familiar.

Whenever we look at relationships, we need to look at the parent that you're most like – and you'll marry the opposite. So if your personality is very like your father you are in general going to marry somebody with a personality more like your mother, someone with the same traits. Remember we're not talking carbon copies here, we are looking at familiar traits.

It's like if you get someone who's been battered in a relationship, and by some miracle they get away from it, they will often meet someone else who again seems lovely at first, but after some time they find they are being abused again at the hands of their new partner.

This isn't because they want to be battered, far from it. But the problem is they don't realise they are attracted to this type of personality, that there is something in the person's personality that is attractive, because it's familiar.

D: How about, often, as well you can have siblings growing up in the same house, treated the same way, badly, and yet it seems to affect one more than the other? For instance, you might have two siblings who have got a really angry father and it affects one more than the other.

W: It affects them differently. You know perhaps one dies of cancer and one becomes an alcoholic. It depends on the person's personality and the way they respond to the situation.

D: I know someone in recovery from alcoholism doing very well after reaching a total rock bottom that included prison, and her brother took his own life. Or there's another I know of, a recovering addict who is creative but never yet made much money but who has three lovely children, and his sister who owns loads of stocks and shares and all the material things and who works nearly all the time, yet she has never had a decent or normal relationship and she is childless despite saying she'd like to have had children…

W: If a family comes to me and there are four kids with an alcoholic parent, then depending on the severity of the impact on the family, I would usually expect to find anxiety, panic, depression, eating disorders or more alcoholism. Nobody is going to live in that environment and be free from symptoms. Alcoholism is a family illness.

D: What should children or partners of an alcoholic or addict do?

W: You need to detach with love. It's like if you go in and find an alcoholic on the floor, what you would do is make sure that person can't choke to death. But don't clear up their vomit and don't put them in bed. Let them feel the consequences of their actions. But of course you make sure they don't die.

D: By feeling the consequences they're more likely to grow spiritually by seeking help because the pain will get too much?

W: Someone will get sick of what they're doing if they feel the consequences. If every time you drink and drive you've got some policeman in headquarters who can just get you off, then that might kill you and others because you'll carry on doing it. But one day if you're faced with going to jail you may have a hard look at the reasons that got you there.

So love is a very important thing. M Scott Peck said love is nothing to do with biology. And it's nothing to do with what you see on a Hollywood movie. If you really love yourself, then you will do the work on yourself, then you will give yourself the attention it requires. Attention is a huge part of love and most people cannot give it to themselves because they can't sit with themselves and they can't face looking at anything they don't like about themselves. In that shadow side of ourselves, if we don't face up to it, if we don't assimilate that shadow into our personality, then it will bite you on the ass.

D: M Scott Peck also said if you were lacking parental love it's very hard as an adult to love yourself. This is because the child who's not loved by his or her parents will always assume that it is they who are unlovable rather than realise it's their parents who are deficient in their capacity to show love. This belief often continues with that child into adulthood and throughout life.

W: It's difficult to understand what love is if as a child no one has ever given you time, ever given you positive regard. If no one has ever spent time with you, told you good things about yourself, then there's often always going to be something missing in you.

Even if you get into the right relationship as an adult, then you've still got to go back and look at yourself and to replace it. That's why we talk about becoming your own parent – we have to learn how to parent ourselves.

That's what growing up is. If we have good parents we learn how to parent ourselves.

D: By good parents you mean those that show you love and listen to you?

W: Yes, parents who tell you how valuable you are. They show you good things, make sure you have an abundance of love. I mean if you don't get an abundance of love when you're a kid you might find it hard to ever give it to yourself.

D: And some children don't get that love and then they also get an even more negative version of that because they not only don't get shown love, they get the opposite: criticism, anger and no positive attention. So it's not only that they are not getting shown love, they are actually getting shown hatred and contempt, and they are getting taught that they are inadequate, that there is something wrong with them.

W: Exactly. So then when you feel really bad about yourself, you often don't know why you feel really bad about yourself. One of the problems for a lot of people is if, for instance, they were intelligent enough to do well at school and university and get a good job or start their own business – and I've dealt with many people like this – is that they still feel something is wrong, but they have no idea what or why. Problems are showing up in their own relationships, the way they're treating themselves, insecurities, self-doubt, anxiety and depression. Even though on the surface it looks like they're all right.

D: What of those children that have been abandoned by parents as well, who aren't in touch with them, when parents have disappeared?

W: That leaves a huge hole.

D: Or put them up for adoption. There might have been a sound reason – but it still affects them?

W: There's research to show that any child suffers a trauma from being taken away from the mother – and quite often when people are adopted it's more than once because they could be taken from the mother, then put with foster parents and then they're taken away from their foster parents. So there's been two rejections before they ever get anywhere...

D: Even babies can feel this – I read that King's College London research discovered the physiological impacts of depression on pregnant mothers can affect babies while in the womb and lead to changes in the behaviour and biology of newborns. It found that babies born to mothers who were depressed during pregnancy showed altered behaviour soon after birth compared to babies of healthy mothers. Babies born to mothers with depression showed biological changes in response to stress at one year old. The researchers think this could be why children born to mothers with depression have a higher risk of depression as adults.

W: Other research has shown you can measure the influence of a mother's depression on a 12-week-old infant. So if the mother's depressed you can already see the change on the infant at 12 weeks. The child is no longer smiling, it's not looking for its mother, it's not trying to make eye contact.

D: And that can affect them for the rest of their life?

W: Of course. If you're not connecting with someone, if you're not staring into their eyes and smiling and know that you're loved and approved of… Children learn quickly. Every child wants to give you a hug and a kiss, but they soon learn not to… Such as if you're depressed or angry at them or don't want it. Or if you just think there is something wrong with that. You know that sort of thinking that some parents have: "Look at that soft bastard, I'm not having my son like that!"

Look how many boys suffer who are sensitive, so their fathers beat them to "make them into men". They don't like anything "feminine". When I was a child I saw some mates with an Action Man and I really wanted one. I thought Action Man was fantastic! But my father wouldn't let me have one because he thought it was too much like a doll... In lots of other ways he was great. But that was his conditioning.

A fear of silence and stillness

D: What about the many people who always say: "I never seem to have enough time." Those people who are always rushing from one thing to the next. Most of us have probably been there at some time, but there are some people I know who would never even stay still long enough to have a cup of tea, or there are those people whose house you go in and there's a TV blaring in one room, a radio in the next, another radio upstairs... There seems to be a fear of silence and stillness. Is this about them or that the world has sped up or both?

W: It's just keeping busy. I know lots of people who have their televisions on all day. I once had a girlfriend who didn't watch television, but she had one on in every bedroom, the living room and the kitchen – and I'm talking 60-inch televisions! All on full volume all over the house.

D: And the reason is...

W: Never turned it off.

D: ...if there is silence?

W: Drives them crazy!

D: Because they might start to think about what their head needs to deal with?

W: When the silence comes in it triggers a type of thinking and what happens is that thinking triggers a mood, then they start to go back to the default settings. Our default settings were conditioned by our childhood –

what we believe about ourselves and what we believe about our world. And you live in that mood.

People do things to make themselves feel good, many times not realising they are actually trying to feel better. Noise, TV, radio… a constant battle to avoid the default mood. To avoid the issues and anxiety that gave rise to the default settings. And then, unknowingly, the constant practising of anxiety producing thoughts and behaviours, creating an ever-spiralling thought pattern into terror.

Others find a drink or a drug, or food, gambling, shopping, sex… They are all efforts to escape from the inner pain. So often it's not a conscious thing: you do something, you feel better – so you keep doing it. But whatever we practise we get good at, even if it's destroying us.

Remember all these things are progressive, meaning it is making onward movement towards a destination. Nothing in this world stays the same, all the stars, the planets being born or dying… Nothing stays the same.

Everything progresses – it's either getting better or it's getting worse. So if your default settings are that you are depressed or you're unhappy or you're sad, they are your default settings. You keep on coming back to them and every time you come back it will be worse because it's progressing.

That is until in the end it will just be overwhelming. One of the ways to escape the default setting is suicide, but it's no answer.

I've seen many people who say to me they're going to kill themselves. I ask them, what's the point of that? Often they answer that they will have peace. I ask them how do they know that? You know, maybe they're right, but I say: "I really have no idea, and perhaps you're right that maybe you will have peace – but there's a good chance that you won't."

D: Your heart may have stopped beating, but you still have the turmoil.

W: Maybe the moment you kill yourself you will find yourself in a far fucking worse position than you are in now. At least here you are in with a chance. Suicide is no guarantee of escape, absolutely not.

D: So what about anyone who says they feel on the brink of a breakdown because the world at times seems on the brink of a breakdown?

W: But the world is a better place than it's ever been.

D: So this is a perception of the world?

W: It's a perception. The world is a far better place than it's ever been. Lots of people say the world today is a nervous scary place, but if you look at history... For instance, take the Crusaders who went into the Middle East and then they sacked a city, they killed every man, woman and child and then gave thanks to God because they got rid of the infidel. So you know we don't live in those times any longer. But it is not so long ago we did.

Why we're all really little gods

W: It's not our humanity we are struggling with, it's our divinity. It is about who we're becoming.

A lot of people today, from whatever religion, say we're all children of God. So what species of children is God having then? When I had children you know me and my partner didn't say: "Hmmm, I wonder what species this will be, I hope they are children – but maybe it's a dog."

We didn't have that conversation because we knew that as we were human we would have a child after our own species, our own type. So if God has children, then God has divine children. He has little gods.

The Bible talks very clearly about the divinity within us and it talks about what we are to become and what we're growing into – the image of God. You won't hear many churches talk about that, they never talk about it. You won't hear a sermon on your divinity, to be like Jesus Christ. The only time they ever tell you to be like Jesus Christ is when they say we should put up with shit: so be like Christ and put up with the pain, put up with the suffering, but never to get to that resurrection, and never get to realise who you actually are.

D: So we're all really little gods?

W: The fact is if we are God's children and God is divine, then we must all be divine. What does that mean? It means if God is moulding us to his image, as the Bible tells us he is bending and shaping us, he's moulding us into divinity.

D: You once asked me if I was okay after we had a good three-hour chat and I replied that I was – but that it had made me realise how messed up I am. You straightaway and emphatically said: "No, you're perfect in there, right inside in the middle of yourself, you were made perfectly – but there's stuff you've put around that perfectness."

Nearly everything that somebody is, is a product of their reaction to how they were treated and brought up as a child. So many people are nowhere near their true selves, they are instead someone based on their reactions to experiences. The real self is still inside under protection.

It's like that story about the ancient chapel wall painting that was made up of dull colours and they were restoring it, but after a while they discovered under the painting was the actual original – and it was in fact really bright and much more beautiful than anyone could have imagined. Then the dilemma was do they restore it to what everyone always knew, or do they reveal the bright version that was always there all along?

Of course it's a fantastic analogy for humankind. Many of us don't even know what's truly within us because we've never been given the chance to see it or never allowed ourselves the chance to see it. Many people who start recovery say they just want to get back to how they once were – but in fact if you do such as the 12 Steps you can reveal something far greater within than we ever knew. I mean, immensely so.

That's the thing, everyone is created perfectly but as we face stuff in our homes and in the world, we put stuff around us. We put up a defensive wall around the perfect creation. We become an imperfect creation, a toned-down version of the real us inside, but we may never know. And that's really quite tragic.

The perfection in us is the spirit, not the body. That is the part that presses from within us to be born.

W: God doesn't make rubbish.

D: You've mentioned about the church and religion, and this is a book that mentions a lot about spiritual growth, but really I think it could be viewed as anti-religious. There's that saying: religion is for people who are frightened to go into Hell; spirituality is for people who've already been there. The big difference.

W: Well, I don't want to be anti anything. I want to just look at the facts and say we need to know how life works. There's no point in telling me that you can go around calling a kid an idiot all day and that kid will grow up into a healthy, happy human being.

So what we are looking at here are the spiritual laws of life. Just because you can't see how something works doesn't mean it's not happening.

D: Bit like a helicopter's blades – you can't see them but it's keeping the helicopter up. Or the frequency that travels through the air to make broadband work, or television and radio.

W: Or as with electricity. You can't see it, but you see the result of it.

D: That's interesting because this morning my youngest son was watching a Peppa Pig cartoon and I heard

Peppa Pig ask her dad what electricity is. He replied something like: "It makes everything in our house work."

I immediately thought, that's not what it is, that's what it does. I'm not sure anyone entirely knows what it is, but we rely on it, in some cases for life over death. So it's the same with a Higher Power. I don't know what my Higher Power is exactly but I do know it makes everything work. All I have to do is make sure I stay switched on, that I stay connected.

W: I mentioned bacteria earlier and that's one of the best examples for me. A doctor called Ignaz Semmelweis was at his wit's end due to the amount of women dying from puerperal fever after giving birth – that we now know is due to bacterial infection of the female reproductive tract following childbirth.

So while at Vienna General Hospital in 1847 he encouraged all the doctors and nurses to wash their hands with chlorinated lime solutions. They did this and the following year it spread to include thoroughly cleaning any surgical tools that came into contact with the women. The women stopped dying.

Even so, his observations clashed with the scientific and medical views of the era. In fact, he was largely ignored, rejected and even ridiculed.

Just more than a decade later, Semmelweis was suffering with depression. He was lured to a psychiatric asylum under the sham of visiting it for professional reasons, but when there he was beaten by some guards, forced into a straitjacket and locked up in a dark cell. He died two weeks later from a gangrenous wound, possibly caused by the beating. Just a few people attended his funeral. He was aged only 47.

Only a few years after his death, the theories of Semmelweis started to become more accepted and then microbiologist Louis Pasteur confirmed the bacteria theory after which surgeon Joseph Lister operated using hygienic methods with great success. Semmelweis is now recognised as a pioneer of antiseptic procedures.

This shows how up until we could see bacteria, people would say you are just unlucky or it was God's will. Now that we have some education we realise it's nothing to do with luck, it's nothing to do with God's will.

There's a spiritual law that you obey – you know, if you're going to stand in the fast lane of the motorway the chances are you're going to get run over. There's a law you need to obey: keep off the motorway.

It's the same with washing your hands. If you don't want to wash your hands before you eat you're running the risk of infection. So spiritual law is something that we can't see, but we see the results of it.

It's like a 12-Step programme in which Step 12 states: "Having had a spiritual awakening as the result of these steps..." So anyone who has done this programme thoroughly and honestly can see the effects of what they've done – even though they couldn't see anything happening.

It's the same with a child. If you always call the child an idiot and a fool, then you will see the results very quickly.

D: And conversely praise a child and truly love them, then you'll see the results of that too.

W: Yes, give them the right environment.

D: Wayne Dyer – who incidentally spent much of his first ten years in an orphanage after his alcoholic father walked out on the family – said: "My beliefs are that the truth is a truth until you organise it, and then it becomes a lie. I don't think that Jesus was teaching Christianity: Jesus was teaching kindness, love, concern, and peace. What I tell people is don't be a Christian, be Christ-like. Don't be a Muslim, be Muhammad-like. Don't be a Buddhist, be Buddha-like."

W: I would never try to behave Christ-like because I find it impossible. I can't behave like that, and if I could I would have done it years ago.

D: The point I think Wayne Dyer was making was that they were spiritual people, full of love with no fear and this is why they became and still are so revered – and so try your best to live by their way, making choices and decisions through love not fear. They knew this because of their incredible connection.

W: Jesus was a religious man who obeyed all the Jewish holidays and laws. But what Jesus talked about was the fact that it has to be in your hearts. What he said to the Pharisees, the priests of his time, was: you always seem to do everything right, you obey all the laws such as when you pay your tithes, yet you are like whitewashed tombs – you are all shining on the outside and full of dead bones on the inside, because unless it's in your heart, unless it's in you, it means nothing.

And religion over the years for many people has just been about clocking in at the church and then you are fine because you have a relationship with this church and if you follow the rules of the church, then you'll be okay. But Jesus, Muhammad and Buddha are talking about a heart condition.

In the Bible, Paul the Apostle says "circumcision is a matter of the heart" and he said to Christians that you don't need to be circumcised like the Jewish Christians, the original members of the Jewish movement that later became Christianity. Paul said it's your heart that needs spiritually circumcising and it's that circumcision that is a sign you belong to God.

D: "Circumcise" comes from Latin meaning "to cut around", but what do you mean? Is it a metaphor meaning physical circumcision is useless if the heart hasn't also been cut out and handed over to God?

W: He's talking spiritually – your heart must be circumcised, your heart will bear fruit. It's a symbol, it's a symbolic act. If your heart is circumcised, then it will deliver and you will see it in the world. The only way you'll know if someone has Christ in them is by their fruit, is by what you see.

D: Step 3 of AA and the other 12-Step groups says: "Made a decision to turn our will and our lives over to the care of God as we understood Him." I read about this once and it says how the word "decision" is from Latin "caedere" meaning "cut" in the same way as "incision" and "scissors" are connected.

So this Step 3 is perfectly worded, it means to cut your will and life from where it has been and give it to the care of a power greater than yourself. And definitely greater than alcohol, although of course alcohol has the power to isolate, destroy and then kill somebody. There is, of course, another significant connection there that we say spirits for strong booze, but that also is used to describe the non-physical part of a person, the spirit, and it derives from Latin for "breathe".

W: You have to give your whole heart to God. So your heart has to become God's heart, it has to belong to God. When God is in your heart, your heart will be changed forever.

For instance, if somebody tells you they're a Christian or any other religion, and they go to this building every week and they say their prayers and they do everything else, but they tell lies and they steal from you, then you wouldn't trust them. Jesus is talking about the divinity of God being carried within someone; the goodness of somebody flowing through, the goodness of God is flowing through that person and into the world. Divine means "godlike".

So saying I'm doing it myself doesn't work, and if it worked I would have gone and done it years ago. What you're saying is that the heart doesn't belong to God, that it still belongs to you and you're going to do your best.

It's like an alcoholic saying: "I'm not going to come to AA meetings, I'm going to do my best on my own." The first part of the 12-Step programme says nobody comes into a relationship with God until they say: "I'm fucked." Nobody comes into a relationship with God until they say: "I can't do this alone any more…"

D: That's a reason why the 12 Steps are written in the plural then, using the word "we" rather than "I". So taking Step 1, it's not "I admitted I was powerless over alcohol – that my life had become unmanageable" but rather "We admitted we were powerless over alcohol – that our lives had become unmanageable". Is this true beyond the 12-Step programmes, I mean people who aren't alcoholics or addicts of some sort?

W: Yes, and it doesn't matter if it's the Pope or Moses or anybody.

D: And they need to say I'm completely in pieces, I can't do this alone, I need some greater power?

W: Exactly. If you look at Moses, he thought he was the greatest guy on Earth, and for 40 years he lived in a royal palace. So you can imagine the splendour that he lived in and the power that he had, the authority that he had living with an Egyptian ruler. Then he kills a guy and he has to run away and he spends 40 years living on the backside of the desert.

So for the first 40 years of his life, he thinks he's it; for the second 40 years of his life he finds out he's nobody. Then God steps in and he finds out when he's 80 years old that God is everything and he surrenders to God.

Absolute proof

D: I have a friend called Peter James who's one of the bestselling fiction writers alive today. He's had one book published called Absolute Proof about what would happen if someone had absolute proof that God exists and what might the consequences be for the person who finds it. What do you think?

W: I recall when there was a young Irishman sat in front of me. He was aged 24, a new client, an atheist, presenting with chronic anxiety and desperate shyness. That's an acute spiritual condition, an ego problem. What else can it be when you believe that you are the focus of everyone's attention, that everyone is solely focussed on you, that you are therefore the most important person in the room?

I like to stir the mind, so I told him he could prove the existence of God.

"Fuck off!" he said.

"You can."

"Fuck off. No one can do that."

"Are you open to an experiment?"

In fairness to him he was, where others haven't been so willing. So I told him to begin every morning for a week with half an hour of prayer and meditation.

"How can I if I don't believe?" he asked.

"Pretend – fake it to make it. You say: 'Okay, if there is a God, show yourself to me... I don't believe you exist... but if there's the slightest chance you do, then I'm interested in getting to know you. Even if it's only to ask you why you're such a bastard.' But whatever happens you are going to sit still for 30 minutes, not a second less... discipline yourself to do this... Even if it's in total silence."

The next week he came in. "What you told me to do last week was really scary."

I smiled. "Why?"

"Because I only did it for three days, but those three days were so different to all the other days."

Having had a glimpse he sought more. He practised the half an hour of prayer and meditation first thing every day. He was with me for two years working on his issues, his soul... he recovered from his fears.

My own experience was different, but again experiential. Not long after I'd stopped drinking I had a panic attack while I was sat waiting for my car at a garage, and I thought: "Oh my God I'm going to drink against my own will again." To manage my panic attacks for years I used to carry a half bottle of vodka around and prescription drugs in my pocket, but I didn't have that.

If ever in the past for some reason I didn't have that I had to get into a pub and ask for three large vodkas. They'd think that a couple of people were coming to meet me, but I'd drink the three of them straight down one after the other, just to get rid of the terror.

So this day I sat there thinking I was going to drink against my will. Then I remembered the serenity prayer that I'd heard: "God grant me the serenity to accept the things I cannot change, courage to change the things I can, and the wisdom to know the difference."

I hardly knew it then, but I said it. I stumbled my way through as I was unfamiliar with the whole process. But I didn't drink. That showed me that despite how I felt, something was working. In the past I would have taken a drink, without any shadow of a doubt, not because I was desperate for a drink but because I was desperate to get rid of the fear, desperate to medicate myself.

Another example is that I was totally and utterly addicted to prescription drugs. Because of the chronic anxiety and panic attacks... Because I used drink to medicate myself, because of the DTs, because my nervous system was shattered by alcohol I could no longer get on a bus, a plane or train. I couldn't even walk down the road.

I was sober a few months when my mentor, who'd also stopped drinking but years ago and was helping me now, asked me how I was finding sobriety.

"A fucking doddle," I replied, arrogantly.

"Why don't you come off those tablets and see how much of a fucking doddle it is then?"

I was rumbled.

There were no treatment centres around in those days, only local alcohol and drug units in hospitals. So I was using these prescription drugs, but when I got sober I knew I needed to get clean from them. After six months of sobriety then I went to see a specialist doctor who told me to cut down half a milligram every six weeks.

I came away, and I had the information. I was supposed to take four of these tablets every day, which was a particularly high dose, but I would always take nine or ten, or I forgot how many I took and I took them because the weather wasn't right, because my wife looked at me the wrong way, because my favourite TV programme wasn't on... I just didn't want to feel anything.

But I couldn't do it, I couldn't get on the same amount every day. I didn't think I could ever cut down as the doctor had told me, and I was sure that I could never give them up.

So one day I walked upstairs. I had the box of tablets in my hand and I knelt down by the side of my bed. I said: "Look, I've heard about this handing it over, this thing they say of 'letting go and letting God'..." And I said as I continued my prayer: "Now I'm going to put these tablets in the drawer and I'm going downstairs."

That's all I said. I put the tablets in the drawer and I went downstairs and I never abused another tablet ever again.

There was something like 84 different side effects with these tablets and they were unbelievable to come off. But I took them as prescribed and came down as the specialist doctor had suggested. Some days I had to scream and life seemed so hard, my brain was fried and I knew all I had to do was go upstairs and open that drawer and put a tablet in my mouth and it would have all gone away for a while. But I didn't do it and I knew Wayne couldn't do that... I'd proved it.

After a year I was completely off those tablets. It was already a proven fact that I couldn't do that when I'd tried on my own. Yet what I had made when I prayed we could call an intention in a certain direction. Something happened, something changed. Bit by bit that faith grew, and I knew I was being looked after.

I managed to get back on buses, trains and fly on planes, and then I learned to fly a plane and I eventually flew a plane solo, alone... it was one of the greatest days of my life. It took time, it took persistence with the programme... but it worked.

One of the big things that I had to do was to get away from my childhood concept of God, what everybody was telling me when I was a kid. Like most people I portrayed God as a bit like my own earthly father or a schoolteacher or some authority figure.

So my impression of God was of a disciplinarian who cared about me, but wasn't going to be too generous a lot of the time and was certainly not going to let me off anything – and apparently according to this god if you did a lot of things wrong you could end up going to Hell. Like apparently you could go to Hell for not chewing your food properly or for running down a corridor and all these sort of things!

I thought when I was first trying to get sober, this is great because God's really helping me – but then I'd do something awful and I'd lose my temper with someone or have road rage or whatever, and I'd think: "Oh fuck, that's it, God's going to turn around and say: 'Right you little bastard I gave you a chance and look at you, look at your behaviour, I'm not helping you any more!'." Then I began to realise that God's not like that, because I had to explore what love was.

So somebody who unconditionally loves anybody is never going to change their mind about that love. And you certainly don't ever arrive at a stage where you say: I'd like to set them on fire, and once you've lit that fire you manage to keep it going forever without them dying. That's not the God of love.

D: My own absolute proof of God came after trying and vowing to stop drinking and other drugs so often that I lost count of the number of times, and I gave up giving up in the end. I was just resigned to all of the never-ending problems and the ill health that were increasingly in my life.

Then I was advised by someone who'd experienced similar addiction to alcohol and other stuff, but who'd been clean and sober for 10 years, to pray on my knees in the morning and ask for a clean and sober day. Then at night before bed pray on my knees and give thanks for a clean and sober day.

Now I had never prayed on my knees and didn't know if I believed in any god. So I didn't even know what I was praying to. I did it though and I haven't touched an alcoholic drink or any mood-altering drug since, and amazingly I've hardly wanted to in the 17 years since then. As well I lost the aloneness I often acutely felt, despite having loads of great friends, and that I felt frequently, even in a crowded room…

Then I had the moment more than 15 years after that when I was on my knees again, but in floods of tears asking God to help me, and I found myself sitting next to you against my will within 24 hours – and since then life has transformed and I've also been able to help quite a few people too. It's some turnaround, and nothing to do with me.

So now if anyone asks me if I believe in God I say to them that's like asking me if I believe in my knees and my legs. Look, I say, they're right here helping to hold me up!

But what if... what would happen if someone did have absolute proof of God? I don't mean the proof we know. But such as everyone heard a message in their minds that the sun was going to set in the east and rise in the west for a week as proof, and it did... or something like that, that everyone had to accept, even the most staunch atheist?

W: Some people no matter what happens, even if God turned up physically in front of them, they wouldn't accept it. They'd still say: but God doesn't exist or it's just some trick. They will never believe it because of arrogance, stubbornness, refusal to see anything greater than themselves. They just believe in a materialistic world.

The person who's open to accepting it, the person who genuinely didn't believe in God and then is confronted and their heart opens – it changes their life. There are lots of people who have been like that over the years.

D: One of the characters in Absolute Proof says cynically about believing in God, and we've all heard the gist of this before: "You can hand over all responsibility – and blame Him for any crap that happens." What do you say to that?

W: When you hand over you have a responsibility to change. It's by seeking to follow spiritual law that things improve, and so-called calamity and shit are the elements mobilised to change the chemistry of your existence.

D: Do you think the world has become more or less closer to God; or more spiritual or less spiritual, whatever way you want to put it?

W: There's a lot more compassion in the world than there used to be. But there's still obviously a lot of evil – the human race is so far away from God. Religion fades as societies become better educated because religion asks us to believe in what the educated find unbelievable – but our need to be connected, to be filled with spirituality, to find meaning and purpose and peace will always be with us. Our experience makes the seemingly mystical and mysterious more concrete as quantum mechanics and the study of atoms opens our natural minds to the incredible nature of existence.

We are always close to God if we are close to ourselves... remember we are using a generic term, a symbol here, a signpost to a reality of being that is beyond comprehension... the knowledge of God is deep within everyone. We awake to that knowledge by calamity, a rock bottom and then a fearless and searching examination of ourselves.... in the mystery of our conscious being is the truth of ourselves.

We connect slowly through the manifestation that something in our lives has changed. Pursuing that change, we experience a new reality of being deep within us as this is the essential difference between spirituality and religion... where we move from a God of tradition to a God of our own experience.

Carl Jung's experience brought him to a God of his own experience. His life's work after that was a study of the psyche of humankind. Other experts have seen it differently: Sigmund Freud said everything was about sex; Alfred Adler the desire to be someone; but Jung said everything we do is a search for God – the great reality deep within us.

Many religious people follow an exterior set of rules and regulations that usually consist of sacraments, rituals and obedience to an authority. While these processes may bring comfort, order, a sense of stability and a way to make meaning and sense of our lives they fundamentally lack the ability to provide the necessary power needed for change.

If religion is something exterior to ourselves it becomes something to defend, the symbols it uses as signposts become external objects of deification to worship, to venerate. This leaves it vulnerable to superstition.

There is no dictatorship of belief in spirituality: it is open, expansive, it is about individual expression and liberty – but essentially freedom from the bondage of ourselves.

We use drugs, alcohol, sex, shopping, medication and so on to free us from ourselves, from our hurts, pain, anxiety and depression, but on all levels this leads only to slavery and servitude to a new master.

By knowing ourselves through turning selfish obsession into selflessness, by being rigorously honest with ourselves, combined with an open mind, we will know a higher power because we will have experienced it.

Most people's concept of God is portrayed by the church, and it's a rather strange one. Until we find God for ourselves, until we seek and try to understand, we will be flapping around in the dark. It has to be experiential.

When I went to my first meeting to try to stop my drinking I walked into the room and I felt so bad, so horrible, so sick, so scared, so guilty, and so ashamed and I felt God wanted nothing to do with me because of the way I was living.

Then this Irishman called Joe started talking about God and I could see that something was shining out of him. His words and his manner and everything about him screamed at me that this man had something. He was obviously spiritual, he had some connection with God.

But when he was talking about God, as some Irish people do, he was "fucking" this and "fucking" that! It had such a profound effect on me because I'd never heard anyone eff and blind and talk about God at the same time. He was just like me, and I thought if he can have a relationship with God, then so can I. That was so important for me.

That was 30 years ago now and I've not had a drink since. But that relationship with a Higher Power was what did it, what got me there, what allowed me to stop and stay stopped. It was nothing to do with me as I'd tried stopping lots and failed every time. Now I've been sober a few years I look back and say how the fuck did I do what I did? I had nothing to do with it.

Sure, I did the shaking, I did the trembling, I suffered all the fears and the panic, the walking into the darkness – but the power came from somewhere else.

I use to think I couldn't have a relationship because I wasn't good, unlike some people who seem to come out of the womb and help their mother with the washing up. I just wasn't like that. Again this keys into my childhood blueprint where good people constantly told me I was naughty, even though I was a well-behaved child. It wasn't intentional, it's a lack of understanding.

Then when I read about the people in the Bible, such as Moses being a murderer, David being a murderer and an adulterer... Previously I thought the Bible was just full of goody-goodies. But far from it! They liked having their own way and they liked wealth and sex and they liked fighting and would kill people if they got in their way. God didn't approve of their actions. But God loved them.

Solomon had 700 wives and 300 concubines, he seriously liked sex! The Bible talks in explicit detail about sex. One book, the Song of Solomon, is devoted to it. But you don't often hear sermons on it. So God is not a prude. I learned more about God.

And when I heard this Irish guy Joe and then I met other suffering and recovering alcoholics I became aware that God loved these people. I realised if God comes for people who are in deep shit like this, the people who fuck up... then people who don't feel they are in deep shit, maybe just don't think they need God.

D: But they do?

W: Of course they do. People who think they can do this themselves have their eyes closed. Many are full of pride as I was – and the word "pride" derives from a word meaning "having a high opinion of one's own worth". Which is not far from narcissistic... having an overinflated view of one's own opinions. So you can lie in a gutter and look down on everybody else!

For many years I thought I should just do it all myself. I thought there was a moral obligation upon me to do it myself. It was only when I realised I couldn't that I sought help.

Finding that out though nearly killed me. I followed self-reliance to the gates of death. Then I learned what the Devil sows for your destruction, God will use for your salvation.

D: What about those people who say they don't believe in God and they look like they are doing really well and even inside themselves they might think: "I'm doing really well, just look at my big house, my brand-new shiny car, my handsome husband or stunning wife, my classy kids, my holiday home in the sun..." Is there something missing?

W: Whatever happens, whatever you do, your body gets older, your body decays, you and your spirit will feel all the things everybody else feels – and then there will come that moment when you face your own demise and you know you're not going to be here any longer.

Also as we have said, no one gets a perfect life, everybody gets something. Our struggles are the development of consciousness. We arrive at many crossroads where we have an opportunity to experience something greater than ourselves. Knock and the door will be opened. But most people slam it shut. So whatever happens, in the human condition, if we say there is no God, sooner or later you'll realise you are not here to stay, that there is no you.

D: I once heard a fantastic story from a speaker at a 12-Step group on YouTube saying that God is often called Father – and he said think of it like this, that it's as if you've got a child and your child has disowned you for 20 years, doesn't even phone you or anything, you've heard that they just think and say that you don't even exist, or that if you do exist that you're shit and you're weak.

Then you are walking past a locked door in a rundown block of flats on a dangerous estate and you hear someone shouting out for help and you immediately recognise it as the voice of your grown-up child. Even though you haven't seen or heard from them for 20 years, at hearing that cry for help you are going to kick the door in without hesitation and you're going to help them at all costs. No doubt, no second thought.

This is why it is that you know when you get on your knees or pray in some way to the God of your understanding, then God is always going to be there – because it's the same, it's a similar relationship – but obviously magnified by an infinite amount. This Father never abandons us. We may abandon, but never the other way round. It's unconditional love.

W: Remember too the Parable of the Prodigal Son who goes to his father and says: "Let me have my inheritance now because I want to go off and enjoy it." So his father gives him his inheritance and he goes off for a life of sex, drugs and rock 'n' roll. But he ends up broke and looking after pigs and even eating the same food as the pigs because he's so hungry.

One day he realises that even his father's servants are better off than him. He decides to go back and ask his father for forgiveness and if he can be a servant in his house.

So he returns and his father sees him coming from a long way off – and that's important – and runs out to him declaring: "My son, my son!" So his father was looking for him. But he knew he had to wait until his son had had enough, that there was no point in fighting with him until he'd seen the error of his ways, until the pain was bad enough.

And it's also so important to see that his father didn't say: "Where the fuck have you been, what have you been up to, have you spent my money wisely or just pissed it away?"

There was none of that. He just wanted his son back, and that's how it is when we return to God.

Everything is progressive

D: Is spiritual sickness progressive?

W: Everything is progressive.

D: So that means spiritual sickness is progressive – unless it's arrested and a daily way of living adopted that continues to arrest it, by growing spiritually every day. So if people have a spiritual sickness that's progressive, is this why many people become more rigid as they get older?

If you're a progressively unspiritual and so a progressively selfish unloving person, and you're not loving thy neighbour as you love yourself, because deep down you don't love yourself despite all appearances to the contrary... I heard that this morning, from the Bible where it says "Love your neighbour as yourself" and I immediately thought of some of the world's leaders...

W: A narcissist has an inflated view of his own opinions. We're talking about ego condition. So there's different expressions of sickness within the ego. There have been many dangerous fanatics – Hitler and Pol Pot spring to mind.

D: Are they like that because otherwise they crumble... they are empty, so there's nothing inside stopping them from easily crumbling?

W: They have no fear of God.

D: Because they think they are God or better than God?

W: I think they just believe that God doesn't exist and that it's their divine right to rule. I don't know that they believe in the afterlife, but they obviously don't care or they don't believe in any retribution in the hereafter for sure.

D: But they often get behind religion as a justification.

W: A lot of these people who have done horrific things will just kill themselves. Because they don't believe in any retribution in the hereafter they just think if they kill themselves they can escape it.

A lot of people think all narcissists love themselves. But the Greek mythology of Narcissus doesn't say that – it says he fell in love with his image reflected in a pool of water.

There's a huge difference between loving yourself or loving your image. Narcissistic personalities are people, like alcoholics, who have an overinflated view of their own importance.

These people, when they give you their views and their expertise, always think they're right and they will fight to the death to be right and tell you why they're right and that's why they are right and they never apologise, unless it suits them – they don't have good relationships.

D: Empty vessels make the most noise...

W: Yeah, but you can't get a good relationship if you're always right about everything, and there's no compromise, there's no diplomacy. These are people who are voting with their emotions. If we go off what we feel we're always acting like young children. But God gave us a brain to work things out. That's why you should never just believe what you're told – God doesn't want you to.

It's like if you were brought up in Japan you might be Shinto, if you're bought up in India you'd be either Muslim or Hindu, if you're brought up in a lot of other countries you'd be Christian... So these religions might well be the basis of your views, this is your blueprint, what you've grown up with. But you can challenge all of that so that you find God for yourself, otherwise you can just be brainwashed and God may not really be in your heart – God gave you your brain to work things out for yourself.

Back to politics, you could say that a lot of people become more right wing as they get older because they're seeking easy simple solutions and they lose the love. People become disillusioned as they get older if they're not growing spiritually.

They develop knee-jerk reactions to complicated problems. Otherwise known as populism. They may keep the religious side of everything, such as going to church and calling themselves Christian or whatever, but if there's no love... then there's no compassion for the misfortune of others.

D: Love your neighbour as yourself means that if you don't love yourself deep down, if you are full of self-loathing despite how you might look and act, then you are going to also loathe your neighbours. You are not going to be able to love your neighbours, other people.

W: The argument about how you treat the poor has been going on for a long time: do you help the poor or do you reject and isolate them? In the British civil service when the famine was taking place in Ireland in the 1840s it was even seen by some that the Irish brought it on themselves because they were Catholics.

D: But was that just a convenient thing hidden behind religion for the British rulers to have power over other people on a neighbouring island?

W: It was a belief, they sincerely believed it. You know, we can be free to pick and choose about what we believe.

D: So books such as the Bible, Quran and Torah have got excellent messages in – spiritual guidance. But you still have to use your brain to work them out and not just be told at school, for instance, what they mean.

W: You were given a brain so that you could go and search and find your own information. To question. You then arrive at a point where you've got to look at what's going on in your heart and soul as well as your brain. Everything needs to be connected, so that you're looking for something. If you don't have a heart then you are never going to look. Our spiritual hunger, our inner emptiness, is our motivator.

What is a thought?

D: Mind experts have worked out that we have between 30,000 and 80,000 thoughts a day. That's a big difference – but even 30,000 thoughts a day is a lot! So what are thoughts?

W: Some people say every thought is a prayer.

D: Even the bad ones?

W: Yeah, be careful what you're praying for.

D: "I want to kill that person."

W: Well Jesus again says if you kill someone in your heart as far as God considers you've already done it; if you commit adultery in your heart as far as God's concerned you've done it.

D: You said to me once to think two words and I did – I thought the words "rock star" and you asked me to tell you when I had, and I did and you said you hadn't heard anything... Our thoughts seem weightless. So where do they come from?

W: If you take any particular phrase and say it in your head and don't say it out aloud, you can hear the words – yet it was never said. So what is it when you can hear something that wasn't said? You heard it said and that's inside your head and that's where everything takes place.

If you look at quantum mechanics it tells you everything is taking place inside your head – whatever you see in the world is an image deep down inside your brain. That's where it's all happening.

Atoms don't exist in just one place, they exist in several places at the same time, giving the appearance of solidity. Yet scientists will tell you there are no solid objects, that everything is just full of vibrations because the only thing an atom's got inside it is a vibration and so it's not solid.

D: So a thought is a prayer to God?

W: As the Bible says: "As a man thinks so he will be." A thought is your computer generating information. So your computer is programmed from the moment you're born. Even before then.

Our thoughts are lots and lots of choices. Our thoughts are not us, unless we decide to believe them and then that's what we become. Whatever you give out you get back. That's a spiritual law, it's called karma – what you sow you will reap.

D: For as he thinks within himself, so he is... In Matt Haig's Notes On A Nervous Planet he writes: "We are mysterious, we don't know why we are here." Why do you think we are here?

W: We're here to find out.

D: We're here to find out why we're here?

W: Of course – and every answer is within you. If you look at your DNA, the history of the entire race is written in your DNA. They can extrapolate where you came from tens of thousands of years ago, so everything is within you. Absolutely everything. And the complexity! No computer will ever be invented that is as complex as your brain.

D: C.S. Lewis' book Mere Christianity said in regards to what's right and wrong that it's all inside us and he was saying that's why we instinctively know right and wrong. It's not written down in a rule book, we're made with it inside us.

He wasn't talking about some of the man-made laws that are made by the financially rich and powerful to help keep them and others financially rich and powerful. He means the moral rules we all know, like how we can never ever get away with something that we know is morally wrong because we feel uncomfortable inside. I might steal some cash from you and think I've got away with it because you didn't see me doing it. But I know from how I feel inside that it's not right.

W: It's put in every person. It's interesting that in the Bible it says that God created the light, and then afterwards created the sun. The light comes from within you. Because that is where you will find God.

D: I spoke to someone who was an atheist, but who was coming round to thinking that there is God because he realised that even before people were in touch with other people on the other side of the world, these people on different sides of the planet were knowing a god and had this feeling within them and they all instinctively knew the same right and wrong, and they all built similar temples and prayed in a similar manner, and the messages of love and compassion were the same.

W: Definitely, we're all connected. Unfortunately it's not always a commonality with peace and love, some parts of man's developing conscious have been quite violent.

This is why Carl Jung studied dreams and concluded that there's a collective subconscious in humanity. Why is it, for instance, that all societies – however unconnected – physically have similar concepts? For example, it seems most societies have a familiar symbolism.

What are dreams?

D: So what are dreams?

W: It's our subconscious contacting us – and what's our subconscious? It's a part of God. Dreams are helping us to become more conscious. If you think of your mind as the size of a beach ball: your conscious mind part, the ego, is the size of a marble – and the rest is making itself known to you. The process of awareness of consciousness can be a painful business, especially if life events such as trauma cause resistance to changing development. This is sometimes wrongly diagnosed as mental illness.

I already mentioned that all growth is turmoil, all growth is painful. If you look at a woman giving birth it's turmoil, it's painful, carrying the baby is painful as it grows. The planet is formed through volcanoes and earthquakes and storms that creates new life.

With our lives when we go through storms we go through development, but nowadays a lot of that development is classed as mental illness. Mental illness is often made much worse by the treatment it's given: if we have no information that what we're going through is normal; if we're put in a situation in a horrible place like asylums; or if we're given loads of medication that stops the opportunity for growth.

You know, there will be times in our life when we feel totally overwhelmed because there's a huge reorganisation going on in our psyche – and resistance to all of that causes the problem. Once we're given the proper information – like with the bacteria story, something we can't see but that affects us – once somebody says to you "what you're going through now is absolutely normal", it eases the overwhelming feeling.

In the therapeutic process the initial stage of my work is to help people arrive at a point where they are able to realise that what they have been going through is normal, that they aren't going to stay there – whatever normal is, and I don't like using that word except as a reference to the human condition. They aren't going to stay where they are, but if they go through it, if they allow themselves to have the feelings, allow themselves to have the disturbance, they will come out on the other side. The disturbance is a conduit.

We've previously said about how Carl Jung had two mental breakdowns, with no medical intervention, and that he was kept in a loving environment. That's very important to note. He went through the breakdowns, and he came out the other side.

When he did he knew he'd been somewhere, he knew he'd been on a journey, he knew he'd been shown something. He was able to then write and study that experiential process for the rest of his life.

D: The pain then is a form of communication. Also you've talked about with addiction and alcoholism that people with these issues need to get rock bottom.

W: Everybody needs rock bottom.

D: Which is the pain, the pain to do something, to hear the noise of pain clearly enough to make change, to grow?

W: Rock bottom is a gift, a gift of desperation. But there are lots of people who were desperate who've killed themselves. Or they take medication. The world's full of desperate people.

Look at people in relationships, and how many people have gone through a divorce and then married somebody else straightaway? People jump from one relationship to another because they'd rather have a bad relationship than the pain of feeling alone. So people are very desperate. We are all desperate.

But we all like to crack on that we're not. You know, nobody likes to say when they're asked how they are: "Oh, I'm desperate!"

There's a huge amount of loneliness in this world. And yet, whatever problem you've got, wherever you are on the planet, if you turn to God and ask for help, sincerely as a surrender of the self, then you will get help.

D: You'll know you're not alone.

W: If you mean it, something will happen. But if you just keep begging God to help you and you're saying the words without feeling and you've no intention of following what it is and you've no intention of surrendering to God and you don't want to change, then you are not going to get the help you require.

You're just using the fire-fighting prayer. When the fire is out, you go back to your old ways that caused the problem in the first place, setting the wood for the new fire.

Sex pleasure & pain

D: Why does sex cause us human beings so much trouble?

W: Because it's a very spiritual thing. You know when two people have sex they start to become one with each other. People miss that and this is where that joining process happens.

Within every human being there are two sides to the personality: the masculine and feminine. These two sides of the personality have to blend together, they have to assimilate, they have to become one... to form the complete individual.

As we become sexual beings, as we go into puberty, that process of assimilation is often mirrored and reflected in our relationships and sexuality. If we are having problems in our relationships then the answer lies within ourselves. What are we trying to make work in our outer world is something we need to change internally.

So our sex lives, as we are sexual beings, are hugely important. It's important we celebrate our sexuality and that we have good sex lives and we have a good sex partner.

D: You once said to me to think about who invented the clitoris and the penis.

W: God invented every part of sex, the clitoris, the penis, the erection, nipples. God developed sexual excitement, anticipation, passion, they are all God-given gifts. Yet you will never hear the church talk about them.

D: In fact I've heard about many Catholics saying they felt guilty for having sex.

W: Of course. Yet the Bible talks about sex very often, very clearly and very openly. So many nations have taboos about sex. When the Christian church got in full flight, as it went all round the world, anywhere they had good open sex lives... then the missionaries were appalled, so they made everyone feel guilty about it and put clothes on.

D: Why did they do that?

W: Because they felt it was God's will, in the same way as Crusaders went to the Middle East and slaughtered everybody because they thought it was God's will. The Christian church genuinely believed it was God's will. Sex though is a God-given gift, including our sexual desire – but when it gets excessive and it becomes lust, that often causes harm and lots of trouble, such as an affair that splits up a family. It is the same as anything: you have a God-given gift to enjoy food...

D: But when you are gluttonous you get fat, then obese and get ill or even die from your gluttony.

W: When you are gluttonous you're going to get overweight and kill yourself through your gluttony. It's the same with anything that gets excessive – alcohol, work, shopping, sex – anything that changes the way you feel has got the path to get you addicted to it.

In Ireland sex was very repressed, something to feel guilty and ashamed about. A young man once came to me very disturbed. "I keep thinking about women," he said. He was quite surprised when I said: "You're 24, you're supposed to."

When you repress something as powerful as sex and make it dirty and shameful, then put men in a position of power over women and children in church and in the home, it twists something natural into abuse.

Generations of children were beaten by the clergy and the civic teachers in schools. The level of physical and mental abuse led to junior schools in Ireland becoming a place of terror. I saw generations of clients suffering from different degrees of PTSD, the same symptoms as soldiers returning from conflict.

Conflict in childhood leads to anxiety in later life. There's a link between PTSD, OCD, schizophrenia and bipolar with trauma and conflict in childhood.

With the church, this was often all seen as the will of God. We had children who were beaten and it was seen as a sign that God loved it if you were cold, fed up, starved, miserable. It paints a picture of God as an ogre and they were told "God loves you". So what do people then imagine love is?

The state and the clergy were one and the same. A great example of absolute power corrupting absolutely.

A client of mine told me he was abused by a priest while his parents were in the other room. I asked him why he didn't tell anybody. He said: "Who would believe me, a kid?" So many children would tell you this: what could they have said? As nobody's going to believe them – the priest had all the control and all the power.

It was totally tragic that in Ireland the priests were all powerful. I had clients who were frightened they would have their children taken off them. A husband and doctor's signature not long ago could put a wife in a psychiatric hospital because she wanted to leave the marriage. There was no divorce in Ireland until the mid-1990s.

It was like the only sin was sex. In Ireland for years it was as if you could shoot someone… but don't you dare fucking sleep with them! As the church's power collapsed in Ireland in the 21st Century the adoption rate dropped by 97 per cent…

D: And you could then buy condoms?

W: Yeah, there used to be no condoms, there was no contraceptive pill, there were no unmarried mothers. I counselled the first unmarried mother to go full-term pregnant in a particular village in Ireland. They still had nuns taking babies off people into the 1990s. There was a whole perversion about things and people had a downer on sex, something people should have been enjoying.

I counselled many couples who – because they weren't allowed to have contraceptives – had no sex life as they didn't want any more children. So they slept in different bedrooms.

A friend of mine went to the priest and asked the priest to help because his father was battering his mother. But the priest told him they must stay together under all circumstances. So he killed his father and he went to prison. Okay, this is your religion for you, you know.

D: That's totally shocking. Then going back to the natural desires we're given, there are the natural desires to eat, to have sex – but when they go too far they become problems, when they are excessive they are natural instincts gone wrong and they will damage us and cause harm to us and those around us?

W: We all need certain things such as breathing and eating, we need security, we need fun, and we need sex to be healthy, happy human beings. Sex is a big one. If we use sex selfishly it becomes a problem, and lots of people do of course. But this whole idea that there is something wrong with sex... There is nothing wrong with sex: sex is wonderful, sex is a little glimpse of Heaven that God let you have.

D: The French call it "la petite mort", the little death, the sensation of orgasm as likened to death, because you lose yourself within it, at that moment, when it's sheer ecstasy. A telling etymology again: "ecstasy" comes from Greek "ekstasis" meaning "standing outside oneself". In the 17th Century an English definition of "ecstasy" was "a state of rapture that stupefied the body while the soul contemplated divine things" and another early English meaning was "implying that the ego is no longer in the physical frame".

W: That's what taking mood-altering drugs is about, that's what doing a bungee jump is about.

D: Which is all comparable to what Carl Jung said in his letter to Bill Wilson, one of AA's co-founders, about a man they knew that "his craving for alcohol was the equivalent, on a low level, of the spiritual thirst of our being for wholeness, expressed in medieval language:

the union with God". And so, maybe, maybe sex addiction, all addiction, is a low-level search for God?

W: It's a low-level thirst for ecstasy.

D: Ecstasy the drug has a connection, as another search for God. It's significant that it became hugely popular in Britain and then around the world as a reaction to the development of far more materialistic thinking in society.

W: One of the good things about psychedelic drugs – and I don't think they are generally good for people – is that they show us what we're capable of experiencing. We're capable of experiencing such ecstasy because that's how we're designed.

All societies find a way to get stoned or drunk, no matter how primitive. To escape from ourselves is a need we all appear to share. An ever more materialistic society is always going to possess a deep spiritual subconscious hunger, which expresses itself in the need for the ecstasy of chemical escape.

But real ecstasy has to come to you through your relationship with your Higher Power. There have been many times in my life since I stopped drinking when I've experienced feelings that have just been unbelievable and amazing – I found within what I was seeking when I was using alcohol.

Growing up in the right environment or not growing at all

D: Our news today is 24 hours every day, reporting on everything from around the world. So we can live forever focussing on the very worst things, and about situations that are taken forward to their worst possible outcomes. An increasing amount of the media that used to report the "news" is now mostly merely political pamphlets, dishing out an agenda aimed at arm-twisting votes that have been forced by fixing on people's fears and making them grow into emotional obsessions. With this constant repetitive stream of information on the same disturbing subjects, it can be difficult to figure out what's real.

W: So don't watch the news. Why give yourself a diet of negative shit? We have free will.

It's very important that you protect your environment. If you take children, they are seeds and if you take a seed and you put it in the right ground with plenty of nutrients and water and the right sunlight, then you've got a beautiful flower. To put it in the wrong ground, then you get a sad-looking one or it won't grow at all.

This is what parents don't realise with their kids, that they are there to provide an environment for the child to grow and there are too many parents interfering in what they think the seed should be, rather than letting the seed develop and see what it is.

There's the thinking that there are only three things you need to know about parenting your children: leave them alone, leave them alone, leave them alone.

Parents just need to provide the right environment. Then let them grow, see who they are. Obviously you have certain ground rules. I wanted my five kids to grow up in Disneyland, I wanted them to be happy. So the rules were that there's no abuse of any description, there's no name calling, and there's no fighting. Don't get me wrong, it happened at times – but we had to deal with it.

D: How did you deal with it?

W: I'd send them to their bedroom and say: "You tell me when you're coming out, and come out when you've got a plan for how this is going to work better and you tell me that plan."

I never said you can't go to football or you can't do this or that. There was no need for any of that because a lot of the times the issues, like the issues when I was growing up, are parents making issues out of things that don't matter because they want to be powerful. The first commandment comes up again: "Thou shalt be right."

To this day if I ask my dad, "Well, why is that?" he will answer: "Because I'm your father." He's aged 89. You know it's because he had that mentality. It's in his blueprint.

When I brought up my kids, we had satellite TV and computer games, and there was no limit – they could play them all they wanted. I see parents as clients who say their children are always on their iPad and it's bad for them, so I ask them how they know it's bad for them because they didn't have one when they were a child. They answer that they were always told to stop watching so much television. We often just repeat the parenting we were given without thinking about if it's actually good for children or not.

So with my children there was a bedtime when they were at school, but during the weekends and holidays they would stay up as long as they wished. They could play the computers, have their friends over, plenty of sleepovers. I tried to create an environment where they could have lots and lots of fun. They have all grown up well, and everybody always compliments me on my kids.

D: And the children of yours who I've met compliment you as well.

W: That's great to hear, thank you. I always made sure my kids learned manners because courtesy is an act of love – how you treat people is very important. I brought my kids up on everything that I've told you, to take everything to God.

But I never ever took my kids to church because I never wanted them to experience God as boring and I've never been in a church that wasn't boring. And I thought: well, if it's boring, then God can't be here because it was God who invented sex, who invented rock 'n' roll and fantastic food and all these beautiful places in the world – so how the heck can God be boring?

D: And you told me that with your prayers every morning you never say the same prayer over and over again because you'll get bored and God will get bored.

W: If I said the same thing over and over again to you how long would you listen to me for? God is real. The Bible describes God's character, and we were made in the image of God, so when I talk to God we have everything: we have arguments, we have a laugh together, we share together, we cry together, we enjoy everything together because that's how the relationship is and at the end of the day I know that I am loved and I know that I'm being looked after.

D: Like a good relationship of daughter or son and father or mother.

W: That's exactly what it is. Jesus called God "Abba", which means "Father". I like the fact that my kids trust me and they can rely on me.

It's where you live – so take a good look ˎ around inside

D: This is a quote from philosopher Alan Watts in his The Book On The Taboo Against Knowing Who You Are: "We seldom realise, for example, that our most private thoughts and emotions are not actually our own. For we think in terms of languages and images which we did not invent, but which were given to us by our society. We copy emotional reactions from our parents…"

W: We're given ways to communicate and we're given symbols and ideas about belief, so we can connect with others. He's talking there in the same way as Carl Jung said that we have to lose our culture and we have to lose our family in order to truly find ourselves.

I'll give you an example – I was listening to a programme on the radio the other night about schizophrenia and this schizophrenic was talking. Now they didn't see this the same way I was listening to it, believe me. The schizophrenic said the voice told her that she had to kill her family and if she didn't kill her family the voice commanded that she must kill herself, and it scared her to death – and they were saying how terrible it was and she needed tablets and she was a threat and could be violent and all of this. That's total nonsense.

Schizophrenia comes around because of trauma, usually sexual abuse. This lady was so suppressed that what this voice was saying to her was that your family is killing you, and if you don't move away from them you'll die.

This doesn't mean you don't have to have a relationship with your family, that you've got to run away from them and never see them again. But you have to detach as a human being. Detach with love. With my kids, they have to detach from what I taught them, they have to check it. One of my sons doesn't believe in God. I can see he's a very spiritual guy, and that's where he is and I'm quite happy with that: I want him to challenge, he's got a brain and I know he'll find what he's looking for.

Sometimes to get to God, we look like we're running away. The novelist C.S. Lewis has been quoted as saying he came "kicking and screaming" to find God.

D: Here's another excellent excerpt from Notes On A Nervous Planet: "When looking at triggers for mental health problems, therapists often identify an intense change in someone's life as a major factor. Change is frequently related to fear." Then a few sentences later Matt Haig continues: "The intensity of the change can be a shock to the system. What, though, when the change isn't just a personal one? What about when change affects everyone?"

W: Would you give me an example?

D: War causes profound change to whole societies.

W: Everybody adapts differently. Wars bring things out in people – a lot of people find out things about themselves that they would never have known. So wars bring out things in us like situations in life bring out things in us that we didn't know were there. As well as trauma it can reveal our strengths.

For myself, many times I've been put in situations to grow me up, to develop me, to show me I can handle things that I didn't think I could. And the reason that I go through these things is because God wants to bless me and the only way that he can bless me with some of the things I want is to get me to a point where I'm mature enough to handle them.

For instance, I would be quite happy to buy one of my children a Ferrari, but not if they couldn't drive it. I want to make sure that if I buy one of my children a Ferrari that they're a good driver and not a lunatic.

So God wants me to have the Ferrari, but I have to be developed enough to have it. I'm not talking about just material possessions, I'm using the symbol to show that if we want a role of responsibility to care for people, to be of use, then we have to be prepared for it.

If this Earth is God's school, then we're like the son of the guy who owns this huge factory. We turn up on our first day at work and we say: "Great! God I'm here – where's the boardroom?"

And God shoves a bucket and a mop in our hand and says: "Go clean the toilets!"

And so cleaning the toilets means we're getting to know everybody and all the people that are on the different jobs and learning how to deal with people for the next 20 or 30 years.

But the day comes when we will walk into that boardroom and then, at that point, we're finally fit and able to be there because we know how to run the place – we know and care about the people and we want it to run right so that these people are looked after, because these are our people, these are our responsibilities.

It's just like when you come here to me for help, for that time here you're my responsibility, but once you leave from here… I'll give you everything that I could possibly have, that's my role, but what you do with it then is up to you.

I'm only the message guy, but that's my responsibility.

How do we feel happy when we're encouraged to be anxious?

D: Without doubt there's been a profound change that we've seen since the internet arrived and social media has boomed. Millions of people now have more digital conversations than face-to-face ones. What sort of consequence is that having on us?

W: Before we developed good roads and transport such as the train, most people lived in villages and they wouldn't go very far from those villages all their lives. So they would only be having conversations with the same people that they'd had conversations with all their lives. When we talk about a profound change it was a profound change for them to get on a train and go somewhere.

I have friends who were brought up in the west of Ireland and they came to Manchester where I moved to Ireland from – and they were overwhelmed when they saw Manchester. The point I'm making is that there were a lot of communities in the world where the development of the train or having a car had the same effect as social media today – it totally changed their lives.

Don't underestimate the first internet – the printing press – that changed Europe dramatically. The church burned Bibles written in anything other than Latin. But when the printing press arrived they could print faster than the church could burn.

English lawyer and social philosopher Thomas More, canonised by the church, burnt people at the stake and tortured them in his own house for having or translating the Bible into English. It is well known that he said he was unwilling to trust the "ploughboy" with God's word.

Because when people read the Bible in their own language for the first time they realised they had been misled and deceived – because the Bible says that God is inside all of us. So we don't need a middle man as we can have a direct relationship… religion and politics were intertwined, they were about the same thing: control. Spirituality is about an individual personal relationship and personal freedom… The church didn't want anybody to know this.

D: Going back to social media today, it does mean that for many people they do not have as much face-to-face contact with others. Some people now feel as if they're in the world without leaving their bedroom. There's an increasing number of people doing that I think, so surely that's not healthy?

W: No, I don't think it's healthy, but then again a lot of our schools and a lot of our societies aren't healthy. Lots of kids get school phobia and have problems with bullying and other things at school, so there are always issues.

Social media is extremely healthy and I also think it's got huge problems that come along with it. It's great for democracy, for instance, because it's undermining the power of the press to set the news agenda and it's undermining governments by making them more transparent and accountable.

D: Although governments are into social media as well now.

W: Of course. When they get quantum computers the governments will be able to control it far more. There may come a time that the only way we can be free of it is if we don't use any electronic devices.

D: It's a good point. But they'll be doing their best to tempt us to buy the latest electronic device, by trying to make it appear indispensable to living in the modern world. We're bombarded with methods devised to make us want the next thing instead of being content with the thing we already have. In the second of the Four Noble Truths, Buddhism says desire is a major cause of suffering and pain.

W: But modern Western life is now geared towards getting it all. Every time you turn on the TV and if you look at an advert or walk down the street and look at the billboards it's always about more.

D: What do we do to counteract it then?

W: I had to say to my kids growing up not to take any notice of it. Recently, I was watching a programme about this teacher and everybody was saying how great he was. He comes on and he says to these 15-year-olds: "This is the most important decision of your life, this will dictate where you're going and what's going to happen to you." Oh my fucking goodness, what a lot of pressure to put on people!

That's nowhere near right – your life is about you. If you get an education, that's great, but if you don't get an education, you get educated somewhere else, you get educated in life. This idea of putting pressure on people is absolutely terrible. We need to be encouraging people and enthusing people. Educate to find your talents and abilities, and you will always teach people to thrive. My father always said to me: "The world is your oyster, you can be anything you want to be, anything you want to be."

Doors will open for you if you expect them to open, and doors that you don't even know are there will open for you when you begin to live spiritually. There's a whole way of living that people just don't know about. This is all going back to doing it yourself and you say: all right, I'll go to the right school and then I'll go to the right college and then I'll marry the right person and I'll get the right job and have the right number of kids – and I wonder why I'm fucked.

Because life is not linear like this. When I sit in the garden I might watch the birds and a sparrow comes zig-zagging all over the place to get to the point it wants to reach. Life is like that. You have to go all the way to the right to come all the way back to the left, to go a little bit to the right and back to the left again. We go all over the place and we're always moving in a direction. But it's not a straight line.

I remember when I got my first degree I was sat on a rock in Wales and somebody phoned me and told me the results. I was looking out at the sea and I thought: "It really doesn't make any difference, I'm exactly the same as I was five minutes ago." It's nice to have, but it didn't make any difference to who I am and where I was.

I still felt fucked, anxious and afraid.

We need to get into a relationship with God so that our lives are guided. In Psalm 91 it says that whoever dwells in God's shelter will be looked after, that "a thousand may fall at your side, ten thousand at your right hand, but it won't come near you". You won't be touched. You don't have any anxiety when you know that.

We relieve anxiety by taking care of who we are and by not allowing ourselves to be infected with anxiety and that when it comes into us we have the answers for it. Many people with anxiety are people who don't have the answers. So the only answer they get is more – because anxiety only creates more of itself, it reproduces after its own kind. More fear, more torment, more pain.

So if you are living with anxiety you are breeding more and more of it. You need to live in the solution, and if you have no solution… then you are just going to have more anxiety.

D: And the solution is?

W: The solution is you've got to find out who you are, look within. This isn't about me telling you to believe in God, this is about me saying to you to look inside yourself, do the work on yourself and you will change. When you get rigorously honest with yourself that you can't do this, that you cannot manage your own life – then you need to find someone who can and maybe that someone who can is deep down within you and deep down within everybody and if it's not there, then what have you lost?

There is no way to happiness; happiness is the way

D: What everyone seeks, just through myriad ways, is happiness.

W: Happiness is a by-product of living the right way. It's not something you can aim for head-on. But people do that all the time – they think I'm going to be happy, so I'm going to do the linear thing: go to the right college, marry the right person and all that lot. Then I'll give myself lots of holidays, I'll buy lots of houses, I'll have nice cars and I will only be happy when I have that and I'll spend my whole life missing it.

Happiness is not about pleasure. The only way to find the right way for you to live is to look inside yourself. You look inside yourself when you get honest with yourself and start writing down how you really feel – and you will most likely need someone to help you with that.

D: Who would you choose to help with it?

W: Buddhists say when the student is ready the teacher will appear. If you really want it, someone will turn up and someone will help you, just like is happening to you now.

D: That's for certain. Although you have to be open to it, be aware and ready for that person.

Another Buddhist phrase that I want to mention here is: "There is no way to happiness; happiness is the way."

I also really like what Jewish psychiatrist Viktor Frankl says in his book Man's Search For Meaning about his time in the heinous Nazi concentration camps and how it was afterwards: that the route to happiness is to find a meaning in life and then that will lead to you being happy. We need meaning.

W: If you ask anybody what they want in life the answer is that they just want to be happy.

D: Although as Frankl said, the pursuit of happiness undermines happiness. But if we find meaning it will lead to happiness. And peace of mind as well?

W: It depends. Because there are lots of people living through shitty horrible conditions who accept where they are and they accept their lives are going to be awful and then they force it on their children. If you're living in some shithole somewhere, you're down a dark, dusty and unhealthy mine every day and you never see anything outside of that, it's hard to have an idea that one day you're going to be happy.

I previously mentioned about when I was in Saint-Tropez, aged 27. I was drinking of course, although I wasn't drunk yet. I stood there watching that yacht come into the harbour and there was that guy on the boat with loads of beautiful women. And I thought: that man has got my life!

Within a few years my world had crashed down, my drinking had come to a head – and I found recovery from my drinking and started a programme for spiritual growth by doing the 12 Steps. I was living in a part of Manchester that I never wanted to go to, let alone live. But anyway I ended up there – and I spent five very happy years there.

So one day I remember I was in my little two-up two-down house. I couldn't work for the first two years when I got sober because my anxiety and my panic was that bad at times, and so I had no money. I had a one-year-old and a four-year-old around my feet. I was washing the pots at the sink and there was never any water pressure, so the water was just dribbling out. There I was with no money, recovering from alcoholism, no job, no yacht with no topless women – and yet I suddenly realised that I was happy.

God looked after me that I never became a professional footballer, that I was never a pop star, that I didn't run the multinational business – I thank God. They were the things that my ego wanted. I mean I used to walk down the streets after being in the pub thinking: where's the person offering me a Hollywood lead part; the record company person running up to sign me for a million quid; where are the football scouts I need to fight away so I can tell them it's City or no one...? But I wasn't doing anything for them, I wasn't trying to get them. I just thought they should have been handed to me automatically, I thought they were a certainty.

D: Is there any certainty in life?

W: The only certainty in life is if you follow the laws of life in a particular way you'll get particular results. You know, rich people know if they send their children to Eton the chances are they'll go to Oxford or Cambridge and then that they'll work in the City or somewhere like that. They know where they're going, they know what they're doing. But there's still every chance that something will go wrong along the way – so we have that type of certainty.

You don't know what sickness you're going to get, you don't know how long you're going to live. But we do know with certainty that if you have good self-esteem, you're likely to live longer and if you look after yourself in certain ways you're likely to live longer. And yet people don't look after themselves like this – there was one part of Glasgow in Scotland where the average age of death in men was reported to be 54 because of the gang culture, alcoholism, smoking and the frying pan.

D: What do you think when you see someone at a cafe who's badly overweight or outside a pub smoking lots? I mean, what do you think is going on with them?

W. Obviously I see the addiction: the weight and the smoking is merely a symptom of unhappiness.

I see desperation all around me. I feel compassion and a desire to help, hence my life's work and this book.

Spiritual sickness of judging skin

D: Another aspect of modern society is that so many people seem unhappy with their looks, and with such as Instagram a lot of teenagers and twentysomethings are going on there and they're really allowing it to damage them because they all think they should look like perfect models.

W: With beauty, there's a huge pressure. Why are so many young women smoking for instance? Because they don't want to eat. The fashion with women these days is that they want to be thinner and thinner. Even many women that look perfectly fine think they're fat. Obviously the extreme of that is anorexia.

It's because of the huge pressure from society. Today it's not just women of course. There is huge pressure on men too.

People are desperate for approval. That's why people seek fame: the approval of strangers based on some type of ability. It's very hollow.

If you're in your teens and your 20s those pressures are a thousand times worse. The bonding between a child and parent begins to be released in teenage years and then the bonding with other people becomes so intense, and then in your 20s you're looking to make your way in the world, and a life partner could be part of that.

There's more obese people around as we have access to vast quantities of relatively cheap food, which a lot of people forget is new. Malnutrition was common in many poorer areas in the UK only a couple of generations back. Men from inner cities had to be fed at special camps in order to pass the army medical in the Second World War because of malnutrition.

So food addiction is more prevalent and another leading cause of depression and anxiety. Being overweight in a society demanding perfection is a tough place to be. Many young women smoke and take laxatives in an attempt to be beautiful. It's also important to note what society thinks, as beautiful changes.

The answer is to be immune to the demands of the culture around us. Those who shout "I don't care what others think" are usually the ones who care the most. Self-esteem is the answer. But to become detached from society's pressures is very much a lifetime journey along the spiritual path.

Obviously you've got to come to love yourself, you've got to become happy with yourself and you've got to treat yourself properly. That's all to do with self-perception. Anxiety and depression are based on the perception of ourselves and thus consequently how we see the world.

Of course, we all want to look well and we all want people to think we look well and it's important we take care of ourselves, such as that we dress properly. But a lot of people don't know how to do any of this. Lots of people just don't know how to take care of themselves. It's often because they've never been shown properly and their self-esteem is so low that it becomes an effort they cannot handle.

D: And the key to stop this damage caused by society's pressure?

W: You should not give a fuck. That's far more simply said than done! But that is quite simply what it is. It is never God's will to compare yourself and categorise yourself in relation to somebody else.

We are designed individually. Nobody else can play our role. We must seek – and be encouraged to seek – our talents and abilities.

D: So don't look at the magazines, the Instagram pictures…?

W: All of these things come back to the same thing, and you can't just snap your fingers and say you're going to do it – it's all about the journey within, learning to find yourself and the more you find yourself the better you'll be.

I've spoken to many people who the world would say are very good-looking people, but they think they're ugly. They think there's something wrong with them because they can only see their imperfection or they're anorexic and yet they still think they are fat.

This is all to do with the view people have of themselves. Everything is to do with what you believe. I remember a plumber coming round to me one time. He was aged 24. He said: "I know I'll never be rich." What a thing to say when you're only 24 and you've said you'll never be rich in your life!

The words you say over your life are extremely important. But it's not abracadabra, you have to follow it up with stuff. You've got to be able to "walk in it". If you want to be wealthy in your life, first of all you've got to declare: "I am going to be wealthy, I am going to be prosperous."

I've asked many clients if they have ever made a decision to be successful. They say no, so I say to them that not making a decision is still a decision – so you made a decision that you won't be successful. Then I say to them to make one now, can you say to me right now: "I am making a decision to be successful." But there are some people who won't do it, because it scares them.

People who fail are often people who give up. Successful people are those that can fall along the way, but they keep getting up. Exactly like when we learn to walk.

D: It's interesting because Step 3 of the 12 Steps is: "Made a decision to turn our will and our lives over to the care of God as we understood God." So it doesn't say we are turning our will and lives over to God, only that we have decided to make a decision. So deciding is what comes first...

W: And a decision is only a beginning because if I make a decision to go to the toilet, I'm going to get a wet leg if I don't follow it with some action!

Most financially successful people know that they will fail, that it comes with the territory of trying businesses and so on – but the difference is they get up and they keep going. A lot of people with low self-esteem will only let themselves fail once and then that's it, they make the decision that they tried that and they'll never try it or anything like it again. So, for instance, they go to counselling that first time and they sit there and think it's shit, and so they walk out having made a decision to never go again.

The decision-making process is informed by our past, our blueprint – and to make a decision outside of that requires an earthquake... a volcano... or pain. Enough pain that we will blast through our own ill-informed programming.

Nations are no different: they have their own collective psyches too. For instance, take into account the impact of the famine on the Irish psyche and the impact of colonisation on the Irish society. If you look at Ireland over the past few years it has at long last developed a self-confidence, much thanks to that period of rapid economic growth in the 1990s and early 21st Century that's dubbed the "Celtic Tiger". In some ways before that many people in Ireland I think had a bit of an inferiority complex about themselves. Thank God that has changed.

So if we look at Britain, it has a legacy of empire and all empire is about superiority, about being better. Perceptions of superiority in a society invariably lead to war.

In the UK the psychological transition in the nation's self-perception has manifested with division in society. But this will produce a new synthesis in society – if the institutions and democratic structures are strong enough. Many societies when in turmoil hark back to some previous mythical age of a golden era, yet a healthy society will overcome this and the myth will stay as myth. In the case of 1930s Germany the myth of superiority and a golden Teutonic era, and the scapegoating of Jewish people, overwhelmed the fragile institutions of the Weimar Republic, leading to the horrors of Nazism.

Individuals are no different as we are like mini-societies in our thoughts and belief structures. We have our myths and beliefs built into the blueprint, enforced by deep moral conviction in their sanctity, which acts as the psychological police force making sure the blueprint line is toed.

If we don't live in the truth about ourselves we will suffer. Our complexes, our disturbances, anxieties and depression are the symptoms of the resistance to the truth and reality of ourselves. It is essential that this truth about ourselves leads us to become what we are designed to be.

It says it in the Bible: "Do not copy the behaviour and customs of this world, but let God transform you into a new person by changing the way you think. Then you will learn to know God's will for you, which is good and pleasing and perfect."

D: Do you think racism is a form of a spiritual sickness then? If you believe in a Higher Power or God or whatever else you want to call it, you know that anyone put on Earth here is in the image of that creator, is of a part of God and has God within, and yet some people think that some people are not as good as them because they have a different skin colour or they're from a different country or they have a different religion.

If it wasn't so serious it would be considered childish. Except that also discredits children, who are never racist unless they've been taught by a sick adult. It's like Albert Einstein said: "Nationalism is an infantile disease. It is the measles of mankind."

W: Racism is a total spiritual sickness. If when you walk down the road you think you're better than the guy sweeping the road or that, say, you are better than somebody with a disability, then you are spiritually sick. These nationalist leaders are manipulating for their own purposes to gain power.

D: But maybe they do truly believe they're doing good for the world. It reminds me that Nazi belt buckles had the words "Gott mit uns" written on them, which translated into English means "God with us".

W: When we talk about Christianity, most people have never properly read the instruction book – the Bible. In fact, historically they were encouraged not to read the rule book. As we mentioned, even possession of the Bible with a partial translation into English used to be punished with the owner of it getting burnt at the stake.

Yet if you read the rule book, it says the most important thing, the "first and greatest commandment" is to "love God with all your heart and with all your soul and with all your mind" and then to "love your neighbour as yourself".

That's Christ talking and that sums it all up: love God and love your neighbour. If you've got a good definition of love it's very difficult to really escape from that.

D: Love your neighbour obviously doesn't just mean your next-door neighbour, it means your neighbour from another town, another country, from another part of the world – basically love other people.

W: Of course. You know, if you think you're better than anybody then you are spiritually sick.

But people do think like this, all over the world. Frequently, it tends to be if you've got money: a person with money thinking they're better than other people who haven't got any. The thing is many people who haven't got money will agree that the rich person is better because they've got money.

For example, have you ever been in a room with someone and there's three of you sitting there and you've just been introduced to somebody and you're all having a nice chat and one of them goes to the toilet and while they are at the bathroom the other person whispers: "Did you know he was a millionaire?" and when he comes back you treat him totally differently to the way you treated him before he went to the loo.

D: Even before you know how he made his million, which might have been from dishonest, ruthless ways.

W: But what we say about people making money – that's another thing that stops people being prosperous because they think a lot of rich people made their money by being ruthless or dishonest. It's not true as most wealthy people have a great integrity because that's often a necessary quality in acquiring wealth.

But because a lot of people believe they don't, it stops them from prospering because they're already putting a blocker up to it. If you want to grow in life you have got to use your imagination, you've got to see yourself there, you've got to learn how to prosper.

Success has to be across the board though, otherwise it's just not success. If you're a success with money but you're a lonely sad bugger who sits in your big house all day and you've got nothing going on in your life and you have no kids or nobody who cares about you, then I wouldn't call that very successful.

D: Exactly – the word "wealth" derives from "well" and "health", but now of course if you say someone's wealthy it means they have lots of money.

W: Paul says in the Bible: "I pray that in every way you may prosper and enjoy good health, as your soul also prospers."

If we don't look within we'll never change

D: Sometimes in today's world it seems as though there's too much choice, and not enough time. For example, with books I have hundreds on my iPhone and still my "to read" list goes up by five or six a week. Even if I could stay awake for 18 hours a day and only read I'm never going to finish what I have lined up to read.

Then when I was 19 I had about ten cassette tapes, maybe in total that was about 200 tracks. Now I have more than 20,000 digital tracks! And yet sometimes I really can't think what to listen to, and it frustrates me and so I end up listening to no music, actually feeling deflated by the array I've just put into my mind, whereas when I was in my teens I never had that problem. Even so, I still get new tracks every week…

W: We can certainly be overwhelmed in today's society by the quantity of what is available. When I was a kid we looked forward to Christmas because we had special food and new movies. Now that stuff is common everyday stuff – people drink wine with their beans on toast.

Too much can bring about greed and a lack of gratitude. Many people lack gratitude when they have plenty. But you can never be happy until you practise – and I mean practise – gratitude. Many of us take things for granted and are not naturally grateful. A morning meditation should always begin with gratitude.

Living in the abundance of everything as we do can also be a great blessing if we are in balance. You have a design on the inside of you and the most important thing in your journey in life is to find out what you were designed to do – and that design can change as you go on.

When I was growing up I loved playing with my toy soldiers and then one day they just went off me and as much as I tried to get it back I couldn't, it had gone and I had to find something else to play with that I loved. The next stage of life was beginning. This continues throughout our lives.

Although often in life this process gets thwarted because people get stuck in jobs and careers where nothing changes or grows. Boredom and frustration will be the signals and, if ignored, depression and anxiety will follow.

I mean, I have a big thing now for flowers that I didn't have at one stage. There are many countries I want to visit and some countries appeal to me more than others even though that's for no logical reason, because what it's doing is reflecting what's inside me. The whole purpose of everything we do is to go inside ourselves because when we change on the inside our outside will change. It doesn't work the other way round.

My interests can change and certainly develop... making conscious life changes... if I don't facilitate them, I feel frustration.

So frustration and boredom are good things as they make us change. If you try to just get rid of the feeling – for example, drink, take drugs or smoke, then you are creating additional problems and only going to produce ever increasing stress and anxiety.

There is no escape from growth. All resistance to growth will be painful and eventually catastrophic. When we embrace growth and change we will be on the way to healthier, happier lives.

D: It makes me remember that Rumi big question when the 13th-Century Muslim man asked: "When will you begin that long journey into yourself?"

Although I would say it's important to care for your appearance. I don't mean to be vain – that comes from a word meaning "empty" – but, for example, when I met you I was complaining I had holes in some of my clothes and you encouraged me to throw them all out to replace with new ones, and you quite rightly pointed out that, for instance, I had on a T-shirt with some holes in it and that I could buy a new T-shirt for just a few quid.

So I did and I felt much better for it. Like having a shower, it just freshens you up.

I'm aware as well not to let the big ego take over with this though. And I like that joke: what's an egotist's favourite song? I Was Always On My Mind... So I need to remember that hardly anyone cares what the great David is wearing!

What I have come to realise is that letting myself have clothes with holes in, when I could afford some new ones, was so that I could focus on lack and wallow in some self-pity, all very familiar.

W: It's important David cares about what he is wearing, and although you may feel the world doesn't care about what you're wearing, don't ever underestimate the power of example and perception.

There was a psychologist and counsellor called Carl Rogers in America who believed the reasons for juvenile delinquency were poverty in the family. He couldn't do the research himself because you have to get another group to do the research otherwise it's prejudiced. So the results of the research came back and he didn't believe it. He had the research carried out a few more times before he would accept that juvenile delinquency was actually caused by the person's perception of who they were.

How you see yourself and what you believe about yourself is the key to your life. It's the key to crime, it's the key to love, it's the key to everything. If we don't look within we'll never change.

It's like some people say it's hard for them to find a reason for their anxiety. But it's not... so long as you know where to look. There's a spiritual law that says "seek and you will find". We have to search inside and we will always find the reasons for our anxiety there. Always. It may take time and it may take effort, but we will find the reason.

More on anxiety – do you believe the negative or do you believe the positive?

D: It seems pervasive today: anxiety. We spoke already about how it's a form of fear, a fear of one's own demise or at least that you're afraid of something.

On anxiety the phrase that I really like is: "I've lived through some terrible things; some of them have actually happened!"

So try this, look at newspaper headlines from a year ago, and see how many of the headlines have become reality. This is such as "Freak winter to freeze Britain". Tell me, has Britain thawed out yet, and did anyone survive that particular apocalypse? Of course, they're playing on anxiety to sell the newspaper.

W: It tells you in the Bible that the thing you fear most will come upon you if you keep focussing on it. Also that how you think, that's how you'll be.

D: There's another quote, this one from 16th-Century author and philosopher Michel de Montaigne: "A man who fears suffering is already suffering from what he fears."

W: Your thinking is everything. The battle between Heaven and Hell is a battle that takes place in your head, between your ears: do you believe the negative or do you believe the positive?

D: And everyone has this?

W: Every human being has it. People can say they don't believe in Satan, but remember the word Satan comes from Hebrew meaning "the adversary" – the opponent. The adversary that's in your own head.

D: The word "adverse" means "preventing success or development"; and it derives from words meaning "to turn against"... So the voice between your ears that loudly criticises your every move.

W: The self-condemning voice, the voice that says to you: who do you think you are, you'll never get anywhere, this isn't for the likes of you.

D: The voice that says to the successful author: you're not very good. I know an author who's had more than 25 bestselling novels and she once said to me that every new story she sends off she is worried that people, starting with her agent of a couple of decades, are going to say: "Okay, now we've found you out with this one, that you are actually no good and in fact you never have been..."

W: Yeah, that voice. It's the voice when a very talented footballer goes to take a penalty and a voice inside his head says: "You are going to miss this." There's always that voice in our head that is trying to destroy us and trying to stop us.

Just look at the voice of drinking or drugging or overeating. You know, I don't want to be fat any longer, I'm sick of when I roll over my stomach hitting the bed, so I am really going to stop. And then you sit down and you're watching the TV and you can hear the doughnut in the fridge calling your name and chanting "come and get me!", and the voice says: "Okay, I'll start my diet tomorrow." Where does that come from?

So when we talk about temptation as well, it's that voice. It wants to create Hell.

We talked about Odysseus being strapped to the mast and all his crew's ears were filled up with wax because he wanted to hear the Siren song. The Greek myths attempt to explain the human psyche like this, as does the Bible.

Many people dismiss the Bible because they think it's just an old book and people have made religion out of it. Jesus Christ didn't come to give anyone a religion, that's for sure, they already had that and he followed it himself as did all the apostles. He came to teach people about love.

But a lot of people who are religious tell you that this God loves you, but that if you do anything God doesn't like – from misbehaving at school, not going to bed on time to telling lies and stealing – then you're going to get burned in Hell for all eternity. That's a load of bollocks! You can't tell me a loving God would put you in Hell, a loving God couldn't do that.

The amount of neurosis people develop from some religious backgrounds because of what God apparently does and doesn't approve of can be life destroying.

D: But what's the purpose of this adversary?

W. Life is about contrasts and extremes. How will you ever understand the meaning of forgiveness if you've never done anything wrong or nobody has ever done anything wrong against you?

D: So we need this in us?

W: Of course, how would you appreciate the day if you've never seen the night? How could you ever enjoy success unless it could have gone wrong?

D: How would we fully appreciate life without death? And the Crucifixion, you say that represents something in the human mind?

W: That's the battle within us between Heaven and Hell. So think of your body as like that pod we mentioned before, that pod you are put in – and no one alive has a choice about that: you were put in that body and you don't know how you got there. Then it doesn't matter how much money you've got: nobody can go to the toilet for you; nobody can eat your dinner for you; nobody can feel your hurt, your pain and your disappointments. Or breathe for you… only you can do that.

You've got to do and feel all of that. So you are crucified in that body. You are fixed there. No human being escapes this. Just think of the pain you've suffered in this life – go and talk to any human being about pain, loss, disappointment or resentment and they know exactly what you mean because they've experienced that.

Now you have a choice, okay? This is what the Crucifixion in the Bible is about, what it symbolises for every human being. So when you see Jesus on the cross, there is a thief being crucified either side of him – that have become known as the Good Thief and the Bad Thief.

The Bad Thief taunts Jesus: "You're supposed to be a master, you should save us, get us down" and he starts insulting him. He doubts Jesus.

But the other thief says: "This man Jesus has done nothing wrong." And then he asks that Jesus remembers him when they have died, he asks for mercy. He trusts Jesus.

Now it's very important to remember that Jesus didn't have to be there. He could have got away easily, but he didn't because it's an act of love. He was there for us, he was there for that thief. He said to that thief: "Truly I tell you, today you will be with me in Paradise."

So many people blame God for all their troubles. But God doesn't even have to be here. We are here living in this world with a self-will, we have a choice. Do we open our heart to the love of God? Do we want help, do we realise we can't make it alone and it's okay to admit that?

Our crucifixion is on the cross of the lives we lead – in the here and now. So that crucifixion within will bring you to a resurrection. Every human being has to be crucified, we are constantly being crucified in our lives, and so then we have to ask for mercy and have trust and if we hand our lives over to the care of our Creator we have our resurrection and we can be restored to life.

Or we can face the hell of progressive pain we create for ourselves due to our powerlessness over the forces of life.

The temple in Jerusalem was designed specifically with the instructions of God. There was an area for women, an area for Gentiles, an area for the priest, and there was the Holy Of Holies and nobody was allowed there, except the High Priest on one day of the year.

When Jesus was crucified it says the curtain – that was hanging from the high ceiling to the floor separating the Holy Of Holies from the rest of the temple and the people – was torn from top to bottom, to show that no man could have done it.

That temple is the design within you, God is within you in the Holy Of Holies within every person. Only a messiah, a saviour, can tear that veil within you: it's too much for us alone.

Then your resurrection will come. The crucifixion has to come to an end, and it's not when you die. Paul says in the New Testament that he has been resurrected to life even though he's still in his body, and then the other thing he says is that he met a woman so selfish that she was dead even though she was still in her body.

It's important to remember that selfishness is a disease, a spiritual sickness.

D: And you were saying something to me once, about how the soul only comes into the body at the last minute because the body is so basic?

W: There was a mystic healer and he said something like: "This is such an awful place to come compared to where we come from, that the soul doesn't enter the body until the absolute last second that it has to at the moment of birth." That was his view and I can't say whether that's right or wrong.

D: Many people may have started glazing over at the story of Jesus and the crucifixion, but I hope are sitting up at least a little bit now because until you explained its symbolism to me I was the same: I'd had the story rammed into my ears, at school mostly, but with no explanation that it represented the human condition, that it was about the being or state of all of us who live and who have ever lived.

You've explained to me before that Jesus is on the cross in the middle of our minds, that's where the crucifixion takes place in all of us. Then to one side we have belief and trust, like the Good Thief, and on the other side is doubt and fear, like the Bad Thief.

And what we call mental illness in its various forms comes because people continue to be crucified rather than seek and find the resurrection that their crucifixion is a lead towards?

W: If someone's got heart disease or lung disease and you study the affected organ you'll find evidence of what's wrong. If you studied someone's brain with mental illness you won't be able to see anything wrong with it.

So physically it's the same as in someone who's not fighting, say, depression. People talk about chemical imbalance and there's no evidence that chemical imbalance exists – it's a theory that sells drugs.

Question why you keep taking the tablets

D: So there's no lessening of serotonin in a depressed person?

W: Every message we get is an electrical or chemical impulse in our brain. So if you sat here right now and you got hungry and I split your head open and we have a look at your brain we could find out the exact place where you're getting the message in your brain that you're hungry and that message will be delivered by chemical signals. So we have a choice: I can either change the chemicals in the signal by increasing the chemical or decreasing the chemical. Or I could leave your head in one piece and just give you a sandwich.

It's exactly the same with depression. If we are going to feel this pain of depression, then there has to be a signal towards depression that is telling you something is wrong. For instance, if I have a broken leg, then the pain is telling me to get this fixed immediately because if it isn't fixed I cannot use my leg. So I see a doctor and say I've got a broken leg and I'm in a lot of pain and this doctor gives me a morphine shot, prescribes some painkilling tablets and then he says goodbye and tells me I can go home.

I would say: "But doc, are you going to fix my leg?"

And he'd reply: "What's the point, you don't feel the pain any longer do you?"

Of course, I'd be horrified! I'd say: "But you know there's something wrong, that it needs fixing, and this is only a temporary relief you're giving me. Why won't you fix it? If you don't actually fix it then it will only get worse…"

Depression is telling you there's something wrong with your life: the soul is saying that it cannot live like this; that it cannot live with this woman or man any longer; it can't live in this society any longer; it can't do this job any longer; it can't be unfulfilled any longer. It is there to allow you to realise: there is something I have to do and when I deal with what's causing the pain the pain will go away.

Your brain manufactures serotonin. If you put more in it, then it has a balancing mechanism, so it won't make it itself. The brain will know there's already serotonin, so it won't make any more. So you can only make a human being feel better as you can take away the pain of the broken leg with some morphine. It doesn't mean you've fixed anything, and it doesn't mean that the pain isn't going to come back.

Human beings have a natural tendency to be well: if you cut yourself you don't have to do anything apart from make sure the environment it's in is good, that your cut is clean, that you protect it – then it heals itself. Your mind is the same. It has a natural tendency to wellness.

The problem with our minds when they are unwell is that most people do the equivalent of wanting a cut to heal and yet every day they jab their fingers in it to make it worse, stick some dirt in it, and then they wonder why it never heals and just gets increasingly septic every day. That's what people do to their mind – if every day you introduce another drug or another day of living in this horrific situation or another day of living in resentment, pride and terror, how are you ever going to get better?

It's very simple: if you've got a child in front of you that you adore, but you say to that child that he or she is a pile of shit, that they are no fucking good, that you can't stand them – then how do you think that child is going to turn out? Yet you have human beings who speak to themselves like that all day because their blueprint tells them to speak this way.

Depression and anxiety have their own language – it's important to come to recognise the voice.

D: The blueprint and Satan?

W: The blueprint and Satan do the same job. A blueprint like this has been set up so that Satan can sit in the chair and read the newspaper. Because of the blueprint, Satan doesn't have to do anything. Satan may have achieved what it set out to do many generations before, and the blueprint being passed on and on and on just keeps it going.

The only time that Satan has to do anything is if you begin to recover, and the newspaper will go down and then there will be a battle. But there's no battle if you're not trying to recover. All you've got is the suffering. But when you find the answer, then the battle will commence.

D: This battle could be in the form of the voice coming into your head saying: "I don't need to go to see a psychotherapist" or "I don't need to go to my AA meeting" or "My kids don't listen to me and my wife doesn't love me, so I'll cheat on her and leave them all"?

W: I'll tell you a very good example – I've seen lots of alcoholics over the years who have gone to AA. To get to

AA they are doing really well, but they've not had a girlfriend for a while, then all of sudden they get a girlfriend. Wonderful, but she doesn't like him going to meetings. She says to him that he's not drunk for a while, and together they decide he doesn't need the meetings any longer. So he stops going and soon enough he drinks again, with all the terror and bewilderment that brings.

Then you might get another alcoholic who goes to AA. He's doing really well, then he gets a job, and he hasn't had a job for a few years. But doing the job means he cannot get to meetings…

You see, when Jesus was in the desert for 40 days and 40 nights, the first thing Satan did was lead Jesus up to a high place and showed off all the kingdoms of the world. Satan said: "I will give you authority over all these kingdoms and all their glory. For it has been relinquished to me, and I can give it to anyone I wish. So if you worship me, it will all be yours."

D: They were Satan's to give?

W: Of course. The "system" in this world belongs to Satan, the wicked one, the Devil – call it whatever you like. If you look at the "system" in the world, it's the system that's the problem. You know the Bible says very clearly that the world belongs to God and everything in it belongs to God. But the system, people invent the system.

What the world spends on arms in a month would feed, clothe and house the entire planet.

D: And if those people are the not very well ones... Or the utterly sick ones... Without a doubt politics attracts some of the biggest egos, some of the most spiritually sick.

I think of it as well, this battle that goes on in our minds, as love versus fear, or love versus anti-love.

W: Love versus no-love. You know the opposite of cat is no-cat.

D: So if God is inside us all do we really need churches?

W: Jesus says time and time again that God is inside us. This is why people should read the Bible. It says very clearly in the Quran too that Allah is in us.

D: It says Allah is closer to us than our own jugular vein, and how Allah breathed from His Spirit into Adam.

The church is created by men, so it is part of the system...?

W: The church has been the biggest part of the horror. The whole concept with religions when they tell you you're going to be looked after and go to Heaven, that's not biblical. The Kingdom of God is here now. And it's the greatest trick in the world isn't it for any religion when they can tell you that you're going to be all right in Heaven, it's the greatest controlling therapy in the world. The church has told people that if you have a relationship with us, because we know God, then you'll be fine.

But it's like in the Monty Python And The Holy Grail film where the king goes past and there are two peasants and one says that's the king. The other one asks how he knows it's the king and the first one says: "Because he hasn't got shit all over him." And that's how it is.

What the church has said is that if you have a relationship with us we can intervene on your behalf with the God who created the universe because we know God and God can be pretty nasty because he's loving you in a very fickle way. And there's also this place called Purgatory that you might get stuck in for 300,000 years before you get into Heaven...

Everybody's got talent!

D: So if God is within us all, and God is the Great Creator of everything, we should know that, and feel confident in any of our abilities. Any doubting that comes is through fear – or no-love – rather than love.

W: There's a biblical story about a master with three servants and he gave them a "talent" each to look after because he was going away. A talent was a unit of currency then that was worth a great deal – equal to about 20 years of wages for an average person. But it's from this story that our present meaning of "talent" comes from – "having a natural skill".

So when this master returned after a long time away he asked them what they had done with the talents they had been given. The first and the second servants told him they had each put their talents to work, and doubled their value. The master was very happy and rewarded them.

But the third one said that he knew the master was a hard man and had hidden it in the ground because he was afraid. The master was furious and called him "evil and lazy", and said that he could have at least just taken it to the bank to make some money from it. He took the talent away from him.

This story is saying to us that God will be angry if we do not live to our full potential. Yet the church in many ways has told us not to, it encourages people to know their place… the church always cooperated with the state.

Where the church and state are as one, those countries are held back economically and socially. Such as

Ireland, Spain and in South America, although now thankfully many of those countries have moved on.

D: So the talent story is really saying that we're all given a God-given talent and not to have any fear and to fully go for it with that talent.

W: Nelson Mandela said: "There is no passion to be found playing small – in settling for a life that is less than the one you are capable of living."

So who are you to hide and stay small – we need you! If someone plays safe then they're not contributing what they should be contributing to the world, what was put in them. Unfortunately, fear limits people.

D: And fear comes from this no-love?

W: The word "enthusiasm" is from Greek meaning "God within, possessed by God, inspired". So we need people around who enthuse us. Many societies stop us from developing by telling us that we should know our place. They are undemocratic and do not allow for careers that are open to talent or they block the progress of women meaning that 50 per cent of the talent in the country is wasted. These are usually religious societies.

Where Christianity is no longer enmeshed with the state those societies have improved economically and have far more social freedom to become conscious. Jung talked about visiting certain countries where he felt disturbed by the people as they were so restrained in their deep-seated need to individuate.

To hold back people from their God-given destinies, whether within the family or society is an evil: it's the policies of Hitler and Stalin who needed obedience not self-expression. In many ways communism in the Soviet Union became a state religion. Evil comes in many different ways.

D: The Devil wears many cloaks.

W: Exactly. The evil of destroying somebody's talent. If you bring up a child and you tell them that they are useless or you marry somebody and you tell them they are nothing and that without you they will never be any good, then that's evil – you're destroying that person's life.

D: Bad teachers can do this too. I've met someone who was told when they were nine that they were useless at reading and when I met them they were in their late 30s and that's what they told me, that they were useless at reading. And yet we were doing a bit of recovery work together and that usually involved reading aloud to a small group of people, so I asked him to try it first, just in front of me. He agreed, read very hesitantly at first because he really believed he was useless at reading as he always had, for nearly 30 years... But when I encouraged him he got going. He could read as well as anyone who can read. Now he has gone on to read out loud in front of hundreds of people on many occasions and there won't be one person who thinks anything other than, this guy can read aloud really well.

W: When I was 13 we had to write a short story for English class. My teacher kept saying she didn't believe I'd written the story I handed in. She didn't turn around and say it was brilliant or whatever, she just kept asking me: "Did you write this yourself?"

D: So that was more subtle, a criticism that was saying: I can't believe you could have written something this good.

W: But she didn't actually say whether it was good or bad. All the whole thing did was make me feel bad about me. If she had said to me that she thought I was really good at writing, then I would have been writing more from when I was 13, instead of waiting until I was 50. From school, as well, I didn't think I was particularly good at art, yet I have recently completed some paintings that people have asked to put in a gallery.

D: What about that Eleanor Roosevelt quote: "No one can make you feel inferior without your consent"?

W: That's correct and I know it helped you, but it's still a very glib quote and a lot of these types of motivational quotes are just damaging when you are very ill. They have their place in the world of the people who are feeling okay, but when you hear statements like that and you're suffering from acute anxiety or chronic depression... then these statements can just make you feel worse. Because it's like your legs are broken and someone tells you to run – not walk but run! It can make a person slink back into the shadows.

When I was in early recovery, someone said to me we were just as happy as we made our minds up to be. I was suffering from acute anxiety and panic attacks, totally uncontrollable at that time as I hadn't learned then what I know now. So I spent the next 90 minutes thinking how I should kill him... not literally of course.

Rip up your blueprint – rip it up and start again

D: There's something else Matt Haig wrote that resonated with many people when he put that sometimes he feels like his head is a computer with too many windows open, and that sometimes we have to disconnect in order to reconnect.

W: I remember when I was first getting sober, I was living in a small house and I was in the kitchen at the back and there was one job that needed doing and I needed a screwdriver for it that was in the car. So I walked through the kitchen, spotting some other things that needed doing, I went through the lounge and saw some more jobs that needed doing, then I opened the front door and noticed that the door needed fixing. In my mind these all had to be done now and all by me, only me. I walked across my small front lawn and spotted a few more jobs I needed to do in the garden.

My head was now totally overloaded and by the time I got to the car I headbutted the bonnet, headbutted it loudly and violently in full view of everyone along my street. I couldn't take the pressure, there was too much to do.

That's the ego out of control. Neurotic, responsibility gone mad, trying to take on everything at once. Instead, make a list: you need to narrow it down.

But because the ego was in control then, the sickness was telling me you should be doing this, you should be doing that, you should be doing this, you should be doing it better, quicker, NOW! Whenever you hear the word "should", then you know you're in trouble. "Should" makes you feel guilty straightaway, and my life was riddled with guilt.

Guilt always has a cause. It's inadequacy – we don't feel good enough for the planet, we don't feel good enough for the people, we don't feel good enough for God. We certainly don't feel good enough for our egos.

It's all going back to your blueprint. Once you've got that blueprint, you then go out and practise it and there's tens of thousands of behaviours programmed in it, from brushing your teeth, to getting dressed, to how you think about different topics to driving your car. We practise all these things.

So what happens is you get very good at making yourself guilty, very good at making yourself depressed... It's not that you're doing it voluntarily, nobody can tell you to snap out of it, that's not going to do it. But it's understanding you can change you.

D: Rip up the blueprint.

W: You've got to examine the blueprint and see where it can change, and the reason we talk about God as we talk about the power is because the blueprint is more powerful than you are: you can't just change it by wishing it away. You need a greater power.

You have to learn how to connect with that Holy Of Holies within you. There is your answer, there is your resurrection. The sole purpose of your depression, your anxiety, your addiction, your pain and everything is to get you to rip the curtain, to take away the veil between you and the Holy Of Holies within you that needs to be born, that's your resurrection.

When that happens you'll be "rocketed into a fourth dimension of existence of which he had not even dreamed" as written about in the book Alcoholics Anonymous and as Carl Jung also talks about.

D: To nirvana?

W: Nirvana, Heaven, Shangri-La – you know, to enter the Kingdom of God you have to take it with you, you won't find it when you die.

D: It figures then that Hell is when we haven't ripped that veil. So we are living in Hell here if we've not worked through it.

W: Lots of people live in Hell.

D: Sure, just ask the alcoholic, the addict, the depressed person, the person too anxious to go to the shopping centre or even leave their bedroom.

W: It's to do with the blueprint. That satanic self-condemning voice always asking: who do you think you are?

I used to get told that a lot by my old man: "Who do you think you are?" That was one of his ways of controlling me. I don't think he meant anything bad by it, it was just a way to shut me up. The problem was I used to think: I wonder what I am really like? Is there something wrong? There must be something wrong with me. What is everybody seeing about me for my dad to ask this so often?

D: It's like the monster in the wardrobe, it's more scary because you can't see what it is.

W: Then it becomes a secret and you're only as sick as your secrets. I had a lot of secrets and the main secret was that no one must know. And so many people have secrets. It killed my mother.

She died because she had a heart attack and instead of phoning for an ambulance, she phoned her doctor and it took three hours for the doctor to get there rather than ten minutes for the ambulance. So when they finally got her to the hospital there had not been enough blood supply to her organs, and we watched her die for three days. The reason she'd not called an ambulance was that she didn't want the neighbours in her apartment block to know her business, no one must know.

D: Which is pride, ego?

W: Yeah, then afterwards one of my relatives insisted that nobody in the apartment block knew she was dead because they didn't want them at the funeral. The funeral wasn't for two weeks and it had to be a secret. So for a fortnight we had to pretend she was still alive. That no one must know – that's a big thing for a lot of people.

It's like there's less shame about mental illness today and although there's a long way to go it's getting better, because at one time it would be that no one must know. No one must know.

There was great stigma about mental illness, huge shame – just as there was with cancer, and people forget that. I had clients in Ireland who never knew their whole lives until the funeral that they had relatives in the local psychiatric hospital.

D: So letting out secrets like this could be like the benefit of confession at church, or Step 5 in the 12-Step programme that says: "Admitted to God, to ourselves, and to another human being the exact nature of our wrongs." So that's letting out your secrets to another human being and to the world, to the universe, the creator of it all.

W: Confession in a church has its place, but also what's the point in telling a seven-year-old that they need to go and confess. Everyone I've ever spoken to who got sent to confession as a kid just made things up!

D: They didn't think that one through! What about if you do it honestly? As in Step 5, which is preceded by Step 4 of course that states: "Made a searching and fearless moral inventory of ourselves." That's a vital help in recovery and has been for millions of people since AA was started in the 1930s, and the other 12-Step groups for such as addicts, gamblers, overeaters and so on followed – so long of course as it is "searching and fearless". That is, don't keep anything inside.

W: Taking a fearless and searching moral inventory of ourselves is essential because we have to clear away the wreckage of the past. Our past conditions, our anxiety and depression, it is the rocket fuel that empowers it to destroy our lives. By writing out our life story with rigorous honesty and examining it, it changes from a liability to an asset, from a curse to a blessing.

Why pain is the communication to change

D: What about someone who's a "catastrophiser", who has worries that seem limitless? What can help here?

W: Catastrophic projection is very common – and it's a big fear, such as that if I allow myself to be angry I'll kill somebody, or if I allow myself to be depressed I'll fall into such a chasm of depression that I'll never get out of it again. Catastrophic projections that are never true. They are just to stop you getting better, they're all part of the moral in the blueprint that makes it so powerful and difficult to overcome.

It's just making love to the negativity, pure and simple. We've talked about it already: as a man thinks, so he will be; the thing I think most I bring on myself. So what is happening is there's a cycle of negativity.

D: But pain can be a great teacher.

W: Pain is attached to growth, it's the touchstone to growth or you can just let it kill you. If you ignore it, it will kill you.

D: Alcoholics do that by running from the pain, which is one of the reasons for excessive drinking.

W: And they die. The majority of alcoholics die. The figures for the UK are something like 25 people die from using ecstasy every year, 700 from heroin, and 40,000 from alcohol.

It's often not listed as alcoholism though because a lot of alcoholics die of heart attacks, liver damage, pancreatic problems or there are lots of accidents, and suicides too.

D: And other addicts run from the pain with other drugs, but just in the same way as those addicted to alcohol. They don't face the pain, yet pain is the communication to change. It's what M Scott Peck described as "legitimate suffering".

W: Pain is telling you something is wrong. Pain is attached to growth, but that doesn't mean everybody who has pain is going to get well – because most people are going to try to get away from pain. They don't believe in recovery.

D: Maybe the correct help isn't there either. I asked my friend who's a GP in England what he does if someone comes to see him who says they're suicidal. He told me: "I only have ten minutes with them, the same as any of my patients, because I've got a waiting room full of impatient unwell people pacing about outside my door. So I will prescribe them some tablets and I give them a helpline phone number – but the tablets won't work for a few weeks if at all and they won't get an appointment through the helpline number for a few weeks…"

We looked at each other then in silence for a few moments. His face was etched with despair. I asked him if he knew some of the people that came in who said they were suicidal. He replied that he often knew their partners and children as well.

W: But your doctor friend is likely not trained in any form of counselling and many doctors repeat what the drug companies have taught them and unfortunately a lot of the time drug companies are like drug dealers – they want to make money.

Thank God for antibiotics, thank God for the drugs that really do help – but unfortunately there are many drugs that do not heal people.

So when somebody has mental illness as we call it, or a spiritual emergency, you have to decide, people need to be given the full information about what's happening. If you want the drugs, then by all means, because when you're depressed or when you're anxious and you're panicking it's horrible and I can understand why anybody would want to get out of it.

I've said to many clients if these work I will buy them for you forever. But the problem is they're not going to work and this is going to be a part of the rest of your life getting worse and worse. If it was purely some chemical imbalance in the brain, then over the years I wouldn't have been able to help as many people as I have helped.

It was a powerful turning point for me with my drinking and prescription drug addiction when I realised in a moment of clarity one day that if I didn't change this was how it was going to be for the rest of my life. My life was going to always be shit like it was.

D: Yet even when some people do acknowledge the pain needs to be faced and they ask for help in the best way they know and that society is saying to do, the good help that works isn't given – such as they're prescribed a drug that's not going to work for a few weeks, if at all. Then the person sits there and thinks I've gone and asked for help, I have faced this pain, I have really tried – but the drug is not working and I phoned the number I was given and I'm still waiting for an appointment two months later…

Or they get to finally see a counsellor and the relationship between them doesn't work. It might be that the counsellor is very good, but they and the client just aren't suited. Or the counsellor is not sufficiently trained in the way that will help them.

So they faced their pain, but now it's even more acute because they've been offered nothing that helps them, any hope they had of ever ending the pain has totally gone... and as a result it's even bigger now. They think there really is no way out. The stuff they've heard about working for other people isn't working for them.

Of course, it could be that the tablets might work, but they are not the real solution, they as you said earlier are just the temporary painkiller. They might mask the pain for a while, but the pain is still there, and underneath the temporary numbing of it, it is progressing, growing bigger.

W: If somebody is suicidal and you hand them a number there's a possibility that the fact they have got the number will give them some reason to stay alive. You've got to remember that there's going to be a huge amount of casualties.

With anyone looking at this, we're talking to people who want to get well. If you want to get well you need desire because you're not going to get well unless you have a desire, unless you have a determination that you really want to live – that's the beginning of how you get well. Once you have that desire, then you need the information, the support and you need to keep applying and keep working at it. There's the spiritual law written down in the Bible that says: "You will seek me and find me when you seek me with all your heart."

D: With all your heart. That's like within the 12-Step programme literature when it says: "Half measures availed us nothing." So you have to give everything. Half effort doesn't get you half success, it gets you nothing. Similarly 90 per cent effort won't get 90 per cent success. As you say, it's a spiritual law, a rule of the universe.

W: It's like if you've got a heart defect and you need four stents to stay alive, but after the operation the doctor says: "We only put in two because we just want to see how you go..." Half measures avail you nothing.

You and your free will

D: I really like this from Matt Haig: "I often sense a metaphorical void inside me that I have at various times in my life tried to fill with all kinds of stuff – alcohol, partying, tweets, prescription drugs, recreational drugs, exercise, food, work, popularity, travel, spending money, earning more money, getting published..." Then he writes about how the things he's thrown in the hole have often just deepened the hole.

W: Mathematician and author Blaise Pascal said: "There's a God-shaped vacuum in the heart of every man which cannot be filled by any created thing, but only by God, the Creator..."

D: So you have to fill the God-shaped hole?

W: People throw everything at it, but the only thing that will fit it is God. Until then it's a black hole that just sucks it all up, it's limitless and bottomless. But once you fit God into it, then the hole is filled, end of story. It's as simple as that.

D: But what do you think when people say such as "God is only for empty people who haven't got anything going on in their life" or Lenin's: "Religion is opium for the people. Religion is a sort of spiritual booze, in which the slaves of capital drown their human image, their demand for a life more or less worthy of man."

W: I have every sympathy with Lenin saying what he said because people were not educated, people were easily manipulated. If you look now people have become more educated and they don't believe this rubbish that the church has told them. Ireland is a classic example: if you look at church attendance it was almost everyone up until around the year 2000. Then came the Celtic Tiger, the huge revolution in the country. Now much of the younger generation don't go, the younger generation has thrown off the concept of God and I don't blame them because you couldn't believe in the nonsense the church was trying to peddle.

D: Or could it just be that the love of money is their new God? And I want to emphasise here that it's the love of money that's the root of all evil, not money itself.

W: Many people seek materialism in an attempt to fill a spiritual hole. In any revolution there is going to be an extreme swing of the pendulum... before it returns to an equilibrium.

The younger generation has dismissed the concept of God, they have thrown the baby out with the bath water. What you can't throw away though is our innate spiritual need and hunger.

D: With less God in their lives due to not going to church won't there be more mental health issues, as it's a spiritual emptiness and sickness that leads to these?

W: The Catholic Church in Ireland created more mental health issues than anything – with the sexual abuse, the way children were battered in schools, the belief system that they put into the country, the low self-esteem. The mental health issues in Ireland were absolutely huge, the psychiatric hospitals were completely full – I mean, even if you were an unmarried mother you were put in one and some of them are still there. The mental health issues were definitely there, they just weren't talked about.

So if you look at what Lenin was trying to achieve, they took away the idea of religion and created a new one and if you look at what drives people, it's a belief system. They replaced the belief system with that they were building, a brave new world: the Soviet state. The people there gave their lives to build this new state. They were the new converts, they believed people would be free and there would be equality, prosperity and people really believed in it.

Like a religion it's a belief system, a desire to change the world. It's about hope and something deep within us that longs to create perfection, paradise, heaven.

It's like the Nazis believed in what they were doing and believed they were right that the Slavs and the Jews were inferior people and they needed to be wiped out. These disgusting hateful concepts are belief systems that are not based on truth, they are based on fear... sooner or later they will collapse.

D: Many churches seem to tell you what God it is that you have to believe in, whereas the 12-Step groups are the opposite, saying you believe in whatever you want to – a God of your understanding, and you'll be right, whatever that is, whether it's the sun or the moon or the others there in the meeting with God standing for Group Of Drunks, Grow Or Die, Gift Of Desperation or Good Orderly Direction – there's a few to choose!

There is free will, and yet many people are put off such as AA or NA because they see in the books or hear a mention of the word God at a meeting. They are put off because of how they've been told they have to know God, because of their experience at school or church.

When I lived in some flats in London once I had a neighbour who I really liked who was drinking every day. I asked him if he'd tried AA and he told me he'd been once and was put off because he'd heard the word God mentioned there. He was an extremely smart man, a former newspaper editor. One morning our postman knocked on my door and said he'd seen through the letterbox that my neighbour was dead in his bath. He was aged just 62. Despite going to the pub every day, I suspect he died feeling desperately lonely. It was very tragic and extremely sad.

W: When we talk about God we're looking to find evidence of the laws of life, the laws of our being. So you can believe in anything, you can believe in the Pope, you can believe in all the different religions that are around, you can believe in little green men if you want to. I mean some people killed themselves years ago because they believed a spaceship was flying past Earth and if they killed themselves they would go and join them.

So you can believe anything, but what we're looking at is if you believe something and move in a particular direction, then can you see that belief produces a result? For instance, studies have shown that when you take certain groups of sick people and one half of the group is prayed for and the other half is not, those who were prayed for tend to get better quicker.

Now that doesn't prove there is a God, that proves that if you take a certain mental intention – and intentions are an important thing – then something seems to happen. So we're looking in that area.

So if I say to you that I pray and meditate first thing every morning for half an hour and what I found is that it has changed my life, then that's verifiable because since the first time I started doing it I stopped drinking – after trying to stop countless times by myself and failing every time.

People ask why does this God of love let all the bad stuff happen on Earth. I think it's because we live on a planet that is about free will, we have a total free will and it's up to each one of us what we do, including whether we ask God for help or we don't.

D: God of your understanding.

W: Yeah, the God of your understanding. Read the Bible and God talks about everything. You know, many people have a downer on sex – yet the Bible is very explicit on sex.

D: I mentioned the Bible to someone the other day and they immediately threw back at me that it says that gay sex is wrong and so they were not reading or believing any of that book. I asked them if they had read that bit, and they replied that they hadn't, but they had heard about it. So is there this part in there?

W: There is a bit where it says that and it also says in there that if you have a son who is an alcoholic and he is not responding to what you say, then take him to the elders and if he doesn't respond to the elders take him outside and stone him to death so that it doesn't spread into others. There are lots of things it says in the Bible, but it needs to be put in its context for the era it was written, when a society was being forged at a particular time.

So I don't know, I'm just saying maybe that was it. Obviously I wasn't stoned to death for my alcoholism. If God loves us, then God loves every part of us. He might not like what we do, but that's not because God's a prude.

Let's be clear – we all sin, go wrong, fuck up. It seems strange how we grade it, how one looks down on another, such as the alcoholic on the drug addict or the wife beater on the adulterer.

The Bible is full of stories that are telling us something about our psyche, that is symbolising the journey of the soul and how we develop.

D: So it doesn't always have to be taken literally, it's a story of the human condition that then has to include our relationship with God?

W: It's a story of the development of a tribe of people into a nation. This is one of the interesting things – in Jesus' day a woman's evidence was no good in court and yet you have Mary Magdalene who was the first witness to the Resurrection. If you were going to fake a story back then you wouldn't have written it like that. Jesus elevated women to a position of real equality. The Roman Catholic Church under Constantine knocked them back down again, and then what they did is discredit Mary Magdalene, such as saying she was a prostitute. It's only in recent years that the Pope actually came out and said there's no evidence she ever was.

D: There's something I read from Carl Jung that for me says it all so perfectly, talking about a plant's rhizome, which is its stem that is continuously growing underground: "Life has always seemed to me like a plant that lives on its rhizome. Its true life is invisible, hidden in the rhizome. The part that appears above ground lasts only a single summer. Then it withers away — an ephemeral apparition. When we think of the unending growth and decay of life and civilisations, we cannot escape the impression of absolute nullity. Yet I have never lost a sense of something that lives and endures underneath the eternal flux. What we see is the blossom, which passes. The rhizome remains."

This is so fantastic – underneath the soil we know there are roots, there's the soil, there are nutrients in the soil, the things we might not even know about the soil, and stuff happens in the soil when it rains. Then above and around the plant there's the air and oxygen, you have the sunshine, you get the rain, you have the breeze and the wind, you have night and day. And if the plant ignores all those other parts of it, and just relies on itself, then it's going to wither and die.

That's exactly the same with us – if we just rely on ourselves and just keep within our bodies, instead of connection with other people, and not connecting with all around us, including a Higher Power.

For me that's a perfect comparison: this plant might be big and bushy and tall and beautiful and it has been growing for years, but if it starts to ignore the stuff around it, if it cuts itself off, then it's going to wither and die. Same for us.

I think it's what can lead people into depression and then to take their life. It's when they get within themselves too much, when they lose connection with this world, with who they are, and with a power greater than they are. They feel desperately alone and small and hopeless, and are left with only themselves, and yet this self of theirs, the sick part of self, cannot see a way away from the pain except one tragic way…

Portugal's decriminalisation and changed policy on illegal drugs in the past decade shows this. Instead of spending money on the "war on drugs", the country – that had one of the highest number of drug users in Europe – started to spend that money on rehabilitation and to allow users to integrate in society again.

For instance, a group of three guys who'd been carpenters until their drug use had put them out of action, were encouraged, and with financial help available, to start up as a small carpentry company and to do their work around their community. This gave them a connection again. And there's a strong point that for many addicts the connection they have with their drug replaces any other connection. You know that thing you hear when an alcoholic sits with his pint glass, almost talking to it. Booze becomes the alcoholic's best friend, at least that's what they think until it turns round and bites them.

Within a few years Portugal saw a massive improvement and, for example, Portugal's drug death toll plummeted to three per million compared to the European average of 17.3 per million. Why other countries haven't followed suit, I don't know.

It's also one of the reasons the 12-Step group meetings work so well. There's connection between people and what they think and feel. I've heard it said that people going to their first meeting are encouraged to listen for the similarities not the differences. I imagine there will be some people who have ditched this book before now, or who will be reading it with the critical chatter in their head, coming up with reasons why this or that isn't true or why this or that would never work for them.

It's very difficult to know when it's the sick ego's drive for power that is the dominant voice in our mind. That's the sick part of the mind doing the thinking, the mental illness doing the reasoning and the decision-making, and consequently leading the feelings and the subsequent actions. Every feeling and action is preceded by a thought.

As I see it, the sick part of anyone's mind, wants to get them alone, feeling alone, isolated and disconnected. It's just like any abusive relationship in that its aim is to realise: I'll get you away from your family and friends, those that care for you, those that can warn you away from me because they can see I'm wrecking your life – and then I have total control over you.

That's why it's essential to ask for help, but you need to choose wisely. Look at someone who has something you'd like, and I'm not talking material things: I mean a sparkle in their eyes, a serenity about them, a tranquility, an assurance.

Because the ego gone wrong is cunning, baffling and powerful. It will tell you its thinking and its way is the solution – but while leading you further into the abyss.

You know the word "dependent" – whether that's on drink, drugs, work, gambling, sex, shopping or on another person – comes from Old French, meaning "hanging down from". It's also where the words "pendant" and "pendulum" derive from. And so anything that has you depending on it can swing you at its will, just like you have a noose round your neck that it has tightened there.

W: We're all part of the same thing. Look at a mountain, that mountain isn't separate from anything else: it's joined to everything else. And it's the same with us. But because we've got legs and we walk around we tend to think we're separate to things, yet we're totally not separate to it. This world all works together. For instance, without the insects there's nothing, yet none of us are particularly happy with insects a lot of time.

D: We all know now what will happen if there are no bees left... So it's all very intricate. Then obviously you get the man-made disconnection from other people, such as borders on countries that have been created by man and not by whatever created this planet and people.

W: That's what's meant by: the Earth belongs to the Lord, but the system belongs to the Devil.

D: The system belongs to the Devil... which is why you get a lot of corrupt self-centred politicians?

W: Well, the Bible says that when the Antichrist, the supreme evil, comes that the Antichrist will be hugely popular and everyone will love him and they will think he's great. And it's funny how things are these days because it says the Antichrist will control the financial system. And that nobody will be able to work in the financial system if they don't have the Antichrist's mark...

D: I think many of us already realise that the people with the true wisdom don't become the political leaders, one reason being because they don't want to as they don't seek to have that power and control over others, because they have more humility.

W: So once again that's a symbol of our lives: when we let God be the architect of our life, then we begin to get somewhere because that's to me the only way it works. We aren't designed to live independently of God.

D: There's one of those fantastic spiritual paradoxes here: we become more independent when we are more dependent on God. I know I just said about the word dependent meaning "hanging down from", but of course God isn't going to swing us around like a play thing! This comes back to Carl Jung saying that excessive drinking is a low-level thirst for God, and all those addictions are an attempt to fill the God-shaped hole…

An example of this increased dependence is when I asked you if I could take some Valium before flying to a best friend's funeral this summer because I was scared of flying for more than a decade and didn't fly once in that time, although I loved travelling. So my fear stopped me doing that.

Anyway, I was concerned that if that fear struck me at the airport that I'd miss the funeral. You said to me that meant I wasn't trusting my Higher Power to look after me, and you reminded me that my Higher Power has amazing plans for me and that meant I wouldn't be going down in a plane!

So I took that belief and knowing instead of any pill, and at the plane's take-off and ascent, which was always previously my most anxious moment, I checked my heart rate and it was normal and also my palms were completely dry when previously on flights you could have wrung a litre of sweat out of them!

So by being more dependent on God I was actually more independent than when I'd been depending on myself, which meant I'd not flown for ten years. Tragically that fear meant I'd not been to visit for quite a number of years this brilliant friend of mine Colin, who lived in Ibiza, and yet I flew to see him in a hospital before he went into a hospice and then I flew to his funeral…

W: When we connect, then we begin to realise the design inside of us. I remember some years ago thinking when I was very professionally successful and my kids were younger, when will I go and work with the stars and the important people then? I was praying one day and God just said to me: "Well, what about these people here, who's going to work with them then, do you think I think it's more important for you to be working with some Hollywood film star or that you're here in this community that needs help?"

You know, if we want to be Prime Minister or go off to work with the stars it's only ego. The people that we're working with are every bit as important as everybody else. It's only our ego, those thoughts I had were only so I could boast: "So last week there I was counselling somebody famous…"

Is suicide selfish? (Asking for a friend)

D: On the subject of the ego and coming back to people who are going to dismiss God or a Higher Power, isn't that because the ego is doing their main thinking, has the loudest voice in their head, and the ego wants to be the ruler – so of course it's going to tell somebody to dismiss God...? It's a bit like when a teenager rebels against their parents.

W: Everybody's got an ego, and then it's a question of whether you are open to finding out about why, about whether you have an open mind. I've met atheists who are totally close-minded, they are atheist and that's that and even if God turned up and tapped them on the shoulder and made everything disappear and come back again and did three somersaults with them through the universe, they'd still say: "I don't believe you exist, but how did you do that you clever bastard?" So some people are never going to ever see anything like God. The ego is self-will.

D: In the AA literature, which I can recommend to everyone not just people who might have a drink problem, it describes how an active alcoholic displays "self-will run riot". So the 12-Step programme is about ego reduction and spiritual growth, and to my mind they go together, are on opposite sides of the scales: when ego goes up spiritual growth goes down; the same as with self-esteem and jealousy because they are connected like this too.

That means, for instance, when someone turns to recovery and the 12 Steps, then the ego is going to try its bloody damnedest to resist that because it knows it's going to get pushed away, not be the ruler any longer.

W: Yes, the ego is frightened. You only go to an AA meeting if you have a bloody good reason to – nobody gets up one morning and goes "I'm feeling a little bit off today, think I'll go to a meeting of Alcoholics Anonymous..."

D: There is the need for a rock bottom, and everyone's rock bottom looks different. It's what's going on inside, which is why you get such as world-famous multimillionaire musicians or sports stars at 12-Step meetings. For sure, I have heard it put that no one comes bouncing happily through the door to a 12-Step group meeting.

But there is that lovely paradox as well and this comes when you get well enough, when ego is reduced enough that you are thinking of what you can do to help others rather than always about yourself; and the paradox is that when someone who's new going to the meetings asks when they can stop going to the meetings to someone who's been going every week for years, and the long-time clean and sober person answers: "You can stop going to the meetings when you want to go to the meetings."

Because by then they will have realised the benefit of them and that going there to help others is all part of the process of filling that emptiness that led to the addiction and their troubles in the first place. We need to give away freely what we have in order to keep it.

W: Well I would say to them, just come today, that you need to learn how to live in the day and that takes time.

People are only going to surrender when they really have to. When people come into such as AA they come in because they're in crisis or they come in because they're pushed in by the courts or family or a treatment centre.

The word "crisis" in Greek means "decisive moment", which means opportunity. So those in crisis come in, they are in crisis and they have made a decision, and they tend to do the programme. But those pushed in are not necessarily in crisis.

Originally I went to a 12-Step meeting for my family. It was nothing to do with me even though my life was down the toilet and things were very, very bad. I still had a few ideas about how to fix myself, I was not bankrupt of ideas then...

But when I came back three years later I was totally bankrupt of ideas on how to fix myself. So I was at that point of total crisis and I was ready to surrender.

D: Here's a big question – and you know I lost my best friend to suicide six years ago after he reached out to me and we chatted so much for two months – why do people take their own lives? How do they get to that point, how does it get so desperate? How do they reach the darkest chambers of Hell?

W: I can't pretend to be an expert on why somebody takes their own life because you could find all the reasons in the world why somebody killed themselves and then you'll find a thousand people with far worse reasons who don't.

D: What's the difference do you think?

W: Maybe it's ego again, maybe the ego wants to be in charge right to the very end. I'm only suggesting, I'm not saying it is.

But I do see the disease of "self" affecting and hurting people in many ways. People often become selfish because they never learned how to get their needs met healthily as a child. They tend then to go off their feelings, as I did, rather than a knowing maturity in their responses to life. As people become more absorbed in themselves they suffer.

It is only through giving of ourselves, of our time and our money that we find happiness. Yet many people who see themselves as giving are doing it for selfish reasons. They want to be liked. That's a selfish motive. Those who play the martyr will not find joy, only misery and futility.

Lots of times when people have killed themselves, people close to them say they were depressed for so long, but then they just seemed to be okay a few days before they did it. That's because they made their mind up to kill themselves and then they have got hope because they've made a decision, they've found an answer to their problems – they're going to kill themselves. Maybe this is a spirit of suicide, something that comes over people and they want to destroy themselves.

Always remember alcohol is a huge factor in suicide. People often kill themselves under the influence of alcohol and they most definitely wouldn't have if sober.

D: It goes against nature though. Nothing else as far as I know kills itself. There is famously lemmings, but that's a myth as when they appear to jump to their deaths it is actually an unfortunate result of their migratory behaviour. So no other living thing kills itself like people do. In fact, life strives to live – like you get a weed growing through a tiny crack in a concrete pavement. Every other thing in life is trying to grow, to be and stay alive.

W: Where humans strive to live, then people tend not to kill themselves. High suicide rates are in the richer countries of the world; in poor countries they have much lower suicide rates – and perhaps it's because if you have to get up in the morning every day and find your food you really don't have time to think about yourself.

But in developed societies the urban poor can find themselves in a very powerless position. If you are reliant on benefits and they are cut, it's very hard to struggle to survive because what can you do? You have no fields to work, you can't go and pull an apple from a tree as it belongs to somebody else. Everything around you is owned by somebody else. People become very desperate.

D: There's that William Blake quote: "The busy bee has no time for sorrow."

W: Exactly. So you can't come up with a definitive answer for why people take their own life. Maybe rich people proportionally kill themselves more than poor people because they don't find an answer to their lives – they've got everything that money can provide and still they're empty. They are sad because they're not growing spiritually, they haven't found anything to fill the God-shaped hole inside themselves.

D: Is suicide selfish?

W: I believe it is in a lot of cases. But there are different reasons why people want to die. There was a case recently of a boy who was attacked by his girlfriend and covered in acid. He was in such a bad condition and constant pain. I could totally understand why he wanted to die, I would too.

A lot of people that I talk to who attempted suicide have said the moment that they jumped they changed their mind. Then frequently there's much evidence of severe scratching around the neck when people have killed themselves with a rope, where they've been trying to get the rope off – so they likely changed their mind.

Over the years I've never had a suicidal client take their own life if they talk honestly about it. Because once you talk about it and you look at the reasons for it, then usually people change their minds.

As I've mentioned before, when you ask someone who's suicidal what they want to achieve, they often say they want peace. So that's great as we all want that, but I always ask them how they know suicide will achieve that? I point out that they don't know if they're going to go to some place far fucking worse. So while you're here I say, at least you're in with a chance, that there are things you can do.

D: I've said a lot of times that my friend was a very selfless person, he was an amazing and very popular guy, an extremely smart person, he adopted a boy who was ten, he always thought of me and everyone else before he thought of himself. He loved to care and help others, and I know he really helped, for instance, his nephew get his life back on track. But I believe his act of suicide was selfish – because he left behind so many distraught people, he badly affected so many people's lives, not least his son who'd already gone through one traumatic rejection in his life...

And there's hardly a day in the years since he did it that I've not thought about it and felt desperately sad that he did it and that I couldn't help him despite my best efforts. Or I question, were they really my best efforts, could I have done more? I think that's the same for anyone left behind after a suicide death.

W: There are no totally selfless people. There's that quote that says: suicide kills more than one person.

D: I know what that means.

W: So when somebody kills themselves they take all their family with them because how do you get over somebody you love just killing themselves? I mean it is a horrible thing to do. I don't get whenever people say to me that it's not selfish and that you shouldn't think like that.

There are solutions, there are answers – but many were just too proud to go and seek them and they decided in a stubborn way that only they knew all the answers and this was the best one. But all they've done now is ruined all these other people's fucking lives. Someone with children who takes their own life has told their children they don't think it's worth staying alive for them, they've told their own mother and father to fuck off, and goodness knows what they're saying to their wife or husband and to their friends and colleagues.

All of these messages have gone into these people, especially the children, that they were not worth staying alive for. The children left behind can dress it up as they go along by saying such as my father was this and that – but that's the message: that they were not worth staying alive for, and that's what goes into their blueprint.

D: What do you think about when people say that the person who ended their life was very ill, that they had no other option because mental illness is not a choice? And that they felt so depressed and worthless and utterly useless that they really believed they were doing their family, friends and colleagues – the world – a favour by ending their life?

W: Anxiety, depression and all the so-called mental illnesses are a problem deep within the person. These pathologies have their own language. For example, you just quoted about depression "people would be better off without me".

They are sicknesses of the soul, which is the mind, the will and the emotions – and as with any illness, if not treated it will get worse. It's progressive.

So the disease of selfishness has the capacity to bring a person to the depths of despair and hopelessness. But also I have come across suicide cases where anger and revenge was the motivation.

D: There is this way to look at it too. In the 1950s the World Health Organization (WHO) agreed with the declaration of the American Medical Association (AMA) that alcoholism was a "disease", so if someone is an alcoholic they too have no choice in that (but they do have a choice to recover as we outline in this book). So then if an alcoholic gets into their car when they are drunk and drives that car fast and erratically and without any rational thought and they crash it killing three children, wouldn't everyone say without doubt that the drunken driver was extremely selfish? I think of course they would because there's no other way to see that.

So there I think is some way to the confusion of why people say suicide is not selfish. They are saying that the person who takes their life has no choice over the fact that they have depression and such anxiety that they feel as if they cannot live any more, that they need to stop their pain. But neither then does the alcoholic who gets in their car in that case have any choice over their actions.

To my mind, it seems the majority of mental health illnesses are to do with becoming too dependent on the sickened ego, to be driven and controlled by it – and so mental health illnesses are inherently selfish. This is why, as we've proven, that "letting go and letting God" works. Or letting go and knowing whatever else it is you can believe in that is greater than you is what really navigates your world.

This is all still raw for me, and I can vouch for it as a best friend, as someone who was told in an email from my best friend a few weeks before he killed himself in his garden that he'd "had a very full life with lots of amazing places, events and people. Of all of them you are the highlight"… then he took his life. That has left me with a heavy load to carry every single day for the rest of my life.

I am fortunate in that I could write about it as a catharsis and I did, more than 100,000 words into a book, as well as newspaper and magazine articles. Also I have lots of support from many people. I've spoken with others who've lost a close relative or friend and it's the same for them. It affects you massively and that stays: it changes those left behind forever.

Maybe it all simply goes back to what Viktor Frankl wrote in Man's Search For Meaning that the route to happiness is to find a meaning in life and then that will lead to you being happy. Most people with children must know that their children are their ultimate meaning...

W: Why do you think it hurts so much that your friend took his life, why does it make you angry even?

D: It's really difficult to know for sure. It's a huge question. But I do now know that anger at a loved one who's chosen to end their life is a common emotion in those left behind, although it's so terrible to acknowledge, so awkward really, and guilt-inducing. I felt almost ashamed that I was angry at my great mate, after all the emotional pain he'd been in. But I do feel anger, and I think it's because I feel something blood-red raw even now that says to me that I wasn't worth sticking around for... I know he was in a terrible place, but that's what it says: it was the greatest rejection of all time.

I don't want to disrespect anyone who has tried or died by suicide, and I have known that diabolical darkness in my two rock-bottom periods. Eighteen years ago I stood at the top of a limestone cliff at Durdle Door in Dorset on England's south coast, not to jump but to look at the view, yet I felt my legs sway forward when I realised the ending of the misery and pain that could come. Fortunately for me, and not of myself, it was my turning point.

Then last summer was worse, after I became complacent, and I had dark thoughts, such as when walking across a bridge, and fighting the urge; then even worse on some early mornings as I sliced the bread to make sandwiches for my two beautiful little boys... No one knew about all this going on in my head. Fleeting one-second thoughts, but they were there. Over a period of a few weeks. The sense of isolation was omnipresent.

Then I have my personal and raw experience with losing my best friend, my soul mate, to suicide after he'd reached out to me and we'd chatted loads for two months. Maybe I could have done better, but I did my best at the time. I told him I loved him countless times.

So it's not to judge anyone, but to speak from experience and what I've learned from reading and talking about suicide so much in the past 17 years. The definition of "selfish" is: "(Of a person, action, or motive) lacking consideration for other people."

Of course, there are many reasons people end their life, and many are understandable such as if you have a terrible debilitating illness with no known cure. But often I think it's because the diseased ego has taken over and there is a feeling of no hope, with no known solution. It's why the belief in a power greater than ourselves is the solution I believe for all mental illness. Then you can relax, just like my children do when I drive them in our car – because they trust I'm taking care of them wherever we go and however bumpy the journey is...

But if I'd gone through with my dark thoughts, what was that if not utterly selfish? For the rest of their lives they would live with the message that they were not worth living for, that the meaning from the love they abundantly gave me was not enough. Sure, I had thoughts that no one would even notice and that their lives would be better. I was in such a hellish place that I thought no one would even notice for a week. Then when they did that they'd just shrug and all be thinking, well it's kind of better this way anyway…

But, to decide all this in my head, led by the sick part of ego…? It had me and nearly took me.

Life is so precious, and we should never take it for granted and we should always be grateful. We're here for a reason. I can think of no better reason that for me it's to bring up my two little boys and to show them love and to show them how to navigate the world and give to the world and have fun in the world. Is there a greater meaning?

If I didn't have children, it could be my friends, or looking after an elderly or less able person. Those of us in recovery get this meaning too as we are in a unique and privileged and fantastic position to be able to try to help others who are in the seemingly unsolvable mess we were once in. That's an immense meaning.

There's always someone or something. It could be writing this book to help others. Anyone out there now who's feeling depressed for instance could try what's in this book, get to a good place and then use their horrific experience to help others out of that horrific place when they are there, or help stop someone getting to that place.

It's that story of the person being trapped down a dark hole and looking up to see standing there an expert on being stuck down holes who's studied it for years and written 20 books on it – but never actually been stuck down the hole. Then by his side arrives someone who says I've been down there and I'll show you how to get out. If you're down there you will relate immediately to the person who's actually been where you are, and most people will choose that person to help them get out of the hole.

Talking about my experience, I do realise now that a lot of what I thought was depression – and I'm not denying there is depression, but here I'm talking about my head and feelings – was actually self-pity. Things weren't going the way I thought they should. The way I demanded. There was no other way, no acceptance. No inkling that I didn't know what was best for me, no belief that I was being cared for by something much greater than me. "Whence the sullenness, this mounting fear, this quarrel with life..." That's from my favourite poem Little Boy, I Miss You by James Kavanaugh.

For me that's the key part in suicide. The thinking gets driven by the ego. It can drive people to do good or bad things. Obviously good is better, but it's not always that simple. There were always good intentions with what I wanted to do and achieve, but to get there I just wanted the whole universe to dance to my tune, to spin around my arse. If only everyone did as I wanted they would realise how I was going to make the world better. But only my way, on my terms! Yet the universe does as it does, it always has, it always will...

Go and write all your worries in the sand at the shore and watch the tide wash them away. Do it again, and watch the tide wash them away again. The world carries on spinning its way. So even with the very moral and great intentions I had, that was selfish, ego-driven, and that was the start of my downwardness that might have led to me being washed over by waves on the beach at Durdle Door.

There's an amazing thing here too as about 18 months after standing at the top of that cliff I was down on the beach at Durdle Door. I was 12 months into recovery and I'd started dating, and on that beach myself and the girl I was seeing first told each other we loved each other. Now Debs is my wife and the mother of our brilliant two little boys. The message: don't give up. Ever.

I'd say to anyone who's struggling to try the things suggested in this book. To be humble and try them. You can find yourself and know happiness and peace again, then so much more. Everyone deserves this. Of course. Give yourself a try. Become the person you're supposed to be.

Often people think of ego as being the big I am, but it's also that voice in the head constantly, constantly, going on at you, the accuser, the slanderer: telling you you're shit, you're not good enough, that you should have done this and said that, that your wife doesn't love you any more and your kids hardly even listen to you so they wouldn't even notice for a few days if you jumped off the bridge and then in all honesty they'd be relieved to know someone as shit and miserable as you wasn't around to bring them down any longer...

So it's like all recovery, it's about taking responsibility for yourself. Faith without action is dead. And I've heard people say don't judge until you've been down in the depths... I have and so have you. Now I'm totally driven by seeing what I can offer that will stop people feeling suicidal, to stopping suicides, to stopping people losing loved ones to suicide and finding every day harder than the one before.

W: My mate killed himself as well and I had reached out to him many times. I went to his funeral, and his two families and young kids were there crying. His son played football with my lad and he was already a troubled soul. I just looked at him there, lost and bewildered... and the last person in the world he could turn to had fucking killed himself.

D: I think when people are saying it's not selfish, perhaps it's because they are meaning it's mental illness that people don't choose to have that leads to their depression and then their suicide. So saying it's not selfish is said with totally good intention because of the fact that mental illness is not a choice, that the depression is not a choice – although there is a choice to get well if you seek that and can find the solution, and often that means persevering until you find it.

There's also that people are out of their real minds, so clearly there's usually no intention to be selfish. Look at what my friend wrote to me seven weeks before he took his life and you'll see where his mind was: "I have become an impression of a Marcel Duchamp sculpture in which the art object is in every way an exact replica of a utilitarian object but is not that thing because it was made without the requisite utilitarian intent... but in reverse. I have the illusion that I know the world but the connection between the object, intent and meaning has been fractured."

Then some people who do want help don't know where to go for help, or seek advice in the wrong place from the wrong people, or as we've spoken about they might go for help and get sent off for counselling, but the appointment date is too far away for them to survive or the counsellor is not very good in the field they need, the tablets they're prescribed haven't done anything – and so they think what can I do now, I've tried counselling, I've tried the tablets...?

There seems only one way they can think of, in their presently damaged thinking that is led by this self-condemning voice of the ego that we've also spoken about, to be rid of this unbearable pain they feel in every single second.

It's like if your self-will is damaged it's only going to lead you further in the wrong way, deeper into the black hole, then further into isolating because this warped thinking tells you that no one wants to be around someone as miserable and useless as you, that no one has ever felt as low as you do and so nobody can help you anyway. Then you end up on your own in a dark room developing your negatives until the sick part of the mind succeeds in killing its host. So viewed like that, suicide is never a selfish act, it's a seemingly unavoidable act.

But I think if no one got so dependent on themselves in the first place, if they trusted in the way of the universe, the stars aligning, God, a Higher Power or whatever, they would not get to the point of depression. Sadness yes, but not more, and sadness is a million miles away from depression. The getting into themselves is a process as well I think of usually many years, never an overnight thing.

For instance, if my friend had viewed the several things that hit him at once in a different way I have no doubt he would be alive today. Such as he was told he had high blood pressure by his doctor – well that was a message for him to lose weight and live a healthier lifestyle. Then he'd always been a successful "business guy", that's how he defined himself – but his present work was struggling. Thing is, he wasn't as keen on that work as other jobs he'd had, so this was a chance for him to find a job he loved again, and also likely move back to his hometown of Chicago and all the loving family and friends he had left behind there in his recent move to a remote place in another state.

Then he found his partner in bed with a mutual friend, but I think most people who also loved my friend could sense the relationship he was in was damaging for him – for instance, he told me his partner told him that he was getting old and that no one else would want him. That's typical and despicable abuse. So finding his partner in bed with their friend was a stark message for him to change, to get out of that relationship – and lose that friendship – and find the person he was really meant to be with in his life. I just wish he'd realised the universe, a greater power than himself, was actually looking after him in its mysterious way.

W: I found out that a girlfriend had cheated on me and my Higher Power made sure I found out – it was a good thing. We'd had a nice relationship for about 18 months and then she started drinking too much. And there were a couple of incidents that made me a bit suspicious that she was being unfaithful or was planning to be. I prayed and prayed and I said: "God, I need to get out of this relationship and I find myself powerless to do this." Then I went away for a few weeks to Australia and continued praying on it and when I came back she'd left and I found evidence of her unfaithfulness while I'd been away. So it hurt and it was painful and I had to go through the pain, but at the same time I had to go through it, I couldn't go back.

We had a good time and that's it, that's all it was. The problem with some relationships is that we're trying to make them into something they're not.

Let's clarify this because there may be people reading this who've never had any exposure to any help of any sort in this way. So when we said about trying praying, and especially the half-hour prayer and meditation first thing in the morning, seek and you will find, if you are sincerely asking you will find the answer to your problems, as long as you persist in the asking. You can't just walk outside and say: "God help me" and then carry on and never ask again. You've got to persist, you've got to say the next morning: "God I asked you yesterday, so where the fuck are you?"

D: And if after that half an hour, if you're still feeling low and confused, you can always get down on your knees again that day and ask once more, can't you?

W: You don't have to get down on your knees to begin with – however and wherever you do it, what's essential is that you entirely turn your direction and your thinking, all of it, and say: "God I need you."

D: I was advised to get on my knees as it's humbling, it's an admission of submission to something far greater than we are.

W: If you get on your knees, that's great. When I talk about people being selfish I'm talking a lot of time about people who refuse the solution. That's why even if you are getting some education or some opportunity, make sure you are praying, make sure you know that you're seeking that higher power. Know that what you're doing is you are turning to find out if there's a God, if there is anybody who cares about you – that's what we're looking for at the end of the day. Is there a solution?

D: Yes, there is a solution.

Don't worry. Relax.

W: It says 365 times in the Bible to not worry, once for every day of the year – and Jesus asks: "Can any one of you by worrying add a single hour to your life?"

The whole idea is trust. There's a lovely story about Jesus with his disciples in a boat and he's fast asleep and a violent storm comes along, so they wake him up, frightened that they're all going to drown. But Jesus says you guys really don't get it do you... you've got me in the boat with you and you're still scared to death!!

It's like a lot of people when they're frightened on an aeroplane, the first thing they do is look to see how the crew is reacting, do all the stewards and stewardesses look all right? They see that they're not panicking and realise it's okay.

I used to listen to a guy called Jack B who was in recovery from drink and apparently he was a getaway driver in the mob in New York. But anyway he used to say in this New York accent something like: "If you pray don't worry... and if you're going to worry why pray?"

Acceptance of the self is very important. When somebody comes in to see me who's depressed, the first thing that I have to do with them is to get them to accept it's okay to be depressed. Or it's okay to be a schizophrenic, it's okay to be an alcoholic. It doesn't mean you're going to stay there.

We have to accept where we are, the resistance is always a problem. Sometimes somebody comes to see me and they say: "I hate my father." I say: "Okay, let's think of another ten ways you could hate him, how much could you hate him, let's love hating your father, let's hate him properly, get it all out." But often they don't want to say it any more. By not resisting, by exaggerating, it diffuses it.

We have ideas about how we need to be, like many people who say: I don't hate anybody. Often with honesty we find they may.

We need to realise if we get honest with ourselves and we start peeling away the layers of the onion, we begin to see what God sees, not the bullshit that we'd like to see and we begin to see ourselves as we really are. And what God is doing is saying to us, all of this shit you're hanging on to is all the stuff that's making you unhappy. Let's get honest, let's get rid of it and you can get on with your life.

I've had several people come to me when they have lost a close relative – they've been honest and have said that it was the best day of their life. They were free.

D: Because of a sense of relief or that there's going to be no more torment?

W: There was a book called I'm OK – You're OK published in the 1960s written by psychiatrist Thomas Anthony Harris that was basically saying your parents are like gods and so it's like suicide to blame them for your problems because you need them to survive. What you basically do is absorb the problem into yourself, the child blames themselves so that the parents remain as gods.

D: That's very interesting – M Scott Peck wrote in The Road Less Traveled that since we do not have the benefit of comparison when we are young, our parents are god-like figures in our child eyes. So our first, and sadly often our only, notion of God's nature is a conclusion of our parents' natures.

If we had loving and forgiving parents, we're likely to believe in a loving, forgiving God. But if our parents were harsh and punitive, we'll probably have a concept when we grow up of a harsh and punitive "monster-god".

Grow old greatly

D: At the other end of the age scale, how can we deal with ageing?

W: The most important thing with age, first and foremost, is what you are doing in your life. People frequently eat themselves older, drink themselves older, smoke themselves older, worry themselves older and then they have a lack of exercise in their lives. All these things make you older much quicker. Exercise is essential for everyone. Find whatever exercise it is that you enjoy. It's got to be fun.

You need to look at your mental, physical and spiritual way of being. Of course we all get older, but you can get older far healthier than you think. So many people have severe problems when they get older – but you can see why they do from what they eat, what they drink, what they smoke, how little exercise they do and how much they worry about things. So it's very important to get that side of it right.

The other thing is, you have to find the meaning and purpose for your existence and to realise whatever you do, whatever you believe – whether you're an atheist or whatever you are – that you're not here to stay, you're passing through. The meaning and purpose in your life is all within you.

D: And everyone who has been given the gift of life has a meaning and purpose?

W: Nobody is left out, we all have meaning, we all have purpose, talents and abilities – and once you look inside you'll find your answers. Most people's relationship with the feeling that time is ticking down, is running out, is to find an escape from the sensation, a distraction, to take a drink or a drug or shop, work, eat. Alternatively many people just make love to the fear and instead of the pain being seen as a warning it becomes an obsession.

So you have to find meaning and purpose to answer the human condition. I believe that's part of why we are here.

I've met quite a few people who say that when you die that's the end of it, and they do not seem to have any of the same sufferings I have in this world. They don't have the oversensitivity, they don't have the dream about meaning and purpose. That just seems to be how they are. They don't appear to be conscious of any big question.

D: Are too many of us obsessed with time?

W: Human beings are totally obsessed with time, especially in the modern age. Everyone wants to have everything done and dusted by the time they're 30. And if it's not done by 30, then it's going to be done by 35. Then when they get to 40 it becomes 50, and by then if it hasn't happened they give up.

So do not fall for one of the Lower Power's time-traps, such as that you better make up for the lost time – or the really big one that is thinking: I'm too old for this and I'm never going to do it now. You're never too old to develop in life. I've read about people who never did any exercise at all who started running marathons in their 50s and 60s.

Then here I am improving my tennis game, improving my linguistic ability, learning more about science than I've ever learned before, still growing spiritually, and I'm three-quarters of the way through my life, I think, or maybe two-thirds...

D: I like the realisation that actually this isn't our time anyway, that we've been granted this time... There has to be a meaning and purpose for that.

Forgive or die

D: Why are people compulsive?

W: Because they're driven by something. Compulsions are commonly drink or drugs, but anything that changes the way you feel has got the power to get you addicted to it, to feel compelled to do it.

With compulsions you're often thinking about the next time you're going to do it, the planning and everything for the next time – and it takes up everything. You're powerless over this.

So get addicted to doing good things like spiritual growth.

D: I caused some trouble in a shop recently because I had in my head that I had to do an item exchange, but I only had 15 minutes for that to happen before I needed to be five minutes down the road in a Spanish class – and I had to buy a bottle of water from the shop next to the classroom to take in, like I always do, because that's what I always do…

So because of my compulsion that I had to do the exchange right then, to tick it off my very important To Do list and make myself feel better that I'd achieved another of the things on that day's list, I was setting myself up. And so it was, when I waited for five minutes to do the exchange only to be told I was at the wrong till… They sent me upstairs – yes, the "great me"!

By the time I was speaking irately to the manager who I'd demanded to see because the queue for the correct till had four people in front of me – my pride jumping out with my every word! – I was already late for my next very important To Do thing, which was buying the bottle of water before the Spanish class.

Then even after leaving the shop, the pressure was still on, the pressure was even more intense! I could have done that item exchange after the Spanish class, but it was as if I couldn't help myself. I was compelled.

That had to do with time too, and always feeling like there's not enough time. I know that many people in the modern world complain about never having any time, always rushing. What's your suggestion?

W: So many people are so busy earning a living that they never have time to make any money. Most people never understand how to make money apart from going and getting a job, having an hourly rate. We're still working with the slave system, it's just a modern-day slavery. Living from one pay cheque to the next.

The time is coming now because of robotics that less and less people will be at work. Even now we have machines that diagnose better than doctors in some areas. So there is going to be less and less work. One person is going to create the wealth of what 10,000 people can do now. So there will be jobs for certain people and society has really got to look at how it deals with all of this.

Sooner or later we're going to have to understand that people don't have to go out and do a job they hate and live a life of drudgery just to put food on the table. If you've ever talked to people who suddenly give up everything and they go to live somewhere else or they go down the Amazon or whatever, none of those people ever say they regret what they are doing. All of them say they wish they'd done it years earlier.

For all of the people who are in those time-traps where they're rushing around and doing everything, the first thing is to prioritise and make a list of what you're doing and how important is it all and what you're doing it for – ask what are your motives and where is it going to get you? Will it achieve the results you are looking for or do you want to be happy? What are your dreams?

D: Perfectionism plays a part in all of this too, that no one else can do it except for you... And it's got to be done perfectly, the way you do it and only the way you do it!

W: People tend to think they're indispensable, but it's not just a question of being indispensable and being perfect – people are under pressure, the traffic's worse and no one has job security. There's a lot of worry.

D: And outgoings have gone up – bills, rent, property prices, food, healthcare costs...

W: Sometimes a lot of the pressure is created because of the lifestyle that someone aspires to. One of the Irish newspapers ran an article every week where they'd show a picture of a house somewhere and say this house was a million euros, and then they'd show you the equivalent of what you would get in different places around the world. I often said to myself but you've got that house there that isn't particularly nice and it's worth a million euros and yet it could buy you a villa somewhere in the South of France for half the price, and then you've got half a million to live on until you retire.

So people have choices, just that sometimes they don't realise it. We're going back to the blueprint we've been handed: it can stop us, it tells us we can't do things. You may be in a position where you can live the life you want – but you will never ever do it because you can never ever give yourself permission to do it.

D: Viktor Frankl wrote fantastically about choice in Man's Search For Meaning about being in a Nazi concentration camp – "Does man have no choice of action in the face of such circumstances?" He wrote that we do always have a choice, wherever we are in life.

"Everything can be taken from a man but one thing: the last of the human freedoms – to choose one's attitude in any given set of circumstances, to choose one's own way... Fundamentally, therefore, any man can, even under such circumstances, decide what shall become of him – mentally and spiritually... It is this spiritual freedom – which cannot be taken away – that makes life meaningful and purposeful."

W: Yes, people always have choices. It's the attitude. It's like Step 6 in the 12 Steps, which is about are we able to stay in an emotional balance under all circumstances? I am in awe of Frankl, the horrors he went through and yet he managed to maintain that attitude. He's proof of the idea that it's not what happens to us so much, it's how we handle it and how we deal with it, and he chose not to hate. Because he knew it would destroy him.

D: So forgiveness is massive? I heard someone say the clue is in the word "forgive" as it means to give ourselves something...

W: Frankl was choosing not to hate. We are destroying ourselves if we do.

D: Like drinking poison but waiting for the person we hate to die from it?

W: Exactly. That's why you're advised to forgive people because it only destroys you. I knew a guy whose daughter was murdered and it was horrific for him of course, and he tried to get into the prison to kill this man who'd killed his daughter and he was consumed with hatred for him and thoughts of revenge – then one day somebody said to him: "That man who killed your daughter is now killing you, he is now destroying you."

Led by your head

D: It says in Notes On A Nervous Planet – "Feeling you haven't achieved enough doesn't mean you haven't achieved enough. Feeling you lack things doesn't make you less complete."

W: It always comes back to the perception of self that's programmed in the blueprint. No matter how successful we are or how beautiful – we can believe the opposite.

You've got to check your ego in all of those things. People go around saying: "Well, I deserve this and I deserve that" and that's a load of bollocks. Do you deserve more than some poor fucker who is born in a slum in Calcutta or some poor sod born in the middle of bloody nowhere with nothing or living under some oppressive regime? It's not about what we deserve, it's about our whole perception of the thing.

If there is a part on the inside of you that says I am not fulfilling my potential here, then you need to look at that, to know what's stopping you from achieving your potential. But this idea, you know there's guilt inside a lot of people, that I could be doing more, I could be achieving more, sometimes that's getting mixed up with ego and exterior programming: the view of someone else about what you should be doing.

Maybe it's not that you should be making money but that you should be teaching kids with disabilities to play basketball. So once again it's that journey inside, to find out what you're really supposed to be doing.

D: And cutting out the expectations of society and family.

W: Expectations are always a difficult thing. You've got to find out: are you fulfilling your potential, what's the dream, what's the desire in yourself?

I think this is hugely important as we in the Western world stand on the shoulders of giants. None of my grandparents owned a car. But my two grandfathers fought in the First World War and I had an uncle who was a prisoner of the Nazis. They went through an awful lot in the war. In general they went through a lot of poverty and a lot of struggle, but they had courage and a desire to achieve and to get on. They always wanted to make sure their children were better off, that they could provide a better life for them.

So here I am in a situation where I'm living in the lap of luxury that they provided and all the people in the rest of Britain provided, such as through the trade union movement and the National Health Service and better education and increased opportunities. There's a big part of me that thinks this has been provided for me and I have to dress for that and I have to live it and I have to live to my potential and to give as best as I can. We live in an age where we are very blessed, but we are just a small part of the world.

D: It's a very good point. Going back to compulsion and addiction, what about people who say that those who are addicted to alcohol or other drugs have just got weak willpower?

W: It's nothing to do with weak willpower, similarly the recovery has nothing to do with willpower. Willpower is like a booster rocket or an afterburner − it's something you use to get you over the line in a race, an exam or at the top of a mountain. You can't live on willpower because if you do you will always be uncomfortable. Willpower is a strain, it's not a natural state of being.

Many alcoholics and addicts of any description, can in fact be very determined strong-willed people. This is one of the problems in helping people to see their addiction, as they are convinced they don't have a problem... because their self-will tells them they can handle it and of course they can stop any time they want. They just don't want to. Denial is a major killer among addicted people.

People are powerless over true addiction, and it doesn't matter how great the willpower: the addictive disease is far more powerful. This is why it kills the majority.

After I stopped drinking I found I was able to use my will in the direction of the recovery programme and getting well. Like most alcoholics I'm an all-or-nothing person, so if I was going to do something it was going to get my all.

The first thing anyone needs to recover is desire. I had an incredible desire to get well and to be successful, and I don't mean just with money although that has its place. I wanted to be able to live again, to be free from the mental jail I was in.

The success I've found in my life can be measured in many ways to how my relationship has manifested with a Higher Power, God as I understand Him. The experience of God through my recovery from anxiety, low self-belief and panic, has been revealed to me in my life in many ways, especially through my children and through the things I've been able to enjoy – incredible moments.

But there are those seminal moments when everything is different to how it used to be... I became far more conscious in those moments and events of the power of recovery.

I remember one day I designed and built a seven-metre-long shed out of wood and I made it look like a log cabin. The day it was finished was a sunny day and I put a chair on top of its roof and I meditated in the chair. And I was so high looking at the mountains in County Kerry in the South West of Ireland there because I was told I couldn't do anything like that by my woodwork teacher at school years before.

It had always been "I can't do this, I can't do that" – but with this shed a design came in my head, and nobody showed me how to create it. I did it my way and I am sure there are lots of carpenters would have said you should have done it this way or that. But I put that shed up and with the winds that blow over the Atlantic where it stood, if there'd been anything wrong with it, then it would have hit the deck. But it didn't and it stood there for 20 years, and as far as I know it's still there.

So the power of belief can be revealed to us in many different ways, and for me once, it was with that shed. Someone might question how I think the power of God was revealed in a shed. But it's what it means to you, it's about the victory in your own life, your own experience of what was once seemingly impossible for you, and more and more things become possible in my relationship to a Higher Power.

For 23 years it used to be impossible for me to get on a plane because I thought they were going to crash, and I went time after time after time trying to get back on one using my faith, absolutely crapping myself doing it and doing it and doing it and then I did it and since then I have gone on to learn to fly and then the day came when I flew a plane on my own and I didn't have a bad nerve in my body.

D: You were scared of getting on the bus as well?

W: I didn't get on a bus for 12 years. I was afraid I'd be trapped on the bus and have a panic attack, same for getting on a train – how the hell do you get off when they're moving?

What happens in the end is your world closes down and the only time you feel safe is at home and even at home you can have a panic attack, but at least you feel like you're in some form of control in that environment.

D: This sounds to me like a situation that would precede suicide when you're closing in and you are going towards ending up with just yourself...

W: I don't know whether it gets suicidal. In fact, I had a fear of suicide because I had a fear of everything and suicide was just another one of those fears. I thought to myself maybe my mind won't be able to take any more, I will lose control and I will kill myself, against my own will. It was terrifying.

It was similar thinking to how I found myself drinking against my own will because I didn't understand what was happening to me. I didn't understand at the time that a huge reorganisation was trying to take place on the inside. I didn't understand that I was an alcoholic, that I was in a hopeless condition, I didn't understand anything about the pathology of the disease and how it manifests itself.

I knew nothing about life changes or the problems in my past. I had no idea what my anxiety was about – I was bewildered, confused, desperate and petrified.

A thinking problem

D: What defines an alcoholic?

W: Someone who's addicted to alcohol. Now when we talk about addiction many people think you have to do it every day, yet some alcoholics only drink every six months – it just depends where it takes them. The problem is not when or how often they take it, but how it makes them feel and what happens next. An alcoholic is someone who having taken a drink can no longer guarantee their behaviour.

The main thing that defines an alcoholic is somebody who having taken a drink of alcohol can no longer stop drinking because when you put alcohol into their system their body doesn't metabolise alcohol like somebody else. So it creates a craving cycle that means they want more and more of it. It then affects the central nervous system.

Normal drinkers get a headache and a sick stomach. An alcoholic gets the DTs. In the beginning this will show as a nervousness in the morning, a depression, ungrounded fears, remorse maybe accompanied by trembling. But it is progressive and if drinking continues it will get profoundly worse.

I used alcohol to cure my anxiety and it gave me temporary relief, but then went on to create anxiety on an ever increasing scale. It became a nightmare.

I used to wake up in the morning feeling like I was in a condemned cell and somebody was going to put me in the electric chair. I was just totally terrified of I wouldn't know what, but I knew a drink shifted it. And then tablets from the doctors shifted it because you don't want to be drinking all the time...

So an alcoholic is somebody who has this craving cycle, and the obsession for a drink. You see, if I was addicted to honey and I went to the doctor's and I am covered in these blotches all over my head and the doctor said: "Wayne, it's the honey, so leave the honey alone and the blotches will go away" – then no matter how much I loved honey I would give it up, and I probably wouldn't have to go to Honey Anonymous. I'd just give it up.

But this obsession with alcohol would mean that – and this happened to me many times – I'd say I am never drinking again and the next thing I was drinking. I used to say that I couldn't be an alcoholic because I could stop drinking for, say, a week. It wasn't until later that I learned it wasn't stopping that was a problem, it was not starting again – that was the problem.

I couldn't stay away from it and it went on and on and on. It was progressive and it got worse and worse. It started with lots of fun – sex, drugs and rock 'n' roll, being the life and soul of the party... It ended up some years later where I'm on the floor with a bottle of vodka spitting and cursing at the television, and there was no fun or enjoyment and I couldn't stop doing it.

I was always trying to stop drinking and I'd go to the shop for a newspaper in the morning and vow that I was not drinking that day and yet the words "bottle of vodka" came out my mouth rather than asking for a newspaper and the whole thing kicked off again. That's how I began to realise I was totally powerless over alcohol, that I kept putting it in me and I didn't want to put it in me and that the fun days were gone. It was just for oblivion and any form of consciousness was intolerable.

There are lots of people who abuse alcohol that are not alcoholic. An alcoholic is the person who goes to the doctor and the doctor says you'll be dead in five years if you don't stop drinking, and they're still not going to stop. But if the doctor says it to the person who abuses alcohol, who's a big drinker, they may not like it but they will most likely stop.

I've got family members and we'd go out all night drinking and come back to their house and there would be a bottle of whiskey on the side and they wouldn't think about touching it. When I was drinking, nobody was going to bed until everything was finished!

D: Many people say it's a thinking problem, not a drinking problem. That is, people drink excessively because of the way they are thinking, and responding or reacting or feeling to those thoughts. But what's a "dry drunk"?

W: Alcoholism is a disease – the alcohol comes in a bottle and the "ism" is in the person. Alcoholics drink because they can't handle the world. But when you stop drinking you've got no more anaesthetic, you have no more medication, and all of a sudden the stark reality of the world is there.

I was incredibly damaged by my drinking. It took me two years before I could work again. I was also dealing with a prescription drug withdrawal, which was a 13-month programme that I had to go through. It was very difficult, I suffered from panic and anxiety, different forms of depression and I had to find something that could help me, so I went to meetings with other people who thought like me and who wanted to change.

It was then that I began to find something that could help with my condition. If I didn't have that 12-Step programme, then I'd have just been left with all the anger, all the bitterness, all the resentment, all the excessive pride, all the oversensitivity. I'd have been left with this mass of feelings that tells me I'm right about everything all the time, which as you can imagine doesn't help any relationship, especially such as with your kids or your wife – or anybody.

This is a dry drunk. Most dry drunks are full of rage because the world isn't going their way. I remember my wife said to me that I should just stand in the corner all day and shout: "Bollocks!" That's a dry drunk.

D: Alcohol is a depressant and often there's some sort of trauma, a huge pain that an alcoholic cannot face or doesn't want to face, so they're depressing it with drink, trying to press it down and keep it pressed down.

W: They are depressing themselves. Living in a chemically-fuelled denial.

Lots of people come to psychotherapy sessions thinking that one day they can find a magic bullet. But our lives are about lots and lots of things coming together until one day you may get to the stage where you're overwhelmed and you break down. That's not a bad thing because a breakdown takes you somewhere, it takes you on a journey within, it takes you on this incredible journey to the self.

But if you drink on it or medicated another way with such as prescription drugs, street drugs, sex the drug, shopping the drug and so on, and try and stop it or block it – then you create all these other problems.

You seek to escape the legitimate suffering of existence, life, and so create a whole new illegitimate form of suffering through substance abuse. When you stop the addiction there is a whole load of damage and suffering that the addiction caused you that you now have to deal with… and you still have to come back to the legitimate suffering you ran away from.

D: So you think most people shouldn't be prescribed antidepressants, that no one should or that it depends on the individual?

W: When I dealt with someone with schizophrenia, sometimes the drugs helped the person stay rational for a period of time where you can begin to talk with them and begin to do something, but those drugs are a problem because the person is suppressing themself.

It's toxic psychiatry. It's important people have the information, when you're suffering from panic and fear and depression the pain is so awful that you want some relief, so I can understand why people immediately think there might be a magic pill that will cure everything. And there are magic pills: cocaine is one, heroin is one, these are the magic pills that if you take these pills you will not feel it any more, you will be relieved. But obviously they're not good for you, and they're going to cause even bigger problems, in the same way I thought alcohol was my magic pill.

People need the choice to take the chemical route or the recovery route. If antidepressants worked why do we still have a world full of depressed people?

We have to face ourselves, if we want to get well we have to face the pain because the pain is trying to help us, the anxiety is trying to help us. If we pinpoint the source of the anxiety by looking within the anxiety, then we'll begin to grow. It doesn't go instantly, it takes time, you cannot just easily snap out of it.

But by taking pills you're prolonging what you need to do, you're putting off the whole thing and your life will never work out. Some people say they take some pills and they help them and they got better – but what did they get better from? I mean, they're okay, they've relieved a few symptoms, but not what those symptoms were about.

Drugs are a huge market. It's a bit like if we say that we've found a car that runs on water – then what are the oil companies going to do about it? So if tomorrow we find that nobody needs any drugs for mental health problems again, the pharmaceutical companies are not going to take that.

The real courage is not in living with mental health problems – but in facing why they are there.

Ongoing stigma of mental health

D: What about the ongoing stigma of mental health?

W: There is one thing for sure – when people say they've got something wrong with their mental health there is some form of stigma, depending on the society you're in. I remember a woman I knew in Ireland who started to find help for her alcoholism and she was told by her family they'd rather she had cancer because they thought her being an alcoholic brought such a shame to the family. But alcoholism isn't something you choose.

D: And is addiction due to nature or nurture?

W: Alcoholics I've known certainly don't come out of happy, bouncy homes. It may be that more people have the physical propensity to be alcoholics, but they don't have such a bad background that they need a drug to alleviate themselves.

D: So they don't drink alcoholically because they are happy enough, or at least they're not messed up inside?

W: Because they don't need to do it. I'm only speculating, no one can say for sure. With all the alcoholics I've ever dealt with though, when you go into their background, there are reasons. Especially for those who think there are no reasons.

When I talk to people with depression or anxiety or who are bipolar or whatever else and I ask them if they drink to alleviate symptoms, it may be that they say they tried it but it made them sick. It didn't do it for them, it wasn't the right drug for them. But when you examine these people's backgrounds you can see there are always issues in their lives when they were a child.

D: Sometimes you have to dig deep too because I've spoken to a few people who have said that their parents were brilliant, but actually as I got to know them more, they've let a few things out or made a few realisations. Then you get idealisation that we've spoken about.

W: Many people are in such denial. I remember talking to a man once and I asked him how his school life was and he told me it was wonderful. But then as we went along he let slip that four of his classmates had to flee to Australia because they were put on an attempted murder charge as when they grew up they tried to kill their teacher because he battered them and he'd caused them so much misery.

So people put up that barrier because they don't want to go there because of the pain of the hurt, because of the emotions. This man was having physical problems in his life and he had huge relationship problems, but the main problem in life was himself who because of deep pain he kept at a distance. Because he couldn't form a relationship with himself he couldn't with others. What is happening on the inside projects to the outside – it's a mirror.

The sickness in his ego guarded the door of his soul. There was no getting through to him. A lot of people are like that. It's like it says in the Bible that Jesus knocks on the door of everybody's heart and most people slam it shut. I've seen that time after time with people. I've seen people kill themselves rather than come into therapy or accept any sort of help. I've been at a meeting for recovering alcoholics and a lady next to me got up and said she'd had enough of this shit. She walked out and she killed herself in the shower.

D: So it's not the courageous thing to do to live with mental health problems, the bravery is in talking about it and seeking help for it, and then facing and fixing it. A friend of mine helping prisoners in a rehab said many left to go back to prison because it was easier.

W: He who conquers himself is greater than he who conquers a city. So, no it's not brave or great to live with mental health problems. That's just going back to the old martyr syndrome, you know you are putting up with it and struggling through – and that's not what is required. That's like a constant crucifixion forever. Crucifixion is designed to come before resurrection. All these symbols are biblical and they are very clear: crucifixion comes before the resurrection, it's not about constant crucifixion.

Biblical symbolism is hugely important in understanding our journey through this world. Take the religion out of it and look at the process in humanity it is describing.

D: Some people seem to want to carry the cross forever though?

W: They are taught it. A lot of religions tell you that you have to carry the cross all the way through this life and right into your grave and if you do that you're going to Heaven. I don't follow that because for a starter it's not biblical. I mean the Bible talks very little about Heaven anyway, it talks about the Kingdom of God being here now, the Kingdom of God within. Heaven is here within you.

As is Hell, but of course we've already had a taste of that as it's highly unlikely otherwise anyone would read this book.

D: If you live your life in the pain, that's Hell.

W: I never knew how bad a human being could feel until my descent into alcoholism. I did not know those feelings and those fears and that depression, I did not know it was possible that a human being could feel like that. But the other side to that is I didn't know how great you could feel in life, which I've experienced since I stopped drinking 30 years ago and got on a programme of spiritual growth.

My alcoholism forced me to come back and look at the fear and anxiety I had run away from.

D: It's true to say that God didn't put any of us on this Earth to feel crucified all our life – but rather to feel useful, purposeful, happy, in the same way that I've had children and you've had children and we don't want them to feel miserable, useless and unhappy. Like most parents, we hope they feel happy and know their worth.

W: God wants you to be blessed. But we have a free will as I've mentioned before. I'm only speculating, but one of the reasons we were put here might be a lot to do with that free will.

If you consider this world is a place that's sorting something, a training ground, a place where we get to understand who we are, I believe we are here to develop, to grow. It's like being sent to a university. We are here to do a course. It's God's school, and it's realising you're a child of God, you're a little baby God and you are being made into something divine that will live forever.

D: Is the purpose of the course – as each person and each generation ideally gets on it and does as well as they can – to make the world better?

W: Part of the outward manifestation of it is to make that part of the world we live in better. Where we are should be a progression to creating a part of Heaven, part of paradise, that we carry around with us. If everybody prayed for the people around them, then everybody in the world would be prayed for, everyone would be covered. If we treat all the people we meet with love, courtesy, decency and respect, tried to do our best for people and for our family by the grace of God rather than try to do it for ourselves all the time, then the world obviously would be a lot better place.

Everybody should feel a little better for having met you. To compliment someone, to encourage, to enthuse, to tell them they are doing well... rather than saying you've put on weight or you look drained or you messed that up.

D: Love your neighbour as you love yourself.

W: Love God, love your neighbour and love yourself. I came to have a knowing of God because of the love that was shown through events towards me. I wouldn't ever have known that love if I hadn't suffered. I became aware of my crucifixion and I desired a resurrection. My behaviour changed as a response to God's love for me.

I remember my old mentor saying if you rob banks, rob them; if you sleep with other women than your wife, sleep with them – but put these 12 Steps into your life and see what you can live with then. I did, and what I could live with changed. Because I changed.

Psychotherapist Alfred Adler said all failure was as a result of a lack of love. So maybe this whole thing, this world was created as a mercy to us. It gives us a chance. The Bible talks about this spiritual battle that goes on, that there was some form of rebellion against everything and this is our opportunity to put things right: that we rebel against God in this world or do we accept God? The problems in our life reflect the problems within us.

That's why the search for God is so important because it's about love, and then the trouble and the conflict will subside. But this is an inside job, and religion is always on the outside, and that's why one of the Ten Commandments says don't make any idols. That includes anybody.

You can't do everything right on the outside and yet be full of dead parts in the inside. If I go around making sure everybody loves me because I'm some fantastic Christian, but on the inside I'm living in denial of the reality of me, then I guarantee you I would be a phoney and suffer as a result.

Can talking about mental health problems ever just be attention-seeking?

D: C.S. Lewis wrote in The Problem Of Pain: "The frequent attempt to conceal mental pain increases the burden: it is easier to say 'My tooth is aching' than to say 'My heart is broken.'"

Of course I think it's vital and life-saving that people are honest and talk about their mental health issues. I know you wholeheartedly agree and you more than most as you are on the mental health frontline, and we both know that secrets can make and keep us sick. Plus it's absolutely essential that when talking about them, especially with a professional such as yourself, that people are totally honest.

It's like if I went to my doctor with a broken ankle and told him only that my little toe hurt, he'd only be able to fix my little toe... Yet when some people talk about their mental and emotional pain, about their mental health illness, they're accused of being attention-seeking. In your 30-year experience, are there people who talk about their mental health issues just to get attention?

W: Of course there are − I had a guy come to me one time who was involved in a depression group that met and supported each other, although there was no specific programme for change. They were all very depressed and they all identified and that was their thing and good luck to them.

But as soon as I suggested to him that it was possible to get well, that he didn't have to stay depressed, I never saw him again − he fled. With this guy, everybody in his family knew he was depressed, his wife put up with it, and if he got well it was going to change a few things for him.

D: I had similar just recently when I sent some words that I thought would be helpful to a guy I'd been chatting with on Twitter. He identifies himself as someone living with depression. He replied to me that he didn't have time to read what I'd sent him. It would have taken about a minute to read and the time he took in writing his reply that he didn't have time and then justifying why he didn't have time must have taken him about a minute...

I've also known of people who find a way to get out of going to, say, 12-Step groups or a counselling appointment because they'll say such as the medication they're taking for their mental health issue is making them feel dizzy. So not only is that drug possibly masking what they need to be feeling and realising, it is stopping them going to the actual place and people that will help them see the way to recovery.

W: Some people have never had attention apart from when they've been ill. It's not just about mental illness, it can be all sorts of illness – and often that's because the only time someone's parents ever took any notice of them is if they were sick. It's important to understand that for some reason and I believe it's to do with a fear of taking responsibility in one's own life, a lot of people don't seek to get well, and it seems, unfortunately, to be the majority.

D: Is this what it means in Viktor Frankl's Man's Search For Meaning when it says: "Life ultimately means taking the responsibility to find the right answer to its problems and to fulfil the tasks which it constantly sets for each individual."

It's just like sitting in a few 12-Step meetings and thinking, nope I'm still feeling bad. It's great that someone has found the place, but then they have to take responsibility for themselves.

Or when my mum worked in a physio hospital at the end of her nursing career with the NHS, she always said the most frustrating thing was when patients came back for their weekly sessions and told her that they still couldn't put weight on the injured leg or whatever and she'd ask them if they'd done any of the exercises she had explained the week before. Of course they'd make excuses such as I didn't have the time, or I forgot what you said...

W: The reason that many people don't want to get well from mental health problems is because it demands responsibility. That's it – you can get well, but it demands your responsibility, that means you have to do it. Obviously you need the help, you need the guidance. But The Road Less Traveled is titled that because unfortunately most people don't choose to travel the path to recovery.

It's like the people reading this book, some of them will be very challenged by it if they've even got this far because they'll realise that there is an answer – and believe me there is an answer and you can prove it scientifically. That's what we've said from the beginning, all of these things you can test them. But a lot of people won't do it.

Forever pain or infinite change

D: There's the phrase that change only happens when the pain of staying the same is greater than the pain of change. I can understand: it's a painful thought and a painful thing to have to look in the mirror at all the scars that you've been avoiding looking at – but you have to face them in order to know precisely where you have to heal.

W: Most people think they are right even when everyone else sees they are wrong. You have to become bankrupt and you have to arrive at a point where you say to yourself: I don't have a clue how to fix me, I haven't got an idea and not only have I not got an idea but all the people around me seem to have no idea, be it the psychiatrist, psychologist, reflexologist, acupuncturist, hypnotist, whatever.

They all say they have an idea, they all say they understand what's wrong – but here I am still sick. It's not until you arrive at the point of absolute bankruptcy where you have no bright ideas how to fix yourself that you will cry out to the universe: "Help me!" That is the point.

D: I've heard of a lot of alcoholics and other addicts saying: "My very best thinking got me in this complete mess in my life" because they tried and tried to sort things out, but then after years and decades of their "very best thinking" they got to the point where they realised their very best thinking wasn't doing it, so they surrendered, surrendered to win: they asked for help and this time listened to what was said.

W: It's a place of utter despair, it's a place of hopelessness, of bankruptcy and you haven't even got the option of suicide, you're just there. Totally powerless. That's when you cry out and that's when – and only then – that the door you didn't know was there opens.

Then after a while you begin to realise: "Oh my goodness, there are all these doors and every time I open one there's another ten." It's learning that they are there, they always have been, in the same way we talked about that bacteria is there but just because you cannot see it doesn't mean it's not there.

All I can do as a psychotherapist or as someone helping such as an alcoholic is to place their hand on the correct door handle, but I cannot push down the handle to open the door, only they can do that. To solve the problem when you are shown a way out you have to step out, you've got to have some faith in it.

Identity is fascinating because we're all searching for who we are – and you can only do that by finding the self and of course it's without limit. Why would it end? Can you imagine if it did end – how boring would that be!

It's like people want to know the future, but just imagine if there were no surprises in life... If you knew all the time what was going to happen, wouldn't it be just so dull.

The other thing is it doesn't go backwards, it goes forwards, it's a forever unfolding mystery. It's exciting!

When I was a kid I just loved exploring everywhere. It's the same with this once I realised the real exploration was the journey within, to explore the inner world of myself and that the inner world of myself was deeper than looking out into the reaches of space. Isn't it funny that the more the imagination of human beings grows the more we realise space is bigger, it just gets bigger and bigger and bigger and we know there are billions more galaxies than we knew about before.

D: It's also that many mental health illnesses if you don't deal with arresting them, especially perhaps such as alcoholism and other addictions, are progressive illnesses. The illness, the disease, the insane and depressive thinking and consequent behaviour and way of being will get worse. But the good news is you can have a progressive recovery, so you will get well and you can get better and better and better.

W: All the diseases of the mind are progressive. The sickness will continue to get worse, with ever greater anxiety and fear… So your life will continue to get worse.

In recovery the opposite occurs. It's strange most people can understand things getting worse, but to think things can only get better is difficult for a so-called normal person let alone a sick one.

Your life should never stop getting better. Now it doesn't mean things happen along the way that you are not happy about, but the direction of your life or the direction of your wellness should never stop getting better.

I have said the same to couples in a marriage. They say that they get bored sexually with each other or the marriage gets boring. But if you know how to run that marriage and you really love each other your sex life can increase, your intensity in your sex life can increase, your marriage can get better, your desire for each other can get better and your individual worlds can get better.

To have a good marriage you need her world, his world and the joint world. If his world and her world are good and they're thriving, they bring that to the joint world. Everything becomes about growth, everything in life is progressive – nothing stays the same.

So we choose the direction that our life progresses, we create the universe we live in. When people say you have to deal with reality, what they mean is deal with their reality. We have to create the world we live in, the universe we are in.

We live in the universe that we want to live in. When we die, our world dies with us – our world exists between our ears, we are creating machines, we are made in the image of God – and God is a creator. The way we speak, the way we think, it all comes from within. That's why the battle between Heaven and Hell is taking place between your ears.

What you speak over your life, what you think over your life is what you create – so will you create Hell or will you create the Kingdom of God?

The Kingdom of God is here now, it's nothing to do with when you die. You're not going to find it just by doing some sacraments or any other religious ceremonies that the church tells you.

It is within that you will find it. The terminology may sound religious, but these are merely signposts. Unfortunately people start revering the signposts and forget to follow the path.

D: Is it that some people are creating their own Hell on Earth? For example, are there some people who are, maybe subconsciously, wanting and wishing ailments on themselves, so they can get a doctor to prescribe strong prescription drugs, such as opiate ones? Then they feel they have a reason for the drugs, for being off their face, for taking something that means they can avoid the spiritual, mental and emotional pain, in reality, rather than the physical pain they have wished or unknowingly encouraged on themselves? Then it's justified and an officially sanctioned addiction all the same...

For example, I know of several people from a family near London, and I also hear something of their extended family, and there's not one of them – aged from their 20s to their 70s – who isn't drinking too much and too often, using illegal and or prescription drugs, or all of these. It's insane, and one of them even carries around a backpack full of prescription drugs...

Now some of the physical medical conditions they have are not "made up" and certainly wouldn't be wished for, but they are a result of the excessive drinking, smoking and drug-taking as well as eating unhealthily and not exercising. They have these heart problems and stomach issues and other health concerns starting in their 30s, 40s and 50s. And now they have legal drugs.

But it's not just this, it's the amount of their lives taken up by planning and talking about their ailments and the drugs they're taking and when they need to take them and restock and the side effects and so on. They are maestros on addiction and are addicted to drama, just that they don't know it. They have young children and it's being passed down to them by their elder maestros.

Tragically, there is never one mention that their excesses have anything to do with it. They talk about someone having wobbly spells causing them to fall over and lots of severe headaches – when what they are, I think, is drunk or with huge hangovers. That's without, due to the lifestyle, the losing and smashing of mobile phones, the bruises, the breaking of bones...

They're very generous and kind people, and it makes me sad when I hear them, so unaware as they are. Yet part of the problem too is they are all quite financially comfortable. So in the view of South East England and what they've been told to achieve by that society and culture of greed that is around there – thankfully not with everyone but it is quite abundant, and it's where I grew up and it's what I learned – they're doing well. But it's tragic and I feel their loneliness and their emptiness.

W: There is a huge lack of education about these matters, about mental health, including addiction. Most doctors are not trained to deal with it although they can be swamped by it. Drug companies set the agenda with a drug for every diagnosis. It's a backward system and until money and education are directed into mental health it won't change.

D: What's derealisation? Matt Haig writes about it, using a fantastic analogy: "I still knew I was me. I just didn't feel I was me. It is a feeling of disintegration. Like a sand sculpture crumbling away."

W: But that's good, that's all about the reorganisation we go through. As we grow we change, we change on the inside. Some of those periods – such as being born, the terrible twos, teenage years, the turbulent 20s – you know, they're not easy... they are conduits to maturity.

When we talk about reality, we are made in the image of God. God is a creator, we are created, and so we create the universe and the world that we live in, usually with certain parameters. But you have to remember that all things are possible with God. For example, if you say God is in your imagination, then that means your imagination can do anything – so you can imagine being on the bottom of the ocean, you are on the dark side of the moon, your imagination can be anywhere it wants. In my mind I can create more and more and more. Good or bad.

That's why it's important my prayers are always saying to God: your will not mine be done. Because my imagination on its own will get me in a lot of trouble. My imagination created my panic attacks, my imagination created all my anxiety because it was totally out of control.

D: And it can create a lot of temptation in terms of lust, or debilitate us in terms of fears.

W: Exactly. When I was a kid and I went upstairs in the dark, I was terrified of the dark – but I made it worse. It was my imagination that suddenly said to me: imagine there's a witch behind the door, so increasing my already desperate panic by several decibels... If you close your eyes you can create your own panic attack.

For instance, if you're scared to fly you can be sitting in your dining room and imagine you're on a plane and you will recreate the physical symptoms so that you start upping adrenaline, you start sweating, you start scaring yourself to death, and it's powerful stuff.

Now, if you can do that, think of all the other things you can do. Imagine if you concentrated on being happy and joyful all the time.

One of the worst things about talking about mental health – and it is vitally important we talk about it – but one of the worst things is when people say something like: "I am like this because I'm diagnosed with anxiety and that means I'm going to be anxious all my life." People are given or find a label and you could argue about whether any of these things exist at all or are they just a way that the drug companies make money?

But getting a label like this, with drugs to take to control or mask it, just becomes a reason for staying the same, so not growing as intended. Labels as diagnosis can be paralysing… unless followed by a prognosis of recovery.

Sadness & anger

W: Most people will happily talk about their sadness, but they are not happy to talk about their anger. Because if you talk about your sadness you can get pity for it, there is little power in sadness to change and if persisted in it will become the paralysing mire of self-pity... yet when you talk about your anger you will have become challenged to change.

Great anger and great sadness often live side by side. Your anger challenges you to change your life, so most people suppress it. But anger is a God-given emotion for your survival.

I don't mean bad temper and abuse, I mean the identity of who you are. If we didn't get that, nothing would ever change in the world. We saw public executions and slavery stopped and women got the vote, but without people getting angry about those things in society, then nothing would have ever changed.

D: And denying the anger or pushing it down...

W: Is the denial of self, and then you keep doing it. To deny self is a form of suicide.

D: So denial – you once mentioned to me about a 30-stone client sat in front of you who said they didn't eat much.

W: But he ate far too much. It's a psychological fact that people forget 50 per cent of what they eat.

D: Unless he had some sort of physical condition that meant he couldn't metabolise fat or something like that.

W: That's mostly a myth I think. I mean if you're looking where there are famines or such as at prisoner of war camps there isn't any of those people who are overweight. They're all skinny because it's food that puts weight on you.

Okay, maybe certain types of medications could increase weight or bloating. But generally people don't have weight problems, there is no such thing as a weight problem, there is only such a thing as a food problem.

D: And that people are eating food to fill an emptiness the same as people might use alcohol?

W: There was another guy I saw who was going for an operation to have liposuction and he was thinking of having a gastric band put in. I mentioned that he was possibly a compulsive eater and he flatly denied it. Food is addictive to some people. Food addicts are no different from alcoholics in that most live in denial.

D: The denial there, for example, in the 30-stone man came because he would know by admitting it he's got to do something about it, which scares him because what then does he do to try to fill the emptiness he feels.

W: It's just the same as the alcoholic who's drinking methylated spirits who says I'm not alcoholic, I've just got other problems – and that's what people convince themselves with. With all addictions people always convince themselves they've got other problems, and if they could deal with all those problems, they wouldn't be doing the drinking or drug-taking or whatever their addiction is…

It's not until you get to the point with addiction where people begin to realise: hang on, I can't stop doing what I'm doing, I find it impossible to stop and stay stopped. But remember your body cannot lie, whereas your head can think a thousand-and-one ways about the same thing. That's why if you have a gut feeling... follow it because your gut is telling you the truth.

D: Repression – what's that?

W: If you had a repressive regime it's a dictatorship and with a dictatorship, people are repressed. So repression is like that: a dictatorship by the ego, it holds everything down, stiff upper lip. Every human being has to understand if your ego is not subservient to the self – you've got problems. If your ego is not subservient to the self you are spiritually sick, and if you are spiritually sick it progresses to mental and physical sicknesses. Everything's connected.

God doesn't want any of us to be slaves

D: There's a biblical story that I'd heard several times at such as school, but no one had ever explained its symbolism to me or why it is relevant to modern life, the human condition forever, until you did.

W: The Bible is a story about the Saviour and it's also a story about you.

D: Exactly. I'm in a position where I'm looking to a new way to earn a living and for a couple of years I've been a little unsure where to go. Over the past few decades I've made a living from journalism, but for many reasons journalism as I know it is dying. I've also travelled loads with my family over the past few years and we've been working on migrating countries too, to get a better life for us all, especially our children.

When I mentioned all this, you asked me if I knew the story in the Bible called Exodus. I must admit when you first asked me that, I thought: here we go, something that's nothing to do with what I've just been saying, is Wayne even listening!

W: If you take the story of Egypt, the Red Sea, the wilderness and the Promised Land, many people look at that story and think it never happened. Even if it did, they think, it's nothing to do with the modern world... But that story is a symbol of the psyche as a journey of the soul.

D: It's a brilliant story. In summary from what I now know, it's where Moses and the Israelites are slaves in Egypt until the Egyptian ruler allows them to go because there have been plagues and all sorts that the Egyptian ruler can no longer endure. It's because of the ruler's unwillingness to free the Israelites that God brought these plagues on Egypt.

So Moses and around 600,000 Israelites, including women and children, make an exit – the exodus – and reach the Red Sea. But soon after, the ruler in Egypt changes his mind and pursues them, sending his strongest army.

Just as the Israelites are fearing they're trapped by the Red Sea and will be killed or returned to slavery, many of them are up to their neck in the Red Sea in their desperation, and then the Red Sea parts and they flee across it. When they are safely across, the Egyptians are also crossing to catch them – when the sea closes up and the army of Egyptians is drowned.

But now Moses and the Israelites are stuck in the wilderness, and the Israelites fear they'll starve to death. Moses urges them to have faith, that God will look after them, and sure enough they are provided with a foodstuff that grows on the ground every morning. It gives them all the goodness they need to stay alive. It's called manna from Heaven.

Moses is instructed by God and passes on to the Israelites that all they need to do is gather what they need to eat a day at a time. Some ignore this though and get enough food for the next days as they're scared they won't be looked after a day at a time. But by the next morning any of the manna they collected from the day before had turned rotten and it stank. So they have to keep faith that they'll be looked after.

They also have to keep faith that one day they will be guided from the wilderness to the Promised Land. After

40 years of keeping faith, they are granted this area, so rich in natural resources that God calls it "a land flowing with milk and honey".

W: So Egypt signified slavery – you're a slave to alcohol, you're a slave to food, you're a slave to sex addiction, you're a slave to drugs, you're a slave to shopping, you're a slave to anxiety and panic, you're a slave to depression, you're a slave to work... whatever it is, your life is controlled by it, it's your master.

One day something happens – the Red Sea opens – you don't know why, and you find yourself on the far bank. Then you're in the wilderness. But the wilderness isn't a bad place – in fact, it's a great place because if you look at all the people in the Bible such as Moses, David, Joseph, Elijah, they were all there, and that's where you get to know God, that's where you come to know yourself... that's where you come to rely on God.

So the slaves from Egypt were in the wilderness. Every day they got fed with manna from Heaven. But people like to rely on themselves and they want guarantees from their bank accounts and from the future, and nobody has them.

What God was teaching was that this is how you learn faith when you go through these types of things, that the manna from Heaven arrives every day as it's needed and you need to know things on a need-to-know basis.

Then one of the reasons that God kept them there for 40 years was to test them and for them to prove they had faith that their lives were under the care of God. This was so that they'd be ready for the responsibility for what was needed to live in the Promised Land.

Because the promised land that you want in this life will come with amazing responsibility to yourself and to your own personal development and to others. The working out of your own salvation is essential – that's the means of being saved from harm, ruin or loss.

So when you go to the promised land it's not going to be given to you just like that. The 40 years spent in the wilderness is the boxing training camp that teaches you how to take it, because you're going to meet opposition. You've been put in a fit condition and you're now part of an elite squad that can go and take it, and this is the journey of your soul. It's like I was saying earlier about how I'd love to give one of my children a Ferrari, but I have to make sure he or she can drive well first and that they're not just going to crash it.

Then I'm going to add one thing on top that we need to talk about and that is complacency. Okay, you and I have come down that road, on that journey and we realise there is no arrival point, there's no cap and gown, there's no certificate, but you've arrived in the promised land and now you've got to look after it.

If you start to think you did this yourself – then you'll fall into even bigger crises than you ever came from. I have seen that happen to people because once you've been in the Promised Land for a while you've got far more to lose than the day you set off from Egypt.

D: It's just like everyone says addiction is a progressive illness, and anyone who slips, for example after being sober for a few years and so who then goes back drinking, they always – without fail – say it was so much worse than how it was for them before, much worse than how it was when they first came into recovery. It doesn't go back to how it was when they last had a drink, even if that was 20 years ago. It's always hideously worse.

I discovered that when I got complacent after 15 years without a drink or anything else mood-altering: the place I went to was much worse than it had been, horrific as that was, 15 years ago when I started my recovery. The flames of Hell back then were licking the soles of my feet and often reaching to scorch my guts; but then 15 years later my complacency allowed the flames to start burning my brain.

So you also explained to me that the Exodus story states that God doesn't want any of us to be slaves. Like too many people still are. We talked before about that, about just look at how people arrive at such as London Waterloo station every weekday morning, so many not wanting to be doing what they're doing, even dressed how they don't want to be, so many feeling trapped and forced to do it – it's merely another form of slavery. People might kid themselves and say there's no alternative or think it's worth it because of the things they can buy. But is it?

For sure, we all have to provide – but God doesn't want his children to be unhappy. What's the point of that unless God's a God of hate rather than a God of love? It's as we also said before, that's like someone having children just so their children could struggle and suffer and wake up every morning dreading their waking hours ahead.

Bob Marley sang in his song Exodus: "Open your eyes and look within, are you satisfied with the life you're living?"

So the Exodus story I can see completely represents my gradual migration from one place to another – geographically, in terms of work and also spiritually. The success of this book depends on it too, as I have to be capable of handling the responsibility of it. So do you. If God doesn't think we are, it won't be granted.

You told me this story and it's been amazingly comforting, and I've relaxed about where I am going and it's been fantastic because I've got out of my own way. Que sera sera, what will be, will be.

But there can be no complacency. I heard a great former batsman once say that even if a batsman has reached 150 runs, the second he thinks he's got the better of the bowlers he'll be bowled out. I saw it happen, when this former cricketer predicted it. He said: "He's got his century and a few more runs, but I think he's finally thinking he's got these bowlers and that's why I think he's going to get bowled out." Next ball…

It's exactly as in recovery from drink or drugs or whatever under the 12-Step programme. Anyone in recovery has to grow spiritually every day. I've heard it put that people say, just because you ate loads yesterday doesn't mean you won't get hungry today.

Or that the monkey on the back of the addict is always doing press-ups and so every day you have to make sure you're getting stronger too – or monkey's going to get you again! And now monkey is even stronger, so can inflict more damage on you, control you more…

W: It's the same for recovery from anxiety and depression. That opposition, that Satan, will lull you into a sense of false security. If you think you've ever got it sorted and that you don't need to keep your conscious contact with a higher power, that you don't need to pray, that you don't need to meditate, that you don't need to maintain your spiritual condition – then you are going to be in big trouble.

Complacency is a huge killer – in all walks of life.

D: And humility is very important. Being humble.

W: Exactly – one of the definitions of humility is the ability to remain teachable. Humility is truth. To become spiritual you have to become humble. To become humble means an acceptance that you can't do this and that you need help from somebody else, that is the only way you'll find a higher power.

When we're talking about this, if anyone's getting upset with the idea of God, what we're saying is, is there a power in this universe?

This year we watched the lunar eclipse, and it's absolutely amazing when you see the shadow of the Earth pass over the moon. At the same time it went blood-red and we also saw Mars bigger than we've ever seen it for years.

So when you look at all of that do you think, oh it just happened, it just went blood-red, it's just all a big bloody mistake. Well, it's the most amazing big bloody mistake that mathematicians can work it out for it to be mathematically possible using the laws of probability.

If you want, forget the word God and call it whatever you want and simply ask: can I move in a certain direction and get a result, and then having found that result can I again scientifically prove it in other areas of my life? Okay, so the experiment can be redone and redone.

"Fuckin' God!"

George was a Glaswegian communist... that's how he titled himself, but in reality he was an alcoholic who drank in the Jewish graveyard. He came into recovery kicking and screaming, being a good communist he hated Alcoholics Anonymous because it had its roots in the USA.

"Fuckin' Yanks," I often heard him snarl...

"Just keep coming George."

Then George heard the suggestion of a Higher Power, sometimes referred to in the generic term God.

"Fuckin' God is it now, fuckin' God! Well you can all fuck off I'm having none of it!"

God as you understand it, George... Just keep coming...

Fuck off...

God kept smiling George kept coming... George was desperate, at the last chance saloon.

We all live in illusion.

I met another guy who drank in a graveyard and he insisted he was in Russia, even though it looked like central Manchester to me. Who am I to argue?

George said that when he was drinking he thought he was a great lover... but when he got sober he realised he'd only been nodding his head.

George kept coming, he prayed to Father Christmas for a while...

But he kept working the programme, the desperation was his gift.

He did what was suggested.

He changed.

He became a very spiritual man and helped a lot of people and worked with the homeless all over Manchester.

I saw the devastation when that afternoon he held his dead granddaughter in his arms, the tears pouring down his cheeks, the awful sobs... He didn't drink.

Something kept him sober.

When he was dying we spoke often, he was at peace with himself, life and a God of his own understanding.

The changes were profound because he was willing to change.

To open his mind.

"Good morning, God" or "Good God, morning"

D: Here's an excellent and complete chapter from Notes On A Nervous Planet: "1. Wake up. 2. Pick up phone. 3. Stare at phone for 72 minutes. 4. Sigh. 5. Get out of bed. Alternatively, once in a while, try skipping stages two to four."

So Matt Haig is talking about how almost everyone has their phone plugged in by their bed and we look at it first thing when we wake up. What do you think is the best way to get out of bed, the healthiest process to begin a new day?

W: The first thing you should do is say to yourself: thank God I can open my eyes and see, thank God I can get out of this bed. Everyone should get their own formula of what they can say to themselves or how they show gratitude because gratitude needs to be the first thing you do in the morning – and that's because negativity and guilt and regret are often going to come flooding into your head.

So the first thing is you've got to fake it to make it, you've got to say: well, what am I grateful for? Remember, when we talk about fake it to make it, feelings are only telling you how you're experiencing something, they're not telling you the reality of something. It's like people say: I don't feel like it or I don't mean it because I don't feel it. That's bollocks. If you do something because it's the right thing to do even though you don't feel like doing it, that makes it right.

D: And you start your day by praying and meditating for half an hour, no more no less?

W: The first thing I do is talk to my Higher Power, God as I understand God. I continue praying in my bed for a few minutes. I thank God that I've woken up sober, I ask God to keep me sober but to direct my thoughts, to direct my thinking, especially that it be kept from dishonesty and selfishness and resentment.

Then I get up, and I say affirmations as I shave and shower. I take a shower every morning, even though the night before I would likely have had a shower because I've usually been playing sport. Every day starts with a shower because it gets my head straight. With my affirmations I say things such as: I have no anxiety about anything; he who rests under the shadow of the most high God will be kept safe by the Mighty One; all things are possible with God; God has plans for my success; this is the day the Lord has made, let us rejoice and be glad in it.

Whatever it is, you've got to find your own state... When I finish my shower I get a cup of coffee and then I sit down to drink it while I talk to God for half an hour.

I always get on my knees... not because God needs me on my knees, but because I need help.

D: And you chat casually don't you, as if you're having a chat with who?

W: My best mate, my father – who loves me more than I can imagine. I've had to learn over the years what love is – and love is that I am totally accepted. Totally accepted.

D: Exactly how you are.

W: Exactly as I am.

D: And where and when can people pray? It doesn't have to be a church or dressed in your Sunday best, does it?

W: There are all types of prayers. You could pray to God in the middle of anything! There was a head of the church in the Middle Ages who said when a man and a woman make love the Holy Spirit leaves the room – what a load of bollocks! You pray any time. It says in the Bible: pray without ceasing.

Quiet alone time is essential. If you don't spend time in a relationship you won't have one. Same goes with God.

D: What can you suggest to someone who's thinking to shut this book and chuck it away because of the mere mention of the word "God"?

W: Well, get rid of the word God, call whatever you pray to, say, Jimmy.

D: And who is Jimmy to anyone?

W: Jimmy could be anything you want it to be.

D: Just something greater, a higher power that makes the wind blow and puts breath into us – who loves the creation that you are. Maybe this can help someone: the way I came to believe in a greater power is that I was asked by a Glaswegian lad who I'd asked for help to stop drinking if I thought I was the greatest power in the universe and if I did, he said, if I was, then could I stop the wind blowing because it was howling and we were both getting blown down that London street as we walked!

I had to admit that I couldn't stop the wind blowing any more than any other person could, that I wasn't the greatest power around. So he said to me: "Then you believe there is a greater power, you believe in a higher power."

W: Let's get back to the basics here – if you don't believe in God and you think God is a load of crap, and remember God is just a generic term and it's got all sorts of different connotations to everybody…

D: Most people probably think of the fluffy white-bearded giant man, the religious version that's often rammed down people's throat with the demand that they have to believe that and only that.

W: Or they think of some horrible bastard that burns people at the stake or I used to think God was in the shape of England! But what we're actually looking at for this to work, is that it has to be real. It's all very scientific: you suck it and see.

So if you don't believe there's a God, but if you're open to an experiment, then pretend there is a God for a week. You don't even need to call this God. Call it Something That Made The Big Bang Go Bang. Or Something That Made Me Love My Children or Something That Made The Complexity Of An Eye or The Beauty or The Wonder or The Fact That I Can Connect And Look At The Wonder In The World.

D: Sure, I know it as something that created us, through our parents. Something so much bigger than our parents are, something so much greater than we are. Something so much bigger than the sun.

W: Whatever it is, all you need to do is say: I'm going to sit down every day for one week and the first half an hour of every day before I have my breakfast I'm going to get out of bed and I'm going to say: "Thank you that I can see... thank you that I can throw my legs out of the bed." Then think of all the things you are really grateful for, such as that your kids are alive, that you have a roof over your head, that you're not living in a war zone, or even if you are living in a war zone... then thank God that you didn't get bombed last night.

Then go and say aloud something such as: "I don't know whether you are there or not God – or whatever name you choose – but I think if you are there you might be a bit of a bastard. But even so, I'm going to sit here and I'm going to give you the opportunity to prove yourself to me. Okay, so I'm going to pretend you exist and I'm going to talk to you like you do exist and if I don't know what to say I'm just going to sit here for half an hour in silence. But, whatever, I will not do it for 28 or 29 minutes, I will do it for 30 minutes." Anyone doing this needs to discipline themselves – and the word "discipline" is from Latin meaning "instruction given, knowledge, learning".

So say to yourself that you're going to do this every morning for a week, you're going to pretend there is a God... See what happens.

D: And get up half an hour earlier if necessary? Wasn't the man who first showed you this process – this amazing transforming powerful spiritual process that you've done for 30 years now and that's allowed your life to move from being an unemployed drunk to a successful psychotherapist who's brought up five children – wasn't this man someone who did early shifts at a factory making toilet rolls?

W: Yes, and he got up half an hour earlier than he needed, at 5am, every morning to do his prayers and meditation.

Being still and in stillness is best. Although I could meditate in the middle of Piccadilly Circus if I had to, in the rush hour!

D: During the 30 minutes you can chat about any concerns you have, mention any anxieties?

W: Chat about the pimple on the end of your nose, sex, drugs and rock 'n' roll, plumbing, DIY – anything that comes up, but talk to God as though God is there.

D: You mentioned about saying I'm thankful that you're sober, but for people who haven't got a drink or any other drug addiction problem, they can still say something like: "I'm grateful that my eyes are open and I can see."

W: And "Thank you I can taste food... thank you for my family... Thank you I can throw my legs out the bed, thank you I'm breathing. Thank you I have running water. Thank you for the daylight. Thank you for my friends. Thank you for the food I have to eat." And so on.

At the end of the week anyone doing it might be surprised. If you do it honestly then something will happen. You will feel something. You will know something. Something will be different and whatever that is I'm not going to tell you what it is, but something will be different.

If you're open to it, you'll know something that you didn't know at the beginning of the week. Then at the end of the week when you've found that something, you have to develop it and you have to nurture it, you have to find out what it is.

Don't hang on to your shit

D: So I want to mention about hoarding, which is obviously a form of spiritual sickness, and then it's connected with tithing in which you give away ten per cent of what you earn – and that you recommend everyone does. One of the reasons for tithing you explained is as a demonstration that you trust you're going to be looked after by God. Is hoarding then the opposite of that, when a person can't believe they'll be provided for and looked after, because they have no trust?

W: It's not just a question of trust that you are going to be looked after, it's a question of understanding a spiritual law again. If you want plenty of money, give ten per cent of your money away because what you're doing is you are providing the flow for it to come. You see, if you have a lake with an inflow but no outflow it's going to be stagnant. But if you have an outflow you've got a lake that's full of life.

It's like in the film Hello, Dolly! when Barbra Streisand's character Dolly Levi says: "Money, pardon the expression, is like manure. It's not worth a thing unless it's spread around…" If you keep it in one place it stinks.

Hoarding is hanging on to your shit. People who hoard stuff are people who hang on to their shit. I've had many clients who hoarded stuff. What happens is when you forget about the hoarding and deal with the person, they get to the stage where they start to deal with themselves, and many times they come one week to see me and say: "I just suddenly got the urge to clean out one of the rooms last week. I threw this out and I went through that."

All of a sudden they start to get rid of stuff. Because hoarding is a great example of a reflection of what's going on within the person.

It's like when someone comes to see me and says they compulsively wash their hands, I don't take any notice of them washing their hands, I deal with them. I mean I deal with them and they deal with themselves, and then they stop washing their hands because there's no need for that any longer. If people hang on to their shit, it reflects in the outside world.

Sometimes the symptom is that you see there's been no change in a person's life. Sometimes I see someone who's a great person and you know they were hippies when they were younger and you meet them in their 60s and 70s and they're still hippies. Nothing wrong with having that sort of mentality, but they're still wearing the same clothes and same styles and absolutely everything as when they were in their teens and 20s.

I am not saying they should dress like old people, but it's like you hear about bands that produce absolutely fantastic music and then the next thing you hear is exactly the same as the last thing because they're stuck, they're drinking or drugging or whatever it is and they've got a sound and everything they will ever play will be the same because until they change, their creative ability won't produce it. If you look at some of the great artists, writers and musicians, they will say that once they stopped drinking and drugging, which they used to think was their creative muse, they created some of their greatest stuff.

Smoking, gambling and the integrity of the false self

W: Smoking is never a good choice. If you're growing spiritually and you continue to smoke there is obviously something hugely wrong.

D: As with excessive drinking and drug-taking, it's suicide by instalments because you know it's bad for you.

W: It doesn't make any difference what it is, we're just looking at the simple fact that it is the drug of choice. Lots of people stop smoking who were addicted, but there are different types of smokers. There are smokers who use cigarette smoking to deal with themselves, it's the ego's weapon in keeping the self in place, that they don't want to deal with their demons and the monsters within and so the cigarette smoke is doing that job. Then when they try to stop smoking, they find it almost impossible because they're not getting in touch with themselves.

D: There's obviously no self-love there because everyone in the world now knows it's a poison and that you're damaging every bit of your body.

W: Of course it's self-abuse. If you find somebody who is doing a spiritual programme such as the 12 Steps and they're still smoking after a few years you know something's extremely wrong with what they've done and then we've got to go back to denial, repression, idealisation and they are still using a drug. It doesn't mean they haven't attempted the programme, but they've done it on their terms: there is no surrender.

You have to surrender absolutely and that's a process. So if you've been around a few years in a recovery programme and you tried to stop smoking and yet you're still doing it, then you have to realise that you're totally addicted, that you are using it to keep the ego in power, to maintain the integrity of the false self.

The same with gambling, there are people who get clean and sober but they carry on gambling. Now they may not be betting houses away or anything like that, but it can still be a real blockage to spiritual growth.

D: I imagine like all addictions it's all-consuming, they're thinking about the next bet, will they win, looking forward to the next, have I got money for that…

W: It keeps you totally occupied away from yourself – as with all obsessions, it's there to block growth and change.

D: And that stops you looking at the demons, dealing with the big stuff?

W: Of course, because it's purely selfish, like smoking is totally selfish. Smoking is the craziest one of all because you know that smoking will give you the worst death known on the planet and you can never even recall any time when you say something like: "I was smoking on Tuesday 23rd January and what a day we had, it was fantastic!" You won't have that from smoking.

At least with some drugs you will look back and say: hey, I had some good times. You just won't do that with smoking, you'll just have the worst death known on the planet and it doesn't give you any highs at all, it's just a total and utter blocker.

D: There is something that I remember here, with my drinking and drugs I'd given up trying to give up. I just thought this is me and that's how it is and I'll carry on until I most likely die young. This was what I was thinking in my early 30s. But then when I was advised by someone who'd been sober for ten years, and he was a couple of years younger than me, to get on my knees and pray and ask for help to give up, I did it and I've not had a drink or other drug since.

I mean my drinking and my life with it had brought me to my knees, but I still resisted this praying on my knees because I'd never ever done that. I'd prayed as a kid, the usual bless my auntie and grandma sort of stuff, then at school when we just tried to make each other laugh during Christmas services and so on. I didn't really see how this could work, but I was desperate and I had no other smart ideas, or even crap ideas. I had no ideas.

So despite all the rubbish that was going on in my life – the terrible abusive relationship I'd been in, the loss of friendships, the no work and being in increasing debt, the police stuff that was creeping into my life, the general mayhem and the utter complete despair I felt – I still had a lot of resistance and even though I lived in a block of flats two floors up and even with the curtains drawn I still thought it was very weird, that someone might see me... Despite all the mess in my life this praying was weird.

W: So what is this resistance? Pride, call it what it is.

D: Yeah, what would people think if they knew the great me was forced to go down on my knees...But I did and it was very humbling and it had a result. It's still here 17 years later, which is longer than I drank for, there is a proof right here. This works.

Some people talk about not believing this God stuff, that they want an intellectual scientific solution. But here is one. In science you try experiments, observe and then reach a conclusion that is a fact. So here are my experiments: over at least five years I tried the experiment of stopping drinking and taking other drugs, on my own, all sorts of ways. I'm a smart guy with all the qualifications and I've written for most of the British national newspapers about world travel as well as extremely complicated medical procedures. But I couldn't give up for more than three days, I think that was my record doing it alone in those last five years.

Then I try this other experiment where I pray on my knees and simply ask something that I addressed as God for a clean and sober day. Since then I have been clean and sober. So the observation and conclusion of this experiment, the fact, is that praying on your knees stopped this addictive drinker from drinking, for every day that I pray.

Of course I've added to that with reading lots of literature and doing a programme that's enabled me to grow spiritually and that's changed my way of living. But there's intellect and intelligence and scientific fact if that's what you want: give up drinking on my own, it's repeated failure; try it with the power of prayer and it works.

W: There was a surrender.

D: Yes, a surrender and it's symbolic to get on your knees or as you know in Islam they touch their forehead on the floor as they pray, which I do sometimes too because it's very humbling and a submissive thing to do and Islam means "submission" or "submit to God".

Many people who have what they consider valid reasons for not and never believing in a greater power already really believe in one power, and that is the power of their intellect. But I think it could be considered egotistical for someone not to believe in some sort of greater power than themselves: I mean, we are so extremely small, such little specks, on a tiny planet in a vast universe of probably many vast universes – so really, how can any of us say there is no power greater than ourselves?

You have those people who say they prefer science. Yet scientific facts are based on experiment and observation. So let's say that since the 1930s millions of people around the world with a previously hopeless condition of various types of addictions have been able to stop and stay stopped and then to get on in life, very often living a life better than they could ever have imagined. If this was due to them taking a daily pill, we would undoubtedly say that pill works so long as you remember to take it every day.

Yet, this is the result from anyone who has honestly done the 12 Steps and who continues to live what they learn from the 12 Steps – to grow spiritually with a belief in a Higher Power of their own understanding. It is experiential and it is proven. It is scientific. Science comes from a word meaning "knowledge"...

When I first felt a higher power come into me I recall thinking: "Ah! This is how a human being should feel." It was a knowing that this was the right way to be. My loneliness left me and my despair and fears left me. I've heard people say that ego can stand for "edging God out", but I had elbowed God out! There was no room for God with my ego how it was. Yet I was that classic: big ego, low self-esteem.

I read somewhere that getting the spiritual experience was a bit like if you are in a church – and most churches for some reason are quite dark and cold in England, except they have tall arched windows and if the sun shines you get a beautiful shaft of sunlight through – and I read somewhere that getting to know God and finding spirituality is a bit like stepping from that cold darkness, just taking one step to the side, into feeling the warm bright light on you. Or maybe in you.

W: That's why it's called the sunlight of the spirit.

D: That for me is a fantastic description because it was exactly like that when I felt it. I remember being ecstatic. Comfortable, and it was a bloody relief as well because I thought I don't have to drive my life any more, I just have to relax and show up and do my best and it's going where it's going.

W: If you don't get on your knees you'll never get it, never – it's as simple as that. It's not that God needs you on your knees, God doesn't need you on your knees. That's for you, you need that, you need to realise the subjugation of the self is the only way to go. Get on your knees and thank God you are on your feet.

I remember one guy who was desperate to stop drinking say: "I'm not going on my knees for anybody!" He was drinking again within two weeks. You know the arrogance, I'm not getting on my knees for anybody – who are you getting on your knees for? It's for yourself. You are not getting on your knees for God or anybody else, you get on your knees for you because you're the one in dire need.

D: There's a chapter in the book Alcoholics Anonymous called We Agnostics that talks of a suffering alcoholic who doesn't believe in God. It describes though how he had a moment that changed his life.

"Then, like a thunderbolt, a great thought came. It crowded out all else:

'Who are you to say there is no God?'"

W: I had a mate, he couldn't read or write very well and he was a rough-and-ready alcoholic in an alcohol unit in Manchester. He told me that there were others in there with him, professional people such as a solicitor, teacher, police officer, journalist, a business owner, all that. But, you know, he said with a glint in his eye: "I'm the only one still alive."

The arrogance of the intellect is often fatal.

D: Comes back to the quote at the start of this book: "There is a principle that is a bar against all information, which is proof against all arguments, and which cannot fail to keep a man in everlasting ignorance – that principle is contempt prior to investigation."

I also like that it says in the 12–Step literature that humility and intellect can be compatible, provided humility is placed first.

W: Intelligence is just a tool. It's like some people are muscular, and some people have lower IQ, it's just a tool – that's all it is.

But if you think that you're God and that you're right about everything... I mean, if you're really an intelligent person you will realise how little you know. Open-mindedness is essential.

Search for the hero inside yourself

D: Here is something Matt Haig tweeted that caused a big reaction: "Anxiety is my superpower." Then in his book Notes On A Nervous Planet he explained what he'd intended by this statement. "I didn't mean anxiety was a good thing. I meant that anxiety was ridiculously intense, that we people who have an excess of it walk through life like an anxious Clark Kent or a tormented Bruce Wayne knowing the secret of who we are."

And he says he's thankful it forced him to stop smoking, to get physically healthy, that it made him work out what was good for him, who cared for him and to try to help others who have it. So he is saying anxiety can be a force for good.

W: It's a force for good if it changes you – and that's what it's for. All of these things are cathartic if you allow them to be. You know, your alcoholism switches from a curse to a blessing, so does your anxiety. If your anxiety gets you to focus on becoming Superman rather than staying small… I mean, all stories, from Superman and Batman to Beauty And The Beast and The Ugly Duckling, all of them are about transformation. They're all telling us how do we change, that within all of us is that potential. Within all of us is a being that needs to be born. Anxiety and the other problems we have in life are all about that birth.

D: And that's why the superhero type of character has always been so popular throughout history. There's a superhero inside all of us.

W: Of course. Search for the hero inside yourself… Remember that song?

D: I remember it well, from the 1990s, the M People song. Search for the hero inside yourself, Until you find the key to your life... The missing treasure you must find.

W: We all know that and we all pay it lip service and people say my body is a temple and all that sort of stuff. So we all know the terms, but to actually get to the point where you get in touch with that person inside yourself... People don't realise the way to get in touch with the hero inside yourself, the second person that needs to be born, is through devastating pain. It doesn't come any other way.

I said previously that birth is like a volcano, it's an earthquake, it's a storm and then something good is formed. That's how the universe was formed. And it's the same with the second person who needs to be born. Unfortunately we have classed that storm as mental illness and we now medicate it so that the birth won't happen.

D: So it just gets gently subdued or numbed.

W: If you go to the mental health services they will likely medicate your second birth. If you're having problems on your own you will medicate it with alcohol, with drugs, with sex, with work, with shopping, whatever. All of it is about staying safe, stopping this person – yet all the answers, everything you need to get out and enjoy your life, they are inside you and they will only come out through that pain. Once you allow that pain to come through you will find it.

Another symbolic story from the Bible is that like Noah's ark everything you need is inside, everything two by two so that it can multiply. The story says it, everything was put into the ark two by two so that they could multiply, everything you need in this universe is inside you. It's all inside you, it's all there and you will never discover it until there's a great fucking flood. Then everything else is wiped out and the subconscious, signified by the flood, overwhelms you and destroys all life as you know it, to create a new life.

The root of our troubles

D: In the 12 Steps literature there's two very brief sentences and they are written so well, with emphasis and humility: "Selfishness – self-centredness! That, we think, is the root of our troubles."

So this is saying that the biggest thing to be resolved for an alcoholic – and, naturally, that can also apply to anyone who's addicted to whatever: be it heroin, shopping, work, gambling, sex, relationships and so on – is being selfish and self-centred. Someone who's selfish lacks consideration for others and is concerned with their own personal profit and pleasure; a self-centred person is preoccupied with his or herself and their affairs. Very similar definitions and the common word in both is self.

W: If we only focus on ourselves we feel totally uncomfortable.

D: Because the world and human beings aren't designed that way, because the whole world would collapse if we didn't think of others and cooperate.

W: What's in me is for you and what's in you is for me, and when we share of ourselves and give to others we feel better.

D: The gift of giving.

W: A bungee jump is another way of escaping yourself because when you do a bungee jump you're not thinking about your electricity bill or how depressed you are, the only thing you are thinking is: I hope this bloody rope doesn't break. That's an escape from self, though temporary, unless the rope breaks of course.

Driving cars fast, racing motorbikes, all these things are a distraction to get you away from what you feel. We all have this angst, this disturbance within us, all of us – it's the level to which that disturbance gets and we all find ways of dealing with it.

In life we're like sharks condemned to swim forever. If we had everything we need, enough food, the right partner, everything and we just try and stay still... it doesn't work: we feel bored, we feel frustrated. We are condemned to grow, we are in this world and we have to grow, but first of all we have to find out how to grow.

Those who embrace change and realise life is about change are the happiest, because we have to grow.

It's a reason why it's very important that you should never compare yourself to other people. You are who you are and you don't know what role it is you're meant to play. If we keep looking at others we could always see we're deficient in some way or maybe we keep looking at them and think we're superior in some way – and both views are erroneous.

D: That's one reason I think such as Facebook and some other social media is an increasing problem for many people because, for example, people go on Facebook and not many people post their problems... they post their successes... their ideal life.

W: Or you're angry. Social media use is a huge problem for people in relationships as well because at one time if you had a row with your partner it was difficult to go and instantly find somebody else to talk to or find company or whatever – but now you can do it instantly, you just go in the other room and go on social media and you can be chatting to someone instantly.

So there's a huge problem with that: adultery and cheating and unfaithfulness. You know your spouse can be sat there and watching TV and you're on your phone talking to somebody else.

People have always cheated, but it's just so much easier now. It's like if I decided to have a drink and I'm at home, then I've got to go and find one, and that means putting on my coat, walking to the door, walking down the garden, walking along the street, and so I've got loads of time to change my mind.

But if I keep that drink in the fridge there's no time to change my mind. It's the same with this that if you're hurt by your partner and instantly somebody else is there to listen to you, to comfort you… Even if you don't actually meet them, you can see them, you can talk to them... And the feeling you get is similar.

D: Porn addiction has increased immensely since the internet arrived. Similarly before then a person would have to go out to the shop and spend money and possibly be seen buying the magazine…

W: Most men look at porn because they're lonely and because they're dissatisfied with their sex lives. But all that does is make them even more dissatisfied and more lonely. It will isolate them more. Men get turned on visually and porn has power because it changes the way you feel.

I always advise people to stay away from porn because it's far more devious than you think. I counsel men who watch porn 23 hours a day and then smash the computer to pieces and then go and buy a new one two weeks later. Because they are kept totally powerless over it. And it gives them a totally wrong concept of sexuality and of women.

Acceptance is the key

D: It's also always damaging to compare your real self to a supposed self – don't burn yourself to death in flames of shoulds and what ifs.

W: Whenever you hear the word "should" you're immediately invoking guilt because you haven't achieved something, you've not done something or you're putting pressure on yourself to do something.

What we really need to be looking at is how are we progressing with our lives, and there will always be times in our life when we feel like our lives are down the toilet, that we're getting nowhere, that the pain is bad and we are wasting our lives and that can go on for years. But that's part of the process as well, that's definitely a part of the process.

Carl Jung said a wonderful thing along the lines of: There are times I look back on my life and I could have done it much better, but I just have to remember I wasn't able to at the time.

D: So it's often good to accept where you are in life. I remember hearing the story of somebody addressing a large group of recovering alcoholics in AA and he said to that crowd listening to him: "We're all recovering alcoholics now, so put your hand up if you think you could have started your sobriety five years before you actually did…"

He paused and then confirmed that no hands had gone up and in fact the audience collectively murmured and then chuckled together at the realisation he was right.

W: Accepting where you are in life is absolutely essential. It's knowing that wherever we are in life, if we are seeking a higher power, if we are seeking a solution to our problems, then we will find it. If you really desire a solution to your problem, a happy solution, I don't mean a suicide solution, then you will find it. Seek and you will find. Go searching and you will find, just don't expect it to be instant – and it will happen.

One day when you think it's never going to happen, the Red Sea opens. Always remember we're talking about symbolism: crucifixions before resurrections.

When Jesus was being crucified none of the disciples were standing there saying: don't worry, Jesus will be back on Sunday. They all fucked off, they all ran because they were crapping themselves. Even though Jesus had told them what would happen, nobody believed it.

So when you're getting crucified it's very hard to believe, until you have been through it a couple of times, that your resurrection is on the way.

It says in the Bible: "Be not weary in doing the right thing, for in due season we'll reap a great harvest, if we do not give up."

Our faces are the same

D: Is the world getting desensitised by seeing so much violence? I mean I saw the guy shooting in Toronto the other day, but I didn't mean to. I was on Twitter and it just happened where you see the video running without clicking on it. You didn't see anyone getting hit or any blood, but it shocked me.

It stayed in my head of course, when you see images like this and the other sort of diabolical stuff that's happened that you see that you didn't used to see – because most people didn't have cameras on them all the time as they do now. So it puts it into my head that I could be sat at a cafe with my friends and a guy like him is walking past...

W: But the chances of those things happening to you are millions to one. Yet people will sit there and smoke a cigarette and that's not a million to one that it's likely to kill you horribly. So the way these things work on social media to get people to a state where they can't let their kids out – yet the chances of somebody taking your kid is a million to one, the chances of you being shot a million to one. But we'll do all the things that will kill us like having bad diets and drug addiction and smoking and drinking.

Or we are becoming callous, I hope not, but I think we are as I don't think we're anywhere near as shockable as we once were, that's for sure. I was saying to somebody the other day that when I watched animal documentaries when I was a child it was very rare that you ever saw an animal being killed by another animal, but the other night they showed live on this programme where they slaughtered loads of buffaloes and pigs, and most animal programmes you see today seem to be about animals killing each other and ripping each other apart. When I was a kid that was very shockable, but it's not now.

D: I've thought this too about such as Batman, and when you look at Batman from the 1950s or 1960s it used to say "kapow!" when he hit somebody and it was always so theatrical that you knew it was just an act. Now the violence on many films is so realistic and bloodthirsty and violent that I turn the films off with my stomach churning. In fact I've stopped watching a lot of films. These are sometimes films that have been rated okay for children to watch, and as a family we're very cautious what our young children watch as these are things that a child cannot unsee.

W: I think also there is an attitude. There's a lot of violence shown that says it's good to be violent like in some revenge movies or the hero doing something where he kills all these people. We need to educate about racism, about discrimination, about bullying, about violence of all forms.

D: And the mass shootings, especially in America – what do you think those killers are about?

W: They're very very angry people who hate society and have got to a stage where they say: fuck you, I'm going to take all of you out.

D: Because something has happened to them.

W: Because they're disappointed, disillusioned, let down, frustrated, had enough – and they have access to weapons. It is not right to put the power to kill in an instant in a person's hands in civilian life, let alone a vulnerable or unstable one.

D: A spiritual growth would fix that as well.

W: Spiritual growth fixes everything. But change is a process. Human beings make a huge mistake when they think things will change with the passage of time. First and foremost you've got to be broken, you've got to have a desire that you want a better life and that's the process that we've talked about and I don't care who you are – unless you're broken you don't get it.

But the problem is always the resistance to the facts. It's like if someone is anxious and they've accepted they will be anxious forever, that this is them. No it isn't, of course it isn't – you can get rid of it totally, there's no two ways that you can get rid of it. Because anxiety is always about fear. Yet it will go when you find a higher power, when you find there's another way to live in this world where you know that you are being looked after and you know you're being taken care of – but that's only something that can come from within.

As a psychotherapist, I'm only showing people the process of finding what is within them, so that they will know themselves. It's not what I'm telling anyone to believe, I'm only showing them that there is a practical way of doing this and if you take this route you will know it for yourself.

Does it work for everybody? Of course it works for everybody. It's the same way as if we are going to walk into a radioactive cloud, then it kills everybody or if we eat the right food it makes us healthy.

D: So there are rules that are human rules. Things that are facts for anyone with the human condition: they are the laws of nature. We are one and always have been, which is why if explained and told properly the Greek myths and the Bible and the other religious books are relevant today.

But how then do we stop the division that's happening today? How do we rediscover our human commonality?

W: We divide ourselves into families, into tribes, into countries, into states, and we divide ourselves by colour and language and culture and all this is the system. But the more spiritual you get the more you will realise any division is all rubbish – that we are all the same. DNA tells us we all come from the same couple in Africa.

D: Yet I always used to relate to the William Blake poem that says: "Oh! Why was I born with a different face? Why was I not born like the rest of my race?" I always felt like that. Even at parties full of my friends. But that lifted from that moment I went down on my knees and prayed, and I thought from then on: I can never feel alone when there is a Great Creator, Father, Higher Power, God... who is looking after me, who put me here.

W: William Blake was a very spiritual man and people just didn't accept his ideas about spirituality at the time. He knew there was something far more to it than what the churches were talking about and he experienced it. But when he tried to express it to people they just didn't get it.

Ten thousand times the size of us

D: In this modern world we've created, there seems to be so many people consumed with doubt about themselves and full of self-loathing. How can we be kinder to ourselves?

W: You have to have an experience of yourself and then when you're doing that you can begin to practise different things. For instance, one thing that people find very difficult to do is stand in front of the mirror and say: "I delight in you, I really love you, you're wonderful." Try doing that in front of the mirror... a lot of people won't even do it. But they'd love somebody to say it to them. So you have to start saying it yourself because even when somebody does say it to you, maybe one day they'll change their mind, so it's important you do it.

Change the perspective of how you view yourself. Such as looking at photographs of yourself as well. That is a huge one. I've had people come to see me who have actually cut themselves out of photos because they hate themselves and they don't think they are worthy of being in it and they don't want to see themselves.

D: Again my experience of when I got down on my knees and prayed, that changed my perspective, because I felt a great comfort knowing that I was being loved and approved of by God, who created me through my parents.

W: The Parable of the Prodigal Son is a very important story – saying that God totally approves of you, no matter how bad you've been, if your heart is genuine and you come back to God.

God doesn't even care whether you've denied His existence. You know, King David killed, Moses was a murderer, none of them were goody-goodies. Jesus broke all the rules too. He once went in a temple and started smashing things up and he was doing it to the money lenders and those guys weren't wimps. But they were buying and trading in his Father's house, they were turning it into a den of thieves.

He always stood up to authority and yet most people who come into contact with authority of any description tend to be a little in awe of it or subdued by it. He wasn't. Then you think these people had the power of life and death over you, but he wasn't bothered by that. So he was brave. Many people love to claim that Jesus was without sin, but he was in human form you know…

Obviously he had a sense of humour, then he must have gone to the toilet and if he was a man he must have had erections. I don't know why people usually don't like thinking like that, but what we're looking at is that within Jesus is perfect. Maybe the story of Jesus is just a story of us all, that Jesus is showing us the way.

D: When it says that we're made in the image of God I think perhaps a lot of people dismiss that because they take it very literally, that there's a bloke out somewhere in space who's ten thousand times the size of us…

W: It's about your spirit. The Bible describes God's emotions, his feelings, that he gets angry, that he gets sad, that he gets happy, so we are like God in our emotions, we are like God in our desires, we are like God in our creation.

D: And what is called in the addiction world "defects of character" or in the Bible "deadly sins" – these are the natural desires that have become excessive, that have led to addiction, that will block us from growing in the image of God, so will stop us becoming the person we're supposed to be.

W: If this world is God's school where we're being taught to be little gods in the image of God so that one day we'll be in this paradise, this next realm, this other dimension, then we have so much responsibility. You see, we're given so much power in this world and we don't even know what it's about. I mean here I am sat in this body regulating my heartbeat, my temperature, this brain function, this imagination between my ears, digestive function, my blood flow, I'm doing all this stuff but I don't even know I'm bloody doing it. If God gave me full power, I'd probably destroy everywhere. I'd be like a four-year-old that's just been given a fast car and two grenades. So it's limited, what I can handle. As I grow, I'm given greater responsibility.

There's a story about a monk who has an incredibly valuable diamond and there's a guy in the city who hears about this and so he finds this monk and he asks the monk to give him the diamond. The monk gives it to him and the guy from the city goes away and he's jumping up and down in joy that it was so easy, that the monk just handed him the diamond. But a day later he feels differently about it, and so he goes back to the monk and hands back the diamond and he asks the monk for the wealth that allowed the monk to give him this diamond, because that was the real wealth and that's the key to life when you just realise there is no lack. Once you key into that spirit in the universe, you're supplied with everything.

There's abundance, there's an abundance of your kids being looked after and you being protected and your health being looked after, of wonderful things happening to you, an abundance of strength to go through the adversity that you'll face. The faith and the wisdom and the love to do it, all of those things are given to you. A few million quid in the bank won't do that for you. The wealth that God gives us is the wealth of having good friendships and people around us who care about us because of who we are, not what we have.

God gives and God takes and it is understanding not to curse God as you go along. I remember I was a few years sober and my business then was absolutely thriving like I was going to be a multimillionaire in no time – and all of a sudden every company I was dealing with stopped ordering in the same month and it went from you're going to be a multimillionaire in no time to you're going to be in the bankruptcy court sitting on the street in no time.

And I remember driving along in my car one day and I said: "God what the fuck are you doing, what is going on?" and I heard this voice, not out loud but it was as clear as a bell: "You did this, if it wasn't for me things would be a lot worse." It totally shut me up and I realised I was going through something and because of that, because of what I was going through there, the door opened and I moved to Ireland and there for the first time I was introduced to the idea of psychotherapy and counselling and the best thing, my youngest daughter was born there.

So that adversity opened the door. Then years later another door opened with my ending up now in Spain. I came to Spain pissed off, just with cabin luggage because I had a return ticket for ten days. But I was here for two days and said: fuck it, I'm not going anywhere and I got an apartment.

D: So when we get some pain or test in our life it's important to give gratitude while we are in it?

W: Give God thanks for all the things you don't like. When my marriage split up and things were very difficult I thanked God every day.

Let me say this, in the Bible it says that followers of God are "eagles", and it says that God took the people on eagle's wings through the desert. Now of course, it doesn't mean he actually put them on an eagle's wing. What it means is that eagles are birds that love storms, and when an eagle gets in a storm it locks its wings and it soars in the turmoil, loves it, all the other birds are flapping like mad or staying out of the way.

It's like when God has said to me on a few occasions, get up and follow me: one of them was into recovery from drinking, another was to live in Ireland, then to the Middle East and now to Spain.

That's important, that's how our lives work. My decisions have always been made for me because I surrender my will. God has the plan, God orders our steps. God shows us the way, but it isn't like: "Oh should I do this God or should I do that?" Instead God puts me to a position when He makes it abundantly clear to me – and it's usually by my emotion every time that things happen to me and it's usually been another rock bottom, usually been a time when I am sick to bloody death of what's going on and that invariably I say: just fuck it, I couldn't care less God, take the fucking lot, I don't care any longer, do what you fucking want. That's usually the point when all of a sudden everything goes abracadabra-boom!

D: That's where the phrase "we get in our own way" comes from then, when we're trying to bludgeon our way through.

W: God's never stupid enough to leave this up to me and you.

Focussing on abundance

D: A lot of people don't even know they're focussing on lack. It's often handed down the generations isn't it?

W: That's why we've got to become aware. You'll hear people say: "Well, you've got to be realistic..." That's a great way to keep you stuck – you know, stay where you are, you're not going anywhere. If you've got a poverty mentality, then your money is no good to you.

D: Modern society in the West – and increasingly beyond – creates a yearning for things, so maybe this is where the focussing on lack can get to some people too. Because the yearning is only really achieved by the fulfilment of getting the thing and then we start yearning for something else. Really, it's just like addiction, of always wanting more.

Like the phrase I've heard recovering alcoholics use to describe how they drank: "One drink is too many and a thousand is never enough."

W: People have always got addicted to try to make themselves happy in an unhappy world.

D: But why do people keep doing things that don't make them happy? Like that definition of insanity: doing the same thing over and over again but expecting different results.

W: These are distractions that are hiding the truth. Why do people sit and watch TV all day?

D: I don't really know.

W: Because it distracts them. But after a while their body doesn't want to do it any longer, so they find a way to deal with it and it's called a large bag of crisps. What they do then is sit in front of the telly and stuff themselves with food because it's the only way they can keep their body there for that long because their body does not want to stay, and that's because it's not designed to do that.

We are supposed to be full of yearning – it's just that addiction is a bastardisation. We are supposed to grow, so we're designed to have continuous desire. It's like I said when I was playing with my toy soldiers when suddenly one day they didn't interest me and so I moved on and wanted to play with something else. Or it's like you've always wanted to go diving and then when you've dived once or for a few years you want to learn to play chess and then you want to move to another country.

But when it becomes an insatiable desire and your desperation combines with insatiability and you think you've found something that will fix you – that's when you're stuck.

So enjoy it, but when it's over, it's over, and then it's time to let it go, because something else is on its way. What people don't like is those in-between times, the waiting time. But God is always revealing more and more, because everything that happens is a tool for teaching us about what's going on within us.

If we change on the inside the outside changes.

The Ten Commandments are not for keeping

W: One of the reasons we are given the Ten Commandments is to show we can't keep them.

D: Show you can't keep them?

W: It's impossible. Any attempt to keep the Ten Commandments and then believe you've succeeded is pure unadulterated ego, nobody keeps the Ten Commandments. So the Bible says that the wages of sin is death, by living the way we do we destroy our bodies, we destroy our minds and we kill ourselves: that's the wages of sin when we live in pride, resentment, fear and selfishness.

The Ten Commandments are to show us we need saving. They show us the spiritual laws of our being. But they have to be kept in our heart, not with an outward show of behaviour.

If you want to kill or steal or lie in your heart that is the same as doing it because by allowing the evil to fester in our minds it makes us sick – it kills us, not instantly, but totally affectively.

How do we get saved? By surrender to God, by the acceptance we're like naughty children; like the Prodigal Son, we come back to God and say: oh God, actually you were right in the first place – I really can't do this without you, I thought I could but I can't. So I'm sorry about pissing you off or causing you so much upset, but I'd like to start again please, with you at the helm this time.

It's a cooperation, it's a two-way thing. God created us with a free will because God doesn't want us to love Him as if we are robots because nobody wants to be loved robotically. God's upset is like any parent seeing a child destroying themselves – it's heartbreaking – and like any parent, God is desperate to solve the situation.

D: And if you give a gift and then tell someone what they've got to do with it and when they've got to use it, then it is no gift. As if I give one of my sons a new bike and say to him: but you can only ride this between 11am and noon on Fridays and you must not turn left with it ever, don't use the brakes and never do a wheelie...

W: Exactly.

D: Or I tell my other son what job he has to do when he's a young man.

W: My dad used to say to me: go and get a job you love to do and you never have to work another day in your life. But often work is defined as drudgery – and that's another thing to address: why is it in this world that people think those people who aren't as clever as them should do all the jobs they don't like doing? It's just saying: because you're not as clever as me you should do all the dirty shitty jobs, although because you're not as clever as me you won't mind.

D: Also I would say a lot of people saying that those people aren't as clever aren't actually that clever, although they might have gone to a school that educated them better and gave them greater self-belief.

W: There's a huge difference between intelligence and education. What we are saying here, everything we've written in this book, is don't let anything limit you, don't let racism limit you, don't let sexism limit you, don't let your lack of opportunities limit you, don't let culture and family limit you – because when you turn to God and you put God in your life, you are on your way.

If somebody comes to me and says it's all too much, I will say give me a list of all the things that are too much. Then when we have the list, I ask them: so what's making you do all of them? How would it be to pick one... and throw it away? How would it be to tear the list up? So there's a lot of work in just those questions.

It's helping people give themselves permission to get away from all the "shoulds", the "I have to do this" and "I have to do thats". That's the internal rule system from the blueprint and it's a programme to which you never voluntarily subscribed. You know, the day you are dead it won't matter at all.

We need to be educated to know that it's on the inside of us because so many people push that away, they live in the despair, it's never going to happen for them, it's never going to work out – and they have all the excuses.

D: Is it more important for some people to be or feel in control when something in their life has been out of their control, such as child abuse or losing a parent or a brother when they're younger?

W: Human beings only feel good when they're in control, that's just a given. If you feel out of control is it ever possible to feel good? So all our attempts at addiction or all our attempts at life, to buy a house and to decorate it, are all attempts to control and build our world.

They're all illusions, the illusion of control is what we seek. But when we find a higher power, then we find what we're looking for.

When I took alcohol it created a spiritual feeling, it made me feel good, made me feel I was in control, it made me feel tomorrow would be great, I could live in the day and I was not anxious and everybody was my friend. It was wonderful. But it was a chemical short circuit in my brain, it wasn't true and it's the same if you take any form of drug. Any high is followed by a lull and the lulls get lower and the highs never get higher. If these types of drugs worked and you can just live in ecstasy forever and never pay a price, why wouldn't we all take them? Of course we'd take them.

We can give ourselves the illusion of control with OCD… superstition, a career, a position, as a parent, in thousands of ways, which will all eventually be seen to fail.

Every society in the world finds a way to get out of their heads because it's the human condition. We are here, we are put on this planet like some prison island and we suffer from boredom and frustration and fear and the full knowledge that one day we are going to expire. You know it's a crazy frightening place and you are here to solve the puzzle. But any mind-altering drug will destroy you because it's faking it, it's not actually the truth.

If you really want to be an independent person you have to become dependent on your God. If your God supplies all your needs then you're not dependent on anybody or anything else.

D: And actually more of us feel this in our gut than maybe like to admit it.

W: Yeah, because you know in your head you might want to be a people-pleaser, you may be afraid or you may doubt yourself – but your gut tells you something, especially about people if somebody is dangerous or they are not right for you. I've counselled so many women who tell me that when they were walking up the aisle their gut told them they were doing the wrong thing, to get out. Their gut was telling them that they should not be getting married, and they paid the price and ended up with some violent lunatic.

Growing up or dragged up?

D: What's the damage of growing up in an abusive environment?

W: People are affected in different ways. Some are going to become very angry and aggressive, some are going to be very quiet and subdued, some will become total people-pleasers – many will be addicted, all will suffer anxiety and mood problems of some description. All of those actions will be ways that they will attempt in trying to survive.

They will become mood managers, depending upon the type of abuse they're getting or used to get. They will manage the mood of others in an attempt to manage their own.

I dealt with a lady who'd suffered from schizophrenia for a long period, and she had been horrendously sexually abused as a child and so she just developed another world. She would go into this other world where all these fairies existed and she would play in that world while she was being abused.

When she came to me she was in her 50s, but what happened was that whenever she got anxious in life she went back to this other world. So she started talking to people that nobody else could see, she did nothing wrong, she didn't attack people and she wasn't violent in any way, she wouldn't set the house on fire or anything like that – but whenever she got anxious, even such as if she received a large electricity bill, she would go into this other world.

What happened was other people didn't like it that she talked to people they couldn't see. So then people would have her put into a psychiatric hospital and her freedom would be taken away, even though she committed no crime. She lost her civil rights.

D: How did you help her?

W: I adopted the 12-Step programme to schizophrenia to say that it was okay to be schizophrenic, but that she was powerless over schizophrenia, and that it made her life unmanageable. Then we looked at her life, and she did all the 12 Steps.

When she first came to me she said she was looking for her parents because she was adopted. Then after a while it emerged she wasn't adopted – her parents were the ones who had sexually abused her. She just couldn't take that on board. How could her parents, the people who were supposed to love her, do this? So she believed she must be adopted and her illusion kept the pain of reality at bay.

She was creating this fantasy world all the time in order that she never lived in the truth. So the truth was that she had to go back and deal with everything and shine a light on everything and she made huge progress by facing it all and her biggest fear – and her biggest fear was being put back into hospital, having her freedom taken away even though she'd never committed a crime.

Schizophrenics are people who've had horrible trauma somewhere in their childhood. This is how they cope with it. Now that doesn't mean that everyone who has trauma will become a schizophrenic. Some people will become depressed, some will become terribly anxious, some will become alcoholic, some will become huge people-pleasers.

D: So they find a way to cope to stay alive.

W: Yes, and usually the whole family has the disease in some form. When I deal with someone who was brought up in an alcoholic family, it's getting the family to understand that they're all alcoholic. They may not all have a problem with alcohol, but alcoholism, the mental disease as classified by the World Health Organization, is in every one of them. But quite often it will express itself in another way, say, an eating disorder.

D: So even without drinking you can have this?

W: Of course, if you were brought up in a dysfunctional family then you will be hugely influenced and you have those patterns in your blueprint. People will say they thought it was all right, but if they can get honest and shine a light in all the dark corners…

For all those people who say they are all right and everything is fine, maybe it is – but in the majority of cases there is something down in the dark that is attempting to destroy you. When the snake bites, the bite is not the problem… it's the poison it leaves behind.

It doesn't matter where you go, unless you leave your head behind you'll be taking your problems with you. If that virus has been put in you, just because you go to live in another country won't cure it.

It seems that often a dysfunctional family will stay living in the same area, all very enmeshed with each other, always on the phone to each other and talking to each other because there's a huge dependency within them.

You will get some people who'll try to make the break. I remember one lady came to me from an Irish family of 11 people and the father was a terribly abusive man. They were all scared of him. I asked her if there was one in the family that didn't do what the father told them. She said she had a brother who lived in England – and she said her father adored him. Because he stood up to his father, he was the only one his father respected.

We've all heard the expression "earn respect", because respect isn't just given to you, you earn it. You may not like the person but you can respect them. Yet if somebody can boss you around why would they respect you? So sometimes, especially in cases like this, you have to ask yourself: do I want to be liked or respected? Obviously it's nice to be liked and respected, but which do you want most out of the two?

Nobody respects anyone they can dominate and if someone dominates you, then you will fear them and that will lead to resentment that is suppressed anger, which in time will make you mentally or physically ill.

If your neighbour's ignoring you when you complain about them leaving their dog barking in the garden for a week, then maybe it's time you got angry with them. I don't mean abusive, but just a healthy expression of the self. They'll be much more likely to respect you then and so be much more likely to do something about it. They might not like you though.

Or you can stay popular with them and put up with the noise, stench and sight of dog poo whenever you look out of your window. You will have your reward. They will think you're a lovely person and you're likely to acquire a stress-related illness.

Make no mistake, allowing others to control you creates huge stress... the deadliest. I've seen people with IBS, colitis and cancer living in situations where they are being controlled by others either at home or work. Being in control, taking responsibility for your destiny, is essential for good health.

Michael Marmot, an expert in public health, did research in the 1970s on the result of power and health by studying the British civil service. Basically he discovered the opposite of what a lot of people thought: that being at the top was far less stressful than being at the bottom. They concluded the difference was control of destiny – the lower someone is in social class, the less opportunity they have to influence key events that affect life. It's this that is causing stress and sickness.

This life is about change and when we trust that you have to step out into the edge of life to enjoy it, that means you have to push the boundaries and you cannot play safe. I saw a young guy once going on trial for a professional football team. The coach said to him afterwards that he played great, but he said I'm not signing you because you went out there and you played safe and you showed me nothing.

It's the same in life. All of this is about learning what we call the spiritual laws, and those spiritual laws are finding the truth of your existence, about the invisible world that we cannot see but that we see the effects of every day.

It's like if you were driving from London to Manchester at night, your headlights will shine 100 metres in front of the car, they don't need to shine all the way to Manchester. The way will be illuminated as it needs to, the way opens up... trust in that.

But by playing safe, trying to make yourself secure, you've made yourself unhappy. Even if you get millions of pounds and you buy the big house and you have everything you want, you will always be unhappy because your security is based on something that's not real. That's why if you look at very rich famous families some of them have a lot of tragedy.

D: You reminded me there of the phrase that when you get out of your comfort zone the best things happen.

W: It's when you can say my biggest fear is to live in my comfort zone because we are all full of potential, but you'll never fulfil it if you stay in your comfort zone.

D: And if you use a football match analogy it's like a team that just passes in their own half. They're unlikely to lose – but they're never going to win.

W: Sooner or later it's got to go wrong – and it will be incredibly dull to play in and to watch.

D: And to score you have to take the risk of shooting. You might miss and then the other team gets possession of the ball. You might hit a terrible shot that goes out of the ground. But you will never score if you don't shoot.

W: In life you have to take risk and it's learning that risk is good. If you're averse to risk you're never going to be happy.

D: Would it be true to say as well that our modern society tries to discourage that? They want people to be strangled by their mortgages, to be always available between nine and five...

W: Of course – it's slavery! Slavery has never gone away, it's just adapted itself.

But it's still slavery and most people have to get up and go and do things that they don't want to do. For a certain amount of money, they make sure they have to come back next week. And the carrot is always that you can buy your freedom one day. Everybody wants to escape from the pain of having to think about the electricity bill or the mortgage.

What we're talking about here is that freedom. You might not be a multimillionaire, but you will be free and you will prosper in every area of your life. But always remember there will be opposition and the more opposition you get the better because it shows you are doing something right.

Just look around all the time and everybody knows the opponent – it's fear.

A lady working in a hospice recently wrote down what the dying told her they most regret. Number one was working too much, slavery. Another was waiting to allow themselves to be happy. Then there was the regret of not doing and trying things they wanted to try.

D: I remember watching a documentary where a lot of octogenarians said their biggest regret in life was not their trying things that had failed, sometimes spectacularly – but it was not trying things. And now it was too late.

I always find it sad that a lot of people have lived a life that isn't their life, is unfulfilled and yet they put their kids through the same system, wanting their kids to go through the same. That'd be fine to do if their lives at the office or wherever were fantastic, but...

W: Because they don't believe anything else. I've seen people in those circumstances, when their grown-up child tries to get out of what they went through, they get very angry with them. It's because they think their child has to realise this is life, this is how it is, your life is going to be terrible like mine was terrible.

I knew a couple who didn't tell their child they had a scholarship for an art school because they wanted their child to get a "proper job". Why would anyone do that, because our imagination is the most powerful tool that we've got?

The people who get out of this are the people who can see themselves out of it.

The more you can dream, the more you can fantasise, the better you'll be. Your imagination is given to you so you can create. You can heal the sick, make the blind see, you can be anywhere, you can do anything you want in your imagination, anything, it's your creation, it's you. The problem is most people are creating shit with it. The imagination works all the time, but it's up to you to direct it.

Dedication to meditation

D: How do you meditate, and what could you recommend to someone who's never tried it or who needs a bit of help with their meditation?

W: Meditation depends on your dedication. I say this because many, many people have asked me to teach them to meditate, yet only one that I know of in 30 years has really stuck with it.

I tried using a Buddhist meditation at first and it worked for a while. But I started drinking again, and it's no good when you drink.

Then I mentioned earlier about the man who suggested I pray and meditate for 30 minutes every morning, my friend Norman who worked at a factory making toilet rolls. He was a little man – yet he had the guts to come out to see me on his own and sit down and spend time with me. He saved my life.

The ego I had when I first came to recovery from drinking was that I wanted E=mc2. I didn't want steps with numbers one to 12 on them. I didn't think spiritual growth was going to do much.

You see, today we have lots and lots of treatment centres and people with lots of money pay to go and get absolutely the best that they can pay for. But God knew the absolute best for me and it was a guy who made toilet rolls in a factory, and he was the absolute best for me and he didn't cost me a thing and he saved my life. You could have sent me to Harley Street and I could have met the most brilliant intellectual man on the planet and he could have taken £500 an hour off me and I could have ended up dead from alcoholism.

God always knows the right person to help us. God works through people. And after spending time with Norman I met another man. He was a civil engineer called Nick who wasn't a trained guy in anything to do with medicine or psychology, but he was five years sober through the 12 Steps. He took me through the steps and he saved my life.

We think we know the answer, and my answer was that if I had a fantastic mansion in the Lake District I'd take all my mates and we'd play five-a-side football all day and then I'd never drink again. I didn't know what was good for me, but God knows exactly what we need.

I remember people coming to me and I would be showing them the 12 Steps and how they could cure themselves of this disease of alcoholism and depression too if they were depressed. But then the opposition would come in, their adversary in the mind, and it would be that someone had told them about the top man in Dublin, the best expert in the country on depression and they would fly up there to see him, and this guy would see them for about 15 minutes and invariably he'd charge them about €150 for seeing them and sometimes he would even be on his phone in that 15 minutes taking other calls – but this was the top man and this is what they needed, you understand me?

The opposition comes in, and once again people are deceived because they have money or they think that money will buy them something. You know, when God's on your side, you will get absolutely everything you need.

When you invite God. That's the most important thing: the Bible says God knocks on the heart of everybody and most people just keep the door shut.

D: What is the Buddhist meditation you do now?

W: I do a Buddhist meditation called "samatha". I started off only doing it for five minutes and I tell you that it was a bloody struggle. I couldn't do it, just five minutes. I just couldn't sit still, but I persevered and then five minutes went to ten. It's counting and breathing within. If anybody wants to learn it, find a Buddhist or visit a Buddhist retreat.

Another meditation you can do is to just light a candle and find a name that means something to you, some sort of spiritual name or something that's important to you and then repeat it over and over again. So choose this name, and repeat it and repeat it and repeat it while you are staring into the candlelight and repeat it until it becomes nonsense.

Stop when it reaches that point of absolute nonsense and just for a few seconds your mind will be empty. Within a few seconds everything will come rushing back in, but just for those few moments your mind will be empty. This meditation with the candle is a very simple way to start meditating.

One purpose of meditation is to shut up the chatterbox mind, and people go wrong in meditation because they say I was thinking of this and I was thinking of that. But that's fine as the whole idea of meditation is to become an observer of the self, to begin to understand yourself.

So when you're meditating you focus on your breathing and your counting, or a name you're repeating, and you focus on what every part of you is doing. If something comes into your mind – and it might be that you start thinking about sex, drugs, rock 'n' roll, football or DIY – whatever it is, when you're aware of what you're doing, just go: "Ahh, so that's what I was thinking." It's fine and then go back to the breathing and then when that happens again it's okay, it's just an acceptance of it. As you persist more and more you'll grow and more and more will be revealed to you.

Prayer is different as prayer is talking to God. The Bible tells you to not use repetitive prayers: "Do not heap up empty phrases" – if you're talking to somebody and always saying the same thing they're simply going to stick their fingers in their ears. Remember that when you're chatting with God you're dealing with a real being, who you are made in the image of, your spirit and God's spirit are the same. So when you talk to God, talk to God about everything just like you chat to a best friend or a loving parent.

D: And you listen at the same time or is that for meditation?

W: Of course, you have to learn to listen. Listen to the still, small voice. Then you begin to get a knowing, an intuition.

D: Can it also be that it's not only a voice? When I sit with the dawn sunlight shining on my eyelids I've seen various reddish patterns swirling. Sometimes I see something in those patterns, sometimes I think that's something…

W: You are exploring yourself...

D: Also it could be a sound or a smell.

W: Yes, but we've also got to be careful when we look for symbols. We could be grasping at things or making things up. But other times there is a clear synchronicity or through that symbol it will all be very clear.

D: I heard that it's always useful to sound out something that you think is a spiritual message with someone else who is spiritual.

W: Of course and it's got to be someone who's open to listening and someone who if they don't know anything about it can say: I don't know anything about it or I don't understand it or just sit with it or whatever it may be. Things have happened to me that I didn't trust people with or very few people with anyway. But as time has gone on, over the years I've shared more because when we were talking about creating your own universe, the world I live in when I die will die with me and that's the same for everybody. Reality exists between my ears, the way I see the world... I build a universe out of it.

Just to finish with how I meditate, I do a minimum of half an hour every morning. As well, I always get on my knees every morning and I always get on my knees the last thing at night and say thank you. It's best if you create a routine like this, and have an obedience to it.

D: What about someone who is thinking they simply haven't got the time to spare half an hour in the morning? It's a fair point, we live busy lives these days...

W: You can't afford that sort of thinking. It's like saying I haven't got time to breathe. Test it out. Get up earlier.

And in that half an hour, thank God, ask God, make that half an hour the best part of your day. Say to God: "God, I'm interested in you, I'm looking for you." If you think the half an hour is just going to be boring like some church services you may have been to, know then you'll be mistaken.

You know, there is always going to be opposition, the opposition is going to say you're wasting your time, don't do this, go and get your breakfast, go and watch the telly, go and do something – that's always going to happen.

You've got a choice. If you've sowed seeds to your spirit it's going to be difficult, but you're going to have a long-term gain where you are going to feel good.

Sowing to the flesh – eating, drinking and so on – brings a short-term gain followed by long-term pain.

D: I heard this when I first started it and it's my experience now too: that if you spend half an hour every morning doing prayer and meditation, it means the next 23-and-a-half hours are going to be better.

I also do a meditation while I swim. I like it because not only can I hear every breath more clearly, I can see the bubbles of my outward breath under the water. It reminds me that something granted me the chance to breathe.

As I swim, I give gratitude for people and things in my life, and I ask for help with anything I'm having problems with, and I ask for my thoughts and actions to be directed to what I can do to help others, especially those who are suffering.

W: It says in the Bible: "You may ask me for anything in my name, and I will do it." Now if you just go off praying all the time for what you can get off God, if you're asking for money and houses and men or women or whatever it is you're after, then nobody likes anybody who's just in it always for themselves – you will be spotted.

This is about a genuine heart condition. Don't get me wrong, in the days when I was struggling for money and things were difficult, I had a fear of asking God for money because I thought God would get upset with me and sometimes when I cracked under the pressure and I asked Him for money I'd go: "I'm very sorry, please just ignore that, just pretend I never even said it..." But I'm not like that now.

If I need something from God I'll ask for it, but say something such as "if it's not the right thing for me now, then I totally understand". And it's so important to give thanks, to show gratitude, even in such as this way: "I don't mind if you make me a millionaire any time you want really God, you know if you want me to be a multimillionaire that's fine and thank you God that you haven't done so far because I have learned so much because I wasn't a multimillionaire. I've learned how to run businesses, I've learned how to educate myself, I've learned how to make things, I've learned how to enjoy many things that perhaps if I'd had a lot of money I would never have learned."

But you have to ask and it says many times in the Bible that it's God's pleasure to give to us. It's like with my children when they were growing up, they never ever came to me and said: "Dad, please feed us today, and is it okay if we stay the night, have you got a bed?" My children never asked me for any of their needs, they only asked me for their wants. It was my great pleasure to delight them if I could and sometimes I'd just surprise them too.

Every Christmas I used to make sure they had at least 20 presents each because I always wanted to show them God's abundance, that they could believe in abundance. You see, God created everything in the world and we are talking here about abundance. I read once that there are enough raw materials in the United States alone to feed, clothe and house the entire planet. God works in abundance.

D: Anyway, you wouldn't have helped so many people as you have if you'd been given a few million quid 30 years ago because you might have gone off jet-setting...?

W: I was put in a position where I was absolutely broke, my former business had gone bust and then the opportunity came because I was walking around the streets one day, absolutely broke, totally pissed off and I walked into the social services office and just asked them how could I become a counsellor. Until a couple of years earlier I'd never heard of counsellors, although I had been working voluntarily with people for five years.

Anyway, a woman there took some time to help me, and gave me the name of a woman who I wrote a letter to and she told me about a treatment centre, and I went to the treatment centre and there was a counsellor there who told me about a course that I should do and everything just opened up like that and that's how I became a psychotherapist.

But if I had not been in a sort of rock bottom that day when I was wandering the streets wondering what the hell I was going to do and how I was going to feed the kids, how was it going to work out, I wouldn't have become a professional counsellor.

The secrets that keep us well

D: What was it you said to me once about how you hear parents saying they did this, this, this and this for their child?

W: Basically I said in response to any parent saying that: okay, tell me all the things you did that you weren't supposed to as a parent.

D: Because when you're a parent you're supposed to do all this, that's the deal if you have children? All those things that some parents think make them super-parents or martyrs are actually just the normal things that a mum or dad needs to do from the moment their child arrives.

W: You are supposed to do all these things and then you've got to say to yourself but what did you do extra, where did you go out of your way – because a lot of parents don't go out of their way. They like to think they have slaved their fingers to the bone for their children, when you hear those parents saying: I did all this and I did all that.

I know there are some parents who are in very difficult positions that do amazing things to bring up their families, but the ones I'm talking about are the parents who just want their kids to know how lucky they are to have them as parents.

If you give anything to anybody do it in good grace, don't go rubbing it in their noses. God is a rewarding God, and whatever you do God's way will be rewarded. You don't need the world's applause.

There's one thing that stands out in my mind that I did more than 20 years ago and I was dying to tell somebody about it, but I realised I couldn't. And to this day I've never told anyone.

D: I understand the principle, a spiritual one. It's because if you do a good favour and then tell people it could be mostly due to the ego.

Like the person who gives to a charity, but who then tells everyone about it, which is most likely the ego talking, and it's saying: "I want everyone to know what a good guy I am and I'm really kind and I'm saying all this because I'm hoping to get something from my donation, whether that's admiration or positive gossip or some business."

But if you give to charity and don't tell anyone, then you know you've done it, and so does God.

W: It can also be the little things. You know such as there are no pots left for anyone to use because they're all in the sink. So you wash them up and put them away. You don't need to tell anyone.

D: You're welcome round mine any time…

Genetic complications

D: Are there some factors affecting our mental health that are genetic, that are down to an individual's wiring or brain chemistry?

W: I'm not a geneticist, so I can only go off what I've read and I have read a lot of different opinions, but as far as I can see there are very few diseases that are purely just genetic. A lot of the time from what I've read it seems like genetics were looped into possibilities. So, say, with a particular disease you have a particular gene that means you can develop it, and then 100 people have this particular gene but only ten people get the disease, then all the research goes into how to cure those ten people... It doesn't go into why 90 people didn't get the disease because there's no money in that.

Everything is geared by finance. There have, for instance, been hardly any new antibiotics developed since the 1970s because the research goes into drugs that people will use on a daily basis as there's more money in it.

This is one of the big issues in mental health. There is a theory that mental illness is caused by a chemical imbalance in the brain. But it is simply that – a theory. There's no scientific evidence to support it, despite all the brains that have been sliced up. Doctors who have no training in these areas are under extreme pressure to follow the dictates of the drug companies.

If you read the Peter Breggin book Toxic Psychiatry, he explains how a lot of the results are exaggerated or downright fabricated. In my own work over the decades working with people with such as bipolar and schizophrenia there is an awful lot you can do to help these people without having to give them drugs.

They call it medication, but it's not medication. Medication is like an antibiotic or a drug that prevents or cures something. The word "medication" comes from the Latin meaning "remedy" or "heal", and the word heal derives from the word "whole". These drugs given to people with mental health issues do not medicate, they do not heal or make anyone whole – they are just drugs, that's pure and simple.

That's why people don't like taking them – because they can't function with them. The problem with a lot of these pharmaceutical drugs is they deal with symptoms, they're not there to enhance the person's life. Don't get me wrong, when you're in the pain with the horror of depression and anxiety I can understand why you would take anything to get yourself out of it. I know I certainly did. But then I created a whole new set of problems for myself due to my addiction to prescription drugs.

The neuroleptic drugs – these depress nerve functions, they're tranquillisers – that were given to schizophrenics are like the atomic bomb. They can cause tardive dyskinesia. This is a disorder that results in involuntary repetitive body movements that often includes sticking out the tongue, grimacing, smacking the lips, slow writhing movements, head turning awkwardly over the shoulder and rapid sudden movements.

When people see someone like this they often think they must be mentally ill, but it's the drug causing it. Like all drugs taken over a long period of time, it causes problems. Every drug has side effects, no matter how efficacious they are.

D: But we can't do much about what is handed down to us in our genetic composition. Surely it figures that because we often look like our parents that we have stuff on the inside that's passed on as well? Such as my dad was bald and now I'm bald, so it figures I've got some of his insides as well.

W: I'm not saying there are no characteristics or things passed on to us, but what I'm saying is look how different you are to your father. You're a totally different character, you've got a totally different outlook on the world.

We've mentioned epigenetics, that talks about the fact that part of the cell rewrites its DNA in response to the environment. Stem cell biologist Bruce Lipton's work on this is excellent. So, yes you can pass on cancer, you can pass on anxiety, you can pass on a lot of things – but there's also a lot of things you can do to change these things. It's the debate between nature and nurture. It's a balance between the two.

Look at what triggers the DNA – it can't trigger itself. The DNA is a blueprint of possibilities. It has to be applied. A blueprint is something that has to be read, and it doesn't function until put into practice by a protein. The protein operates through a signal. That signal comes from trauma, toxins, or perception – cells either grow or protect. If you are constantly anxious, they are in protection mode, so they won't grow and regenerate healthily.

When you are anxious you are more stressed. Your immune system will be low. Stress hormones are used to stop organ rejection in transplants. You will also be a little slow-witted because if your hypothalamus is in flight-or-fight mode, the brain is going to be bypassed. So your perception of yourself is going to play a huge role in your biology.

D: And if you've got a defect in your brain or heart, from something that has been passed down?

W: A good brain surgeon or heart surgeon may be able to do something...

D: Or a good psychotherapist or a good belief system?

W: A good therapist can help you change your blueprint that will change your self-perception, which will be the key element in living free from anxiety and depression.

D: You can say that people might have been handed the anxiety gene, but maybe they've in actual fact simply been taught it rather than given it?

W: If you look at families, when things go badly wrong they have a tendency to go wrong in a particular way in certain families: some families go schizophrenic, some families go alcoholic, some families seem to have heart problems, other families have problems with cancer.

D: So if things are going badly wrong then they have got a propensity for this, they can become prone to it? No one knows for sure, but it could be that without the terrible stress of a divorce for instance the ill health would not have come along. In fact, the author Peter James attributes his diabetes as coming on in connection with the stress of his divorce. Another friend of mine, Colin Butts, told me he thought his pancreatic cancer was possibly brought on by the stress in his life when he was writing and organising things for a film of one of his books. Tragically, he died aged just 58 after a big battle with it.

W: One of the best examples is tobacco smoking as there's no doubt on this planet that tobacco smoking kills people, no doubt – but it doesn't kill everyone. I saw a guy on the TV once who was still working and he was aged 102, yet he smoked and he drank. If you and I walk into a cloud of radiation it will kill us both, it will kill everyone that walks into it, it won't leave anyone out.

But with tobacco smoking it often seems to need the train-crash scenario, it seems to need a few things coming together to kill you and that's not rare. And I'm in no way defending tobacco smoking, because it will nearly always kill you way before your time.

This hostile beautiful world

D: I love these Wayne Dyer quotes: "Loving people live in a loving world. Hostile people live in a hostile world. Same world. Heaven on Earth is a choice you must make, not a place you must find. Go for it now. The future is promised to no one. Don't die with the music still in you."

W: There's a story about two guys walking along the road between two towns and they bump into each other and one guy says to the other: "What are the people like in the town you just came from?"

"Oh they are all pretty nasty and horrible," replied the other guy. "What are they like in the town where I'm heading?"

"I think you'll find them much the same," came the answer.

D: It reminds me of a guy speaking on YouTube at an AA convention who said that he left one town because of all the spiteful annoying people there, and he settled in his new town and it was great, until after a couple of weeks he started bumping into this town's spiteful annoying people. "It was just the same!" he said.

W: Lots of people live their lives through resentment, fear, pride, selfishness, self-pity, negative thinking and then they wonder why their lives don't work out. What you give out you get back.

So I would talk about forgiveness and repentance before changing attitudes. Repentance means a radical change in attitude.

There's no point in asking a Higher Power into your life and then carrying on being the same. If you live in a slum and you've got cholera and Jesus passes by and you get your miracle and you are healed, what happens when you go back in the slum?

Once you get any healing, you have that road to Damascus moment, and so you can't go backwards or that's when you turn into a pillar of salt. That comes from the story of Lot's wife in the Bible after two angels arrived in Sodom and at dawn the visiting angels urged him to get his family and flee, so as to avoid being caught in an impending disaster to fall on the city due to its iniquity. The command was: "Escape for your life! Do not look behind you, and do not stay anywhere in the valley; escape to the mountains, or you will be swept away." But as they fled, Lot's wife looked behind, and became a pillar of salt.

Salt is a preservative, it symbolises keeping everything the same. No change kills you. When we change it's essential we keep going. When Daniel got out of the lions' den, he didn't go back for his hat.

We always have to go forward and we have to trust we're being looked after if we have God in our hearts. Now I have met a lot of Christians who say that once they had that road to Damascus moment where they've been converted and they've found Christ, that then they think it's all over and that's it. But there's a huge amount of work to do on yourself, to stop you from going backwards.

D: It's like in the 12-Step programme where it advises spiritual growth and to live and grow one day at a time. If you do 50 press-ups one day but then stop, it figures that your muscles are not going to carry on growing.

W: We need spiritual nourishment every day. It's about continuity and maintenance.

D: Shouldn't it all just be beautiful and perfect all the time?

W: We arrive at a point where we create harmony and then something happens and it blows it apart and we go on then through the wilderness until we create a new harmony, which then contains another problem. That's the nature of existence, it's supposed to be there. The big problem in the Western world is we keep thinking it shouldn't be there...

We keep wanting to eliminate symptoms. Of course, we must try to make life better, that's important, such as we have sanitation, good housing, food, good relations, good law and order – all of these things are essential. But it's also understanding the process of human growth and we will make life a lot better when we realise how human beings grow and facilitate that process.

D: Like we have the seasons in nature.

W: Exactly. Of course, when you feel down and when you feel bad you can think the rest of the world is at a party. That's how you feel, that's the nature of it and it's realising that statement is not true.

When you walk down the street and you're depressed you tend to think you're the only one like that and everybody's looking at you. But it's not true, as these other people have been in the chemists for their antidepressants, those others have just scored down the road, that lot are heading for the pub, others are depressed, others are living a life of misery – it's all around us. But when you're depressed or anxious that's how you feel: that you are the only one in the world like that and you feel awful.

When you're happy, when you're in love because you've just met this wonderful partner, you go down the road and you feel like skipping and you want to kiss everyone and say: "Good morning, how are you, isn't life wonderful!"

Love is so important and we need an understanding of what love is and then, if we can begin to love ourselves, our perception changes. Depression and anxiety cannot flourish in that environment.

As mentioned, depression has its own language, as does anxiety. Like all the mental health diseases, they talk to you because you can't feel bad about anything until you think it.

The language of self-love has to be learned. Love is never easy... it's not weak or wimpy... It's a battle in the mind between darkness and light, joy and pain, despair and hope.

D: That reminds me of one of the Buddhist Noble Truths that says: "Life is suffering." It's similar at the beginning of The Road Less Traveled with the first sentence stating: "Life is difficult." But when we realise that in life there is suffering, that it is difficult, it lessens the suffering and the difficulty.

It's like sometimes I've phoned one of my spiritual advisers – someone who's some steps ahead of me in their spiritual growth, but who also got on this path because they'd been to Hell – and told them something that's happened and how I've felt, and they've said they have had a similar experience or that they would be feeling the same as me. Sometimes that's all it takes to feel better.

That's because the self-condemning voice in my head wants me to feel alone, that I am the only one in the history of humankind that has ever felt like this. It wants to isolate me, trap me in a corner alone.

And I'm thinking of all those people drinking too much alone in their bedsits, or alone in their mansions. Trapped in the depths of despair and anxiety.

I think it's a huge reason the group therapies work well in that the self-condemning voice, the ill ego, gets battered away mob-handed by the group, who if they are rigorously honest will share things that the others relate to and they will realise they are not unusual or alone in this world or terminally unique in any way.

Twitter and social media in general is starting to work this way too as people get more honest and open, such as Matt Haig's Twitter stream, where Matt and a lot of people are very honest about their anxiety, depression and other mental health concerns. I gather his book tours are similar too, where a room full of people are being open and honest, and so they're getting a good taste of why group therapy such as the 12 Steps AA or NA and so on meetings work so well.

What a relief it is to hear that other human beings have the same kind of worries and issues and problems as you do, despite the best efforts of that sick part of the mind that doesn't want you to know and wants you to think you're suffering the worst and you're the only one. So the ill ego hates when we hear that honesty from others!

W: All research shows that when you mix in groups it's more therapeutic. Social media is extremely good in that way as it stops a lot of people from being lonely. Then when I was in the Middle East I was using Skype and it was fantastic.

When I was first looking for help in the 1980s, when I didn't know what was wrong with me, I went into the library or a book shop and there was nothing. Yet walk into the library or a book shop now and it's wall-to-wall from ceiling to floor with self-help books. Back in the 1980s I remember I found one book on homeopathy and I couldn't even pronounce it and so I thought I was the only person who was suffering with whatever it was that was wrong with me.

I didn't know anyone else like me and the only time I ever knew that anyone else was like me was when I went to a group working the 12 Steps.

Because before then, when I went to see a psychiatrist and all the other patients were sat in the waiting room, I still didn't think I was like them. I was certain they were all there for different reasons and I was there because I had a brain tumour nobody could find, and if they found the tumour, then I wouldn't be sitting there.

I was actually so unwell that I thought all those other patients would look at me and just know that actually I was there to work with the psychiatrist and I was observing them for him!

Panic dying

D: How can panic attacks stop?

W: Deal with you, deal with your existential angst, find out about your meaning and purpose – and as you deal more and more with you, these things such as panic attacks will go away.

That fear, that panic is a pain that attracted you to it because you have to deal with your inner world – that's why you are here. You are not here to go out and get a mortgage and win prizes for literature, star in this movie or whatever... you are here to grow and that's what you need to look at, and to do so you've got to look at your inner world.

When you walk near the edge of a cliff you get a fear that's healthy. Think of the panic in the same way: your soul is stood gazing down into the chasm, it's dying because of the way you are thinking. You can't live that way... step back... change.

All the things happening in your outer world are triggers to get you to look inside. When you deal with the inside world you will find your outside world automatically changes. Your whole environment will change; and the people around you will change when you deal with your inside world.

D: Why could it be that panic attacks often seem to happen in such as shopping centres? Is it because there is lots of noise, too many people, there is an overwhelm?

W: Because you feel out of control. You can't control it – how are you going to control a shopping centre and everything and all the people in it? It's scary and then the big fear is: what if I crack up here and everyone sees that? That's the big one. If everyone sees me having a panic attack, then I will be mortified. They will know then for certain that there's something wrong with you and nobody must know that.

Sometimes people feel so out of control they're terrified they will take their clothes off, start laughing insanely or sing the Hallelujah chorus... it's catastrophic projection and it's horrendous. Or people can believe they are going to lose control and kill someone or just simply break down into tears.

It is ego. You are not connected to yourself, so when you go into that shopping centre you think you're on a stage and that everybody's looking at you. Everyone – but no one really gives a fuck you're there, no one, and yet you're thinking: they're all looking at me... It's just pure ego. One of the main things I've learned is, and I love it – I'm invisible.

D: It reminds me of this guy I know who was quite a snazzy dresser and he lived in some flats where there were three blocks of flats facing each other, nearly 100 flats in total. And he said after several months of working on himself, the ego reduction and spiritual growth of the 12 Steps, that he felt such ease when he noted something. He was called Peter and he said, referring to himself: "It was one of the greatest reliefs of Peter's life when he realised that no one in the other flats was at all concerned about what Peter was wearing that morning when he stepped outside of his door."

So something like a panic attack could actually be, as you've described to me, a "spiritual test"?

W: Well, you get tests in life that are designed to move you to the next level. Panic attacks are no different – they are giving you an awareness of your spiritual condition.

When we get tests like this it's not God coming down like a schoolmaster, the tests are positive. If you don't take the test you don't mature to the next level of responsibility and remember you cannot receive a blessing if you aren't ready to handle the responsibility. The other thing is you can't avoid it. You can't flunk out of school, you just have to take it again, and if you don't pass it, you just keep getting it and getting it until you do.

D: And it's always to teach you something?

W: Of course, you can't go where you're going without passing the tests. I like the story of Jonah and the whale – when God speaks to Jonah, commanding him to preach repentance to the city of Nineveh or the city will get destroyed.

But Jonah was stubborn and he didn't want to go and see the king he had to see to do this and so he thought I'm not going, you can fuck off. Instead he got on a boat and sailed off in the opposite direction to Nineveh. So God sent a violent storm. Afraid of God, the sailors tossed Jonah into the sea because they knew the storm was his fault. Immediately the storm calmed down.

Instead of drowning though, Jonah was swallowed by a massive fish, and then he's in the belly of this fish and he's begging God to let him out and full of apologies and all of it. So three days later God makes the fish vomit him out. Then Jonah is on the beach and he's walking and says to God something like: "Thanks for getting me out of there, God you're great!" And he's walking along on the beach and God asks him where he thinks he's going. Jonah tells God he's off home. No, no, no, no, no says God – you're going to see the king. God doesn't change his mind.

So he did and the people in the city believed Jonah's message and they repented. God had compassion on them and did not destroy the city.

D: It's a great story. And these tests are often painful like that?

W: Like I've said before, but it's got to be emphasised, the tests are not painful but our resistance is. That's always the problem: resistance, mainly because we are afraid. So we have to learn to overcome fear.

A lot of the tests I take today are exactly the same tests I took many years ago, although I have no resistance to them now and so they are not painful.

I remember when my life was going down the toilet and someone who I asked for help who'd been sober a few years advised me to wash the pots at home. I said to him that my life was shot and he was telling me to wash the fucking pots!

Anyway, I got so desperate that I did it and it worked. Then I learned how to build a day: get up, do half an hour prayer and meditation, make the bed, brush my teeth, clean up the house, eat breakfast, make sure everything's in order the best I can. You've got to learn how to build a day. The Bible says to not despise the day of small beginnings. I had to start at the beginning, but I had a battle because my ego wanted me to start at the top.

D: The other thing you've said to me about the spiritual set-ups or tests is to always ask: what is this teaching me, what is it here for, what are you showing me God?

W: I remember when I was in the Middle East after a relationship broke down and I was in the house on my own in this beautiful place and feeling depressed and I had to remember that I wasn't on my own because I wanted to be, but I was there because there was a message to be passed to me.

And it was about growing up, maturity, strength for the future challenges, it was about how do we go through these things, how do I go through all of this without cracking up, being overwhelmed or using drink or drugs?

God up

D: I've heard of people who in a state of such as anxiety or depression see things, things that seem evil but that are in usually innocuous everyday things we see, such as a car's red tail lights or a painting or photograph on a wall. What's going on there?

W: When you're losing control you often see things. But what's important to understand is when you're breaking down like this there's an attempt on the inside of you at a reorganisation. When that reorganisation takes place it creates chaos in your mind.

It's like if you're redecorating your house and you start in the morning, then have to go out for the day. When you come home in the evening, there's mess everywhere – yet you don't mind because you know what it's going to turn into when the redecorating is finished.

But when you're coming apart at the seams and nobody has told you any of these things about life, that this change and reorganisation is actually part of the human condition, you think there is something seriously wrong with you.

You feel you're going mad.

D: Another house analogy I like is that if your house was knocked down you would obviously be shocked, but you have to go through that to make the space for a better house. And for a moment there's always going to be an empty space where your old house stood. You just have to give time some time and wait for the new better one to be built.

You mentioned losing control. Do you think more men take their lives because they like to be in control more, or because men don't generally talk about emotions as much as women do?

W: Many men don't talk... your mouth is a pressure valve, if you don't let out pressure you will be internally overwhelmed.

D: A lot of people, thankfully, are talking about how terrible the phrase "man up" is, inferring as it does that men should never show their emotions, or talk openly and honestly, or cry.

W: When I was a kid I was told that if you keep crying like that we will give you something to cry about, that big boys don't cry. So it made me more ashamed because I was quite a sensitive kid.

D: So men have to open up here, otherwise they're going to keep it all in and struggle and suffer – and in the UK, men are three times more likely than women to take their own lives; and in the Republic of Ireland they are four times more likely.

W: As I grew up I remember getting this fear when my drinking started going wrong and it was a fear from childhood. I got this fear that I would start crying in front of people. We were talking about panic attacks and one of my fears was that I would just break down in a shopping centre and I would burst into tears and everyone would look at me and I would be totally ashamed. Even though I had nothing to cry about as I saw it, but that was a fear from childhood.

D: There was more pressure because you were male?

W: It was more pressure because I was very good at sports and when I was playing football or rugby or something like that if you hit me I would hit you back twice as hard. I wasn't nasty, I didn't bully people, I didn't attack people, but physically I could look after myself. But still I was a sensitive man and things upset me, and there was always this fear that there is something fucking wrong with me because I can cry.

To this day I don't really like to cry. I always thought I could control tears, but when my mother died I couldn't control them, even though I had my problems with my mother and I didn't really want to, my tears just fell.

I recall I was in the pub one day and two guys were at the bar crying their eyes out. What had happened was their best mate had just killed himself that afternoon. I knew why he did it because he was just like me. I'd seen his drunkenness and what had gone on in his life. I didn't know him, but I'd observed him, his wife leaving, what was going on in him sparked something with me. I had an identification with his distress.

D: It's when someone gets into that distance we spoke about right at the beginning: "that hell thousands of miles away but also right there." He saw no other way out.

W: Let me stop you, there's no way out but that's why when you get up to your neck in the Red Sea it opens, at the last possible moment it opens, if you keep believing and trusting and asking a Higher Power for help. That's how these things work.

But you need to pray, and if you don't yet believe in anything, just try it and say: whoever you are – help me.

Pray, ask for the help and then see what happens because I guarantee you if you mean that from your heart, then something will happen.

I think having a mind like we do is about wholeness. When we get expressions such as "I was in pieces", "I was beside myself" and "I can't live with myself" I think it's about all the conflicts within our mind that make us feel like there's something more. It's about becoming one, about becoming complete as a human being. The mind, body, soul and spirit.

It's our ignorance of these great matters, the turmoil on the road to the ecstasy within us that causes great fear, that seeks our destruction in the storm. When we realise the storm is the natural form of growth, as is the volcano and the earthquake, and soar with it – our freedom from the bondage of anxiety is begun.

God is within us, we are to achieve holiness, oneness with God. God is me but I'm not God.

I think there's a lot in that.

38637502R00216

Printed in Poland
by Amazon Fulfillment
Poland Sp. z o.o., Wrocław